CAPTURE

American Pursuits and the Making of a New Animal Condition

Antoine Traisnel

UNIVERSITY OF MINNESOTA PRESS
MINNEAPOLIS
LONDON

This book is freely available in an open access edition thanks to TOME (Toward an Open Monograph Ecosystem)—a collaboration of the Association of American Universities, the Association of University Presses, and the Association of Research Libraries—and the generous support of the University of Michigan's College of Literature, Science, and the Arts and the Provost Office. Learn more at the TOME website, available at: openmonographs.org.

The University of Minnesota Press gratefully acknowledges financial support from the University of Michigan to contribute to the publication of this book.

Portions of chapter 1 are adapted from "Huntology: Ontological Pursuits and Still Lives," *Diacritics* 40, no. 2 (2012): 4–25; copyright 2013 Cornell University. A portion of chapter 2 was previously published as "American Entrapments: Taxonomic Capture in James Fenimore Cooper's *The Prairie*," *Novel: A Forum on Fiction* 49, no. 1 (2016): 26–48; copyright Duke University. Portions of chapter 4 are adapted from "Le faune et la sirène: la situation de Cuvier dans l'économie de *The Marble Faun*, de Nathaniel Hawthorne," *Transatlantica* 2 (2011); online since June 5, 2012; http://journals.openedition.org/transatlantica/5563.

Published by the University of Minnesota Press
111 Third Avenue South, Suite 290
Minneapolis, MN 55401-2520
http://www.upress.umn.edu

Printed in the United States of America on acid-free paper

27 26 25 24 23 22 21 20 10 9 8 7 6 5 4 3 2 1

LIBRARY OF CONGRESS CATALOGING-IN-PUBLICATION DATA

Names: Traisnel, Antoine, author.
Title: Capture : American pursuits and the making of a new animal condition / Antoine Traisnel.
Description: Minneapolis : University of Minnesota Press, 2020. | Includes bibliographical references and index.
Identifiers: LCCN 2020022352 (print) | ISBN 978-1-5179-0963-5 (hc) | ISBN 978-1-5179-0964-2 (pb)
Subjects: LCSH: American fiction—19th century—History and criticism. | Animals in literature. | Human–animal relationships in literature. | Animals in art. | Photography of animals.
Classification: LCC PS374.A54 T73 2020 (print) | DDC 813/.309362–dc23
LC record available at https://lccn.loc.gov/2020022352

for anna, always

CAPTURE

First paint a cage . . .
When the bird arrives . . .
Gently close the door with the paintbrush . . .
Erase all of the bars one by one
—Jacques Prévert, "To Make the Portrait of a Bird"

CONTENTS

INTRODUCTION

A NEW ANIMAL CONDITION

On October 9, 1883, the United States Patent Office issued a license to Benjamin W. Kilburn for his new invention, an accordion-style instantaneous camera mounted on the end of a shotgun shaft.[1] An advertisement in the *New York Tribune* celebrated Kilburn's apparatus as a more humane method of hunting (Figure 1). The gun camera promised the impossible: to catch the prey even as it escapes. "It never results in the death or even maiming of fish, flesh, or fowl," the ad boasted, "yet all three may be easily bagged."[2] Kilburn's invention makes explicit early photographic technology's indebtedness to the gun.[3] Its conflation of hunting and mediation, moreover, reflects a radical transformation in the way animals were seen during the period. The nineteenth century witnessed an unprecedented surge of experiments with new technologies and scientific methods for pursuing live animals. Privileging knowledge gained through vision, these experiments sought to access the animal's "truth" through its image.[4] However, the effect of these experiments was not the perception of greater intimacy with animals (as many hoped) but the perception of animals as ever more elusive. The gun camera, for example, did this by effectively severing the time of the apprehended animal from that of the viewer, rendering the bird fully visible only after its initial sighting, on the developed film. This book asks, What is the ontological status of these animals left free and untouched while at the same time caught and held by their representation? During a century that saw the mass displacement of wildlife and the accelerated extinction of animals in the United States, how can we account for the emergence, and read the implications, of this new kind of hunt—one that claims no lives, only likenesses?

Capture examines the strange dislocation of these fish, flesh, or fowl that appear at once in and out of the bag and the biopolitical and ethical stakes of the transformation in the representation and treatment of animals over the nineteenth century. I characterize this transformation as a shift from the hunt regime to the capture regime. The bloodless hunt promised by the gun camera is a paradigmatic feature of the period's drive to archive and encase animals, ironically, in order to preserve and study their liveness. This book introduces and theorizes this drive, and its consequences for animals, as capture. Unlike the hunt, which targets individual animals, capture attempts to seize something intangible, something presumably inherent to all animals: vitality, motion, states of change.[5] Rather than simply enabling their preservation and study, new aesthetic, scientific, and technological methods for pursuing live animals produced them as increasingly fleeting and endangered, making them all the more susceptible to new forms of biopolitical management.

Capture names the modern imperative to apprehend animals at the historical moment when they are receding from everyday view. This imperative is both epistemological and ethical: epistemological because it accompanied a turn to scientific objectivity, which demanded that the objects of study be left "untouched"; ethical because its emergence coincided with a crucial transition in human–animal relations in the nineteenth century, as the United States shifted from the western frontier to the industrial city.[6] The phenomenon of species extinction, then only recently theorized by the French naturalist Georges Cuvier, announced the future collapse of animal (and other) species at precisely the moment that the rapid rearrangement of the American landscape and emerging practices of biocapitalist exploitation were making animals newly vulnerable to human action. Insofar

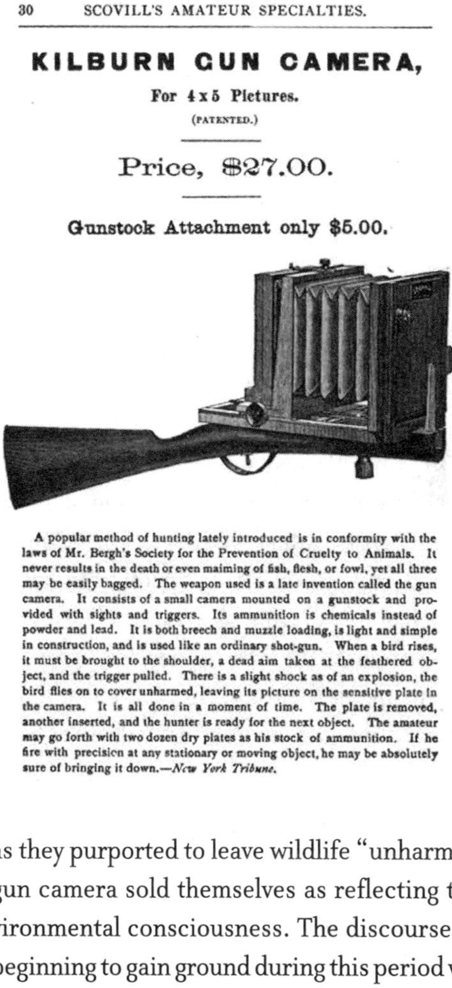

30 SCOVILL'S AMATEUR SPECIALTIES.

KILBURN GUN CAMERA,

For 4 x 5 Pictures.

(PATENTED.)

Price, $27.00.

Gunstock Attachment only $5.00.

A popular method of hunting lately introduced is in conformity with the laws of Mr. Bergh's Society for the Prevention of Cruelty to Animals. It never results in the death or even maiming of fish, flesh, or fowl, yet all three may be easily bagged. The weapon used is a late invention called the gun camera. It consists of a small camera mounted on a gunstock and provided with sights and triggers. Its ammunition is chemicals instead of powder and lead. It is both breech and muzzle loading, is light and simple in construction, and is used like an ordinary shot-gun. When a bird rises, it must be brought to the shoulder, a dead aim taken at the feathered object, and the trigger pulled. There is a slight shock as of an explosion, the bird flies on to cover unharmed, leaving its picture on the sensitive plate in the camera. It is all done in a moment of time. The plate is removed, another inserted, and the hunter is ready for the next object. The amateur may go forth with two dozen dry plates as his stock of ammunition. If he fire with precision at any stationary or moving object, he may be absolutely sure of bringing it down.—*New York Tribune.*

FIGURE 1. Advertisement for Kilburn Gun Camera. Reproduced from Scovill product catalog, New York, 1883.

as they purported to leave wildlife "unharmed," technologies like the gun camera sold themselves as reflecting the country's nascent environmental consciousness. The discourse of conservation that was beginning to gain ground during this period was essential to the uptake of capture, presented as a harmless operation as compared to the explicit violence of hunting.[7] Capture's ability to present itself as a mere taking—of the animal's likeness—in fact conceals a making—of what I call a new animal condition—a making that is all the more efficient because it appears nonintrusive. As a self-effacing form of power, capture is consistent with what Michel Foucault calls biopower, the power to "foster life or disallow it to the point of death."[8] This book displaces Foucauldian biopolitics' center of gravity from Man to the animal and from the European metropolis to U.S. settler territory to recount the story of biopower's early footholds in America.[9] The making of capture as the new animal condition, I argue, is inextricable from the making of the new nation—the construction of a hegemonic American identity and iconography and the consolidation of early capitalism and settler colonialism. Indeed, this book examines how predation was internalized and refashioned both as the tacit logic of Manifest Destiny and as the engine driving the biocapitalist management of human and nonhuman populations in U.S. empire.

Capture's sublimation of the hunt worked to invisibilize and naturalize the violence visited on both animals and animalized human subjects—violence that contributed not only to the extinction of wildlife and the exploitation of animals on an industrial scale but also to the relentless expropriation of black lives under chattel slavery and after the abolition of slavery, as well as the near-eradication of indigenous populations. The regime of capture privileges control over conquest—or rather, folds the explicit violence of conquest into biopolitical protocols of management and regulation. Capture illustrates Alexis de Tocqueville's early insight that power in America "does not break wills, but it softens them, bends them and directs them; it rarely forces action, but it constantly opposes your acting; it does not destroy, it prevents birth; it does not tyrannize, it hinders, it represses, it enervates, it extinguishes, it stupifies [*sic*], and finally it reduces each nation to being nothing more than a flock of timid and industrious animals, of which the government is the shepherd."[10] Power becomes more pervasive and invasive as it moves away from the spectacular and discontinuous display of the scaffold or the hunt ("making die or letting live") toward the continuous and inconspicuous operations of what Foucault calls "pastoral power" ("making live and letting die").[11] This form of power, which addresses not subjects of right but populations at the level of their biological existence, is predicated on an immemorial presupposition of capture: of having the (human) animal already in hand.[12]

Not only was the drive to contain the animal central to the consolidation of U.S. hegemony, but it would define many of the century's most iconic American works. As if to counteract the evanescence of animals, to keep hold of them at the very moment of their disappearance, canonical U.S. writers, artists, and inventors of the period—John James Audubon, James Fenimore Cooper, Edgar Allan Poe, Herman Melville, Nathaniel Hawthorne, Eadweard Muybridge—sought new strategies, devices, and techniques for rendering the vitality of animals visible and lasting. As a logic of mastery through containment, capture is indissociable from the overtly majoritarian status of the white, male, and Euro-oriented canon of nineteenth-century American literature, art, and science from which it emerged. While Kilburn's gun camera is an obvious illustration of the fulfillment of this logic, this book focuses on earlier literary and visual experiments by which capture was prototyped—experiments ranging from Audubon's "still-life" watercolors of hunted animals to Hawthorne's counter-taxonomic poetics to Muybridge's "trip-wire" locomotion studies.[13] Grounded in the study of exemplary artistic and scientific works of the period, *Capture* is, rather than a cultural history, a theoretical, literary, and material analysis of the transformation of animal representation and its lasting biopolitical consequences. This introduction lays out a theory of capture; the chapters that follow elaborate a particular dimension, operation, or effect of the prototyping of capture in U.S. literary and visual experiments bent on understanding, ordering, and taming the natural world.

The rise of capture is an effect of the following concomitant developments: the biopolitical securing of white settler colonial hegemony in relation to animals and animalized human subjects; the automation of animal death and the management of wildlife; and the rise of modern taxonomic and early biocapitalist discourses that viewed life as a principle of commensurability and exchangeability. Together, these developments consolidated the significance of procedures of enclosure and containment to the rise of modern governmentality and industrialization. Material examples of these emergent forms of control include, among others, the isotropic partitioning of space for colonial and capitalist gain that was set in motion by the Land Ordinance of 1785 (explored in chapter 2); the adoption of the gridiron plan for urban centers and its consequences for the tracking and policing of racialized subjects in particular (explored in chapter 3); the development of profiling technologies inspired by modern taxonomy (explored in chapter 4); the mechanization of animal life tested and honed in the second half of the nineteenth century (explored in chapter 5).[14] Representationally, these forms of control found expression in emerging aesthetic protocols that circumscribed animals in space and time. The project examines how these developments informed and reinforced one another and how in the process they contributed to the making of a new conception of the animal as no longer wild yet not quite domesticated, neither present nor fully absent, but instead as thoroughly framed by relations of technology and capital.

Capture's contributions are threefold. First, the book shows how the drive to contain and record disappearing animals was a central feature and organizing pursuit of the nineteenth-century U.S. cultural canon. Second, it examines how this drive motivated the invention of new aesthetic, literary, and medial genres and techniques (lifelike painting, detective fiction, the moving image), which exposed or sought to compensate for the limitations of earlier modes of figuration, and thereby transformed the very nature and project of modern representation. Third, it analyzes how these new representational devices and modalities informed and shaped the modern animal condition and contributed to naturalizing the wide-scale exploitation and erasure of animals as we know it today.[15]

AMERICAN PURSUITS

It is *Moby-Dick,* the "quintessential" American novel, that most famously dramatizes the U.S. project's material and symbolic investment in the workings of capture. Melville's epic chase is the centerpiece of the white masculinist tradition of the hunting narrative in the American literary canon (e.g., Cooper's *The Leatherstocking Tales,* Parkman's *The Oregon Trail,* du Chaillu's *Explorations and Adventures in Equatorial Africa,* Roosevelt's hunting memoirs, Connell's "The Most Dangerous Game," Faulkner's "The Bear," or Hemingway's hunting chronicles, to mention but a few examples). Countless autobiographies of big-game hunters were published during the nineteenth century and the first half of the twentieth century.[16] The use of hunt narratives in the self-fashioning of the United States often promulgated a colonialist agenda that naturalized the reconfiguration of subsistence habitats into potential property. A singularly if not uniquely American subgenre, hunting narratives have monumentalized the mythos of the intrepid and enterprising frontiersman who dominates his natural surroundings, with all its attendant sexual and gendered connotations (animal pursuit as a stand-in for white hegemony, colonial empire, sexual dominance, or the foibles of masculinity).

As D. H. Lawrence observes, *Moby-Dick* chronicles the "last great hunt."[17] But the novel makes clear that hunting is hardly over—rather, it heralds the dawn of a new kind of hunt: the hunt that knows no end. *Moby-Dick*'s full title, *Moby-Dick; or, The Whale,* can be read as oscillating between a logic of the hunt and one of capture.[18] What, exactly, is the novel (named) after? Is it the individual animal called Moby Dick or is it "the Whale" as a taxonomic category? Is the novel a hunt for a particular white whale or an attempt to capture the essence of the category "Whale"? In a chapter he calls "as important a one as will be found in this volume," the narrator, Ishmael, warns the reader against the temptation to subsume the animal under the apparent stability of its name (proper or generic)—a temptation he identifies as intolerably allegorical.[19] The problem of allegory for the animal—its tendency to subordinate the literal to the figural, the singular to the general—is precisely the problem posed by Melville's title: *Moby-Dick; or, The Whale.*[20]

Like Melville's title, the hunt pulls in two directions. It is both fundamentally iterative and (somewhat counterintuitively) sustainable, for the kill is the end of the hunt but not of hunting.[21] As a corollary, the animal is both (but not simultaneously) an individual being and a representative of its species. In the hunt, therefore, the individual animal can acquire a proper name, as with Moby Dick.[22] It is precisely this possibility that the animal is denied when the logic of capture emerges as an apparatus of early biocapitalism. This shift is registered in the novel as the transition between two markedly different, but not incompatible, logics for "accounting" the whale. The first logic—that of the individual animal—is embodied by Captain Ahab, who is driven by his monomaniacal desire for revenge against the white whale; the second logic—that of the animal as species (and as commodity)—is reflected by the ship's proprietors, Peleg and Bildad, who own the *Pequod* along with a number of anonymous shareholders. While these retired captains are ironically introduced as peaceful Quakers, they are "Quakers *with a vengeance,* . . . the most sanguinary of all sailors and whale-hunters."[23] But unlike Ahab, their vengeance is not aimed at any particular whale but at the entire whale species: remaining on shore, ostensibly harmless and comical, they are insatiable entrepreneurs who demand that the whalemen "harvest" as many whales as possible—an insatiability that raises the specter of extinction, while curiously disavowing the possibility of this event.[24]

Peleg and Bildad crystallize the literal and symbolic displacement of violence produced by a biocapitalist rationality that systematically outsources labor and treats natural resources as endlessly reproducible.[25] The proprietors' fixation on the anonymized animal mass of "the whale" condenses the logic of capture; Ahab's fixation on the individual specimen called Moby Dick exemplifies the logic of the hunt.[26] Unlike Ahab, who is obsessed with hunting the one animal, the merchants Bildad and Peleg hunt a profit that is, in theory, without limit (as Ishmael repeatedly notes, the whalemen do not receive a fixed wage; they work on commission, with their pay indexed to the number of whales they kill). With Ahab's disappearance, what vanishes is not hunting but the hunt as a spectacular, singular undertaking; the singularity of the hunt is subsumed into the routinized, systematic regime of capture, under which animals become indifferentiable from one another—exchangeable, like all commodities.[27] This economy of infinite substitutability is premised on the epistemological slide from "Moby Dick" to "the Whale," from animals to "the animal"—from hunt to capture.

FROM HUNT TO CAPTURE

The operations and effects of capture are best understood by examining it alongside the form of pursuit it sublimates (but does not entirely displace)—that of the hunt. The biopolitical regime of capture established itself in the wake of profound transformations in U.S. hunting culture.[28] With the rise of industrialization over the course of the nineteenth century, hunting was gradually rendered obsolete as a subsistence activity and as a technology of conquest by the systematic "taming" and settling of the nation's territories.[29] As more "efficient" means of procuring animals were being promoted, hunting was recast as a primitive anachronism or an occasional pastime. By the late 1800s, technological developments in the production of traps and guns made it increasingly difficult for many game animals to reproduce fast enough to survive; two animals emblematic to the United States, the passenger pigeon and the bison, both thought at the beginning of the century to be so numerous as to be inexhaustible, were hunted respectively into extinction and near-extinction in the space of a few decades.[30] Meanwhile, with the advent of the "technological reproducibility" of animal life under industrial farming, standardized slaughter began to replace hunting for subsistence, and the continually perpetuated pool of livestock supplanted the unpredictability of prey. Both extinction and mass slaughter, then, are phenomena wrought by a shift in notions of animal reproduction, itself subtended by a transformation of what reality the term *animal* designates.[31] Over time, the aleatory practice of the hunt was rechanneled into the biopolitical logistics of capture, which indexes both the will and ability to reproduce animals endlessly and the anxiety prompted by the notion of wildlife as ontologically endangered, inevitably and constantly threatened by disappearance.

Although hunting fell out of common practice, it did not disappear. It simply reappeared in new forms: internalized as an epistemic frame for the new artistic and scientific fervor surrounding the "mute mystery" of animal nature;[32] analogized in legal regulations like the "rule of capture," which legislates the acquisition of "feral" or "spontaneous" resources like gas, oil, and groundwater;[33] and recycled, in the figure of the frontiersman, into a nostalgic trope celebrating the nation's valiant and enterprising early years. The European colonists in America had largely ceased to rely on hunting for sustenance as early as the seventeenth century, but during the nineteenth century, the aforementioned changes (the introduction of livestock and the decline in game animals, caused by overhunting and the reorganization of ecosystems to fit colonial economic regimes) reached a tipping point that altered attitudes toward hunting. This shift, exemplified by the establishment of restrictive game laws as early as 1817, primarily affected those indigenous tribes with nomadic lifestyles, as well as rural and enslaved populations for whom hunting had remained a significant subsistence and cultural activity.[34] Hunting began to be framed as an atavistic practice even as it was being celebrated as the glorious bedrock of the nation (in the paintings of Karl Bodmer and George Catlin, for instance, or in hunting memoirs like Parkman's *Oregon Trail*). It was valorized as a heroic enterprise in the context of an idealized past and prescribed as a prophylactic in an irenic future in which it was no longer a material necessity. This explains why, at the end of the century, Theodore Roosevelt could unironically prompt his fellow (white male) Americans to "return" to "savage virtues" by hunting.[35]

This book identifies in the transition from hunt to capture a profound epistemological shift in the conception of animals. Here, the hunt is less as a ritualized, embodied activity than as a diagram of power-knowledge. Hunting and capture entertain very different relations to their objects. Hunting supposes the copresence, however brief, uneven, and fortuitous, of the hunter and the hunted. Capture, however, disrupts this promise of contemporaneity, converting it to telos. As capture makes the subjection of that which is preyed upon appear predetermined, even preaccomplished, a form of nonpresence comes to saturate the animal's state of being.[36] The availability of animals in capture, then, reverses the conditions presumed by the hunt: for the hunter, encounters cannot be fully anticipated or planned, for they happen in no small part on the hunted animals' terms. The hunter goes after the prey in its own territory, which French poet Jean-Christophe Bailly defines as a network of holes and hideaways where animals can retreat.[37] Under capture, animals are assumed already at hand but fundamentally dislocated. Deprived of a territory, Bailly observes, animals are submitted to a regime of inescapable visibility: they

FIGURE 2. The dynamic of capture is already apparent in this image that accompanies the entry for "Approcher" in Chomel's *Dictionnaire œconomique* (1732), which stages the hunter's disappearance behind the apparatus facilitating the animal pursuit.

cannot hide, but neither can they manifest unexpectedly—they can no longer appear.[38] One of the corollaries of the "dis-appearance" of animals—the loss of their capacity to appear on their own terms—is the effacement of the figure of the hunter (Figure 2).

Capture, which aims to preempt sudden appearances and chance encounters, coincides with what John Berger diagnoses as the systemic "disappearance" of animals under industrial capitalism.[39] Under capture, animals disappear in plain sight. When we see captive animals, they are only superficially available, seeming fundamentally out of place—on display in cages or images, thereby "rendered absolutely marginal." The zoological garden, "where people go to meet animals, to observe them, to see them," Berger argues, is "in fact a monument to the impossibility of such encounters."[40] Captured, animals have become "immunized to encounter."[41] And indeed, zoos in modernity traditionally perform the immunitary function of protecting endangered animals from disappearing at Man's hand. Although modern zoos inherit from earlier menageries a residual sense of colonial pride, exhibiting rare and "exotic" specimens as trophies—including both animal and human specimens—they primarily justify their existence as educational institutions and as sanctuaries for endangered species.[42] What one sees in zoos is not there (for long). Hence "disappearance" does not simply refer to the empirical vanishing of animals precipitated by colonial and capitalist exploitation, but it also indexes a more general difficulty to see animals—their becoming "out of focus" under the modern gaze.[43]

"Everywhere animals disappear," writes Berger, compounding the perpetuity of animal disappearance in a devastating present simple.[44] Akira Mizuta Lippit builds on Berger's thesis by proposing that, with the advancement of modernity, animals come to "exist in a state of perpetual vanishing." In disappearing, Lippit proposes, they nonetheless leave a trace, their nonpresence becoming the paradoxical condition for a new image of animality to emerge.[45] Thus the signifier "disappearance" covers two distinct, if interdependent, realities. On the one hand, it refers to the empirical recession of animals from daily life under industrial capitalism; on the other, it marks their phenomenological vanishing before our very eyes. As a corollary, we can distinguish between two modalities of capture. The first is a constative statement that registers the historical subjection of animals to technologies of enclosure and supervision. The second is a performative utterance: it constitutes something called "the animal" as that which disappears. The transition between the hunt regime and the capture regime has a number of salient implications for the material and symbolic conception of animals, as summarized in Figure 3.

THE MEDIATED ANIMAL: PURSUIT WITHOUT END

What *Capture* tracks, therefore, is a transformation in the way animals were perceived, a rupture between seeing and knowing them. Essential to my theorization of capture is the notion that with the move from hunt to capture, animals become indissociable from their mediation. Hunting narratives are always punctuated by anxious periods of waiting for the prey to manifest itself (*Moby-Dick* is a case in point). But capture upends the temporal logic of hunting, according to which animals exist in their own right before the encounter with the hunter. The hunt supposes a spatial distance (and a shared temporal moment) between hunter and hunted. Capture, however, is asynchronous; it

THE HUNT REGIME	THE CAPTURE REGIME
AXIOM 1 The hunt presumes animals.	AXIOM 1 Capture presumes the animal.
AXIOM 2 Animals are endowed with the capacity to appear on their terms. Animal encounters cannot be fully anticipated or planned.	AXIOM 2 The animal appears already at hand. The animal can no longer be encountered.
AXIOM 3 Animals occupy territories.	AXIOM 3 The animal exists in a milieu.
AXIOM 4 Animals can escape or they can die.	AXIOM 4 The animal cannot escape and it cannot die.
AXIOM 5 The hunt is interminable but each time unique.	AXIOM 5 Capture is repetitive and monotonous.

FIGURE 3. Distinctions between the hunt regime and the capture regime.

supposes the separate temporalities of the original encounter and the later engagements with the reproductions. If we read capture's displacement of the animal's pursuit from spatiality onto temporality through my opening example, we see that the gun camera, which on its face is more humane, inaugurates a hunt without end. While in the moment its life may be spared, the bird viewed through the lens of the gun camera is recast as endlessly reproducible and thus eminently disposable (it is not fortuitous that the animal's loss of aura—what Walter Benjamin calls the "here and now" of an object, "its unique existence in a particular place," that which in principle resists reproducibility and commodification—coincides with the rise of industrial biocapitalism).[46]

Unlike hunting, capture does not anticipate so much as presuppose its object. The verb *capture* is what linguists call a telic verb insofar as it envisions a clear endpoint and, grammatically, demands an object; whereas the verb *hunt* is atelic: one can hunt without knowing in advance what will be hunted or whether the hunt will be successful.[47] The strange temporality of capture is encapsulated in Kafka's aphorism "A cage went in search of a bird." The epigram inverts the expectation that a cage exists in order to confine a given animal, suggesting instead that it searches for a specimen that will conform to its design. This uncanny reversal of cause and effect is the defining paradox of capture. Should the animal not, logically, precede the instrument of its captivity? Does nature not, in principle, come before technology? But to capture something from nature is to sacrifice the very naturalness that one sets out to secure or preserve. Capture is not simply the act of containing an entity that already exists in the world—an entity whose nature or essence precedes the event of its seizure.

As Rey Chow argues, capture is not a neutral aesthetic operation but an act with significant ontological effects. Reading Walter Benjamin, she shows that through the act of capture, something new—a new reality, a new relation to the (natural) world—comes into being:

> *Benjamin has in effect inaugurated a reconfiguration of the conventional logic of capture*: rather than reality being caught in the sense of being contained, detained, or retained in the copy-image (understood as a repository), it is now the machinic act or event of capture, with its capacity for further partitioning (that is, for generating additional copies and images ad infinitum), that sets reality in motion, that invents or makes reality, as it were.[48]

When the value of images (or animals) is no longer a function of their rarity but of their reproducibility, the perception of these realities is radically changed. The object represented (the captive animal) no longer conveys the aura of the original. Unlike the auratic wild animal, which the hunter dislodged from its territory, the domesticated animal appears essentially dislocated; it is a being altogether different, brought into existence through the means of technological reproduction. Capture—the representational modality prompted by technological reproducibility—strips its object of its naturalness, its originality, its singularity. Made into stock, the virtually limitless copy (the farmed or lab animal, the zoo specimen, the photographed beast) supersedes the now-unattainable (extinct or spatially marginalized) original. In capture, the animal is assumed invisible, disappeared, unknowable—a manifestation of something other than what we see. In other words, capture introduces a new phenomenality of appearance, one that indexes something framed as vanished, extinct, no longer encounterable. Thus, while capture presupposes its object, it is nonetheless haunted by an unavowable intransitivity, a secret intranquility.

Consider an early example of capture's visual logic: the thaumatrope (Figure 4). First popularized by Dr. John Paris in 1825, the thaumatrope is an optical device, a small disc with an image on each side. When the disc is twirled, the two sides appear superimposed, giving the impression that they form a single, composite image. Early prototypes of this "philosophical toy," as it was called at the time, often depicted a bird and a cage. When in motion, the bird appeared trapped, captured through an appearance of stillness that was in fact caused by movement too rapid to be registered by the human eye. The thaumatrope stages a displacement of animacy, which shifts from the object studied to the enframing technology that produces it—from the bird to the cage.

According to Dr. Paris, the aim of the thaumatrope was to generate "young Cartesians" by "driving a wedge between what we know and what we see."[49] While you know there are two distinct images, you only see a bird in a cage. If the Cartesian discourse implies that stillness was thought to be the condition for reliable knowledge, as film scholar Tom Gunning argues, the toy also ironically taught that stillness can be manufactured by motion, thereby calling into question the reliability of the human observer.[50] This suspicion in turn contaminates the "real world," robbing it of permanence or stability, rendering it phantasmagoric and its occupants elusive. The thaumatrope has been significant to debates about the phenomenology and temporality of vision in modernity; little attention, however, has been paid to the images it displays, particularly to the persistence with which they represent animals. As a technology in the service of a biopolitics of vision, the thaumatrope functioned to captivate a new generation of viewers

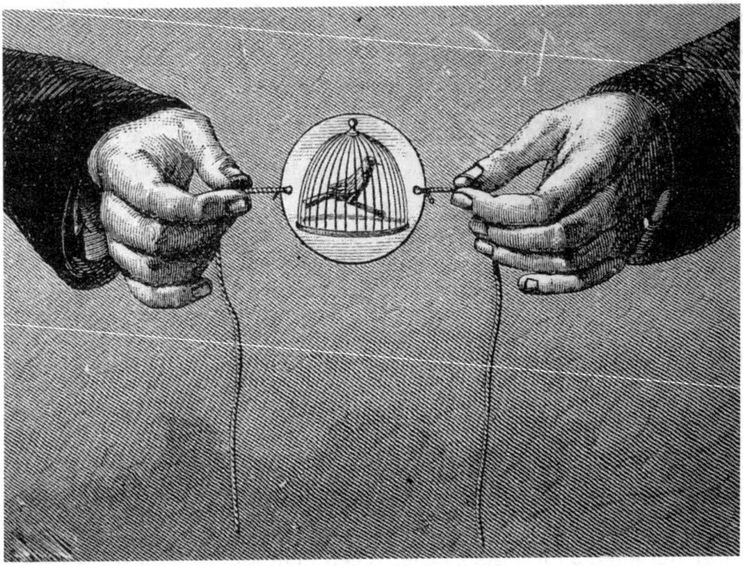

FIGURE 4. Thaumatrope, c. 1825.

and train them to conceive the animal as essentially captured.[51] When the hands that hold and operate the thaumatrope are no longer seen, the capture of the animal appears to be a fact of nature.

Capture coincides with the turn to scientific objectivity in the first half of the nineteenth century as an attempt to remediate this hallucinatory order of things; when the capacities of the naked human eye can no longer be trusted, knowledge must be outsourced to mechanized protocols and technologies of vision. Muybridge's famous motion capture experiments in the last decades of the century, which produced the first successful photographic images of a galloping horse, did precisely this: render motion intelligible without direct human intercession. Muybridge is mostly known today as a pioneer of the moving image, but his primary object was to unravel the "secret" of animal motion, as attested by the title of his massive 1887 photographic catalog, *Animal Locomotion.*

We can contrast Muybridge's work with another monumental collection of animal representations to situate his work in the transition charted in this book: Audubon's *The Birds of America.* Printed between

1827 and 1838, the book gathers 435 life-size watercolors in a "double elephant" folio, thus named for its uncommon size. Audubon's avowed ambition was to paint all the bird species known in North America. Both Audubon and Muybridge seem to partake of the same archival epistemophilia, but they approached their subjects very differently. In *The Birds of America,* Audubon perceives his specimens with the eyes of a hunter: his birds are "out there," in the wild; he immobilizes them in order to draw them; he focuses primarily on their external appearance; and he presumes animals to be knowable in terms of their taxonomic identity, which is visible to the unaided human eye. For Audubon, animals occupy a specific "place"—geographically, in the order of nature, and on the page of the naturalist's book, which promises to render their accurate anatomical proportions. In contrast, Muybridge approaches his subjects with an intent to capture: he aspires to seize not animals but their movement, pursuing in his stop-action studies an invisible economy of forces shared by all animals—*the* animal—if uniquely expressed by each. For him, the comprehension of animals is less a function of space than time; space is subordinated to an immanent principle of transience and transformation, both at the individual level (locomotion) and at the level of the species (evolution).

Capture, to sum up, indexes a passage rather than a presence. It destabilizes the conventional temporality of representation, understood as coming after the object represented; in this new model, the act of capture (its moment) is both distinct and indissociable from that which is represented. Despite the perceived simultaneity, the capturer (or observer) and the animal do not inhabit the same time: they are entangled rather than synchronous. Chow insists that we must refrain from collapsing the temporalities of the trapped and the trapper: if they are "situationally entwined," they are both temporally and "phenomenologically disjointed."[52] We can know "the intent or intelligence of the trap's design," Chow argues, but not "the prey's experience of *being* captured." As a metaphor for representation, capture borrows from hunting the sense of apprehending something endowed with the capacity to escape; but capture converts capacity into ontology, producing its object as essentially fugitive (it "sets reality in motion," as Chow puts it). While hunting envisions fugitivity as a faculty of the prey, capture assumes fugitivity as the property of the animal (as that which is proper to it). This fugitive animal poses an insurmountable challenge to representation when representation is beholden to a logic of presence. Capture, in contrast, assumes the fugacity of its object and produces the animal as it vanishes, as vanishing. In capture, the animal is not made present (re-presented) so much as it is *conjured* by the apparatus. Thus, for Chow, capture is a process of entanglement that comprises irreconcilably heterogeneous temporalities.[53] Yet in these "entanglements" lie the promise of an ethics of capture, which, I argue in the conclusion, offers unsuspected modes of relating with incommensurate life-forms.

Capture is a hunt for likeness, not life. From *capere,* meaning to seize with one's hands, the verb "to capture" was not used as a synonym for "to represent" in English until the twentieth century, previously appearing mainly in hunting and military contexts (e.g., the catching of prey, seizing of land, taking of slaves or prisoners). The *Oxford English Dictionary* dates the semantic repurposing of the term to 1901, when it came to express the action to "catch, or record (something elusive, as a quality) in speech, writing, etc."[54] Yet in the middle decades of the nineteenth century, Daguerre and Edison had already used the lexicon of captivity to describe the archiving of fleeting images and sounds, which suggests that capture-as-representation is indebted to technologies of reproduction like photography and phonography.[55] When successive images can make movement appear (even though this movement resides in none of the images taken in isolation)—when images are given the power to produce a nonimage—the imaging apparatus thus represents that which stubbornly eludes vision. As a hunt for likeness, capture paradoxically opens the possibility of apprehending life as a representational object. In effect, the representation of life's irreducible aphenomenality demands a new technical and cognitive apparatus based on the reproducibility of the image. Just as the reproducible image dreams up the nonimage, the reproducible animal dreams up the nonanimal: a wild, transient creature that appears essentially unknowable, unseeable.

THE BIOPOLITICS OF CAPTURE

When did we stop seeing animals? When did they start becoming "out of focus," as Berger suggests?[56] To answer this question, we must look for changes in the field of vision itself—in the underlying conditions for the appearance of animals. This is a question that Foucault raises in *The Order of Things,* where he identifies a radical transformation in the way natural sciences approached their objects. "In the late eighteenth century," he writes, "a new configuration was to appear that would definitively blur the old space of natural history for modern eyes."[57] The shift in question was the invention of the notion of life. In the classical episteme (which for me encapsulates the logic of the hunt), there are individual living beings but no conception of life as a larger, autonomous force; the natural world is classified according to its external structure. In contrast, the modern episteme situates life below the threshold of the immediately perceptible. In this new configuration, animals appear only insofar as they manifest in a flash the invisible agencies of the life that momentarily supports them; at the moment when life "escapes" the strictures of classical knowledge, animals disappear into *the animal.* In their individual existence, animals are not enough. They are no longer declensions of primordial molds or ur-specimens but transient manifestations of the deeper, invisible principle called life, which does not belong to them but runs through them. Life itself, which is continuous, can only be grasped negatively, indirectly, through the necessarily discontinuous picture drawn by the passage—and passing—of animal figures.[58] New technologies of vision like the gun camera, the thaumatrope, and Muybridge's time-lapse photography invent new ways of seeing, but they also invent new ways of conceiving the "real." By framing it as fleeting and evasive, these technologies prepare us to accept a world in transit, to accept its mutability and manipulability—thereby confirming tautologically the need for apparatuses of capture. Animals (and their captured representations) occupy a special place in that transformation, for they not only emblematize it but also help to produce it. The image of the animal is both the site and the sight of the disappearance of life. "The animal," Foucault writes, "discovers fantastic new powers in the nineteenth century."[59] Or rather, the nineteenth century rediscovers the animal through the prism of the "untamed ontology" of life.[60]

The Order of Things is not, as it has sometimes been read, an account of the disenchantment of the natural world precipitated by enlightened science; Foucault's formulation, crucially, focuses not on loss but on gain: the animal "discovers fantastic new powers." These powers are curious ones because they originate not from the animals themselves but from a life over which animals can claim no ownership. These are powers haunted by what Derrida calls a form of "nonpower [*impouvoir*]"—the power to die, the power to suffer, the power "not to be able"—but they are powers nonetheless, reducible neither to sheer powerlessness nor to the absolute subjugation of animals (though they can facilitate this subjugation).[61] These powers dispose the living to change and being changed, render it susceptible to a number of internal and external "conditions of existence." This concept of "conditions of existence" was central in the transition between natural history and biology, Foucault argues: "In a general way, the object of natural history in the classical age is an ensemble of differences to be observed; in the nineteenth century, the object of biology is that which is capable of living and subject to dying." The notion that what lives comes to be "linked to the possibility of dying," he continues, "refers to two possible systems of conditions of existence."[62] The first system, associated with Cuvier, is anatomo-physiological: it invents a new form of taxonomy preoccupied not by recording visible differences but by inferring correlations between different organs (what are the internal conditions of an individual's existence?). The second, associated with Darwin, is ecological: it binds the living to a milieu more or less favorable to its flourishing (what are the external conditions of an individual's existence?). In both cases, the life of an organism is conjugated in the future perfect as survival, from the point of view of its predictable disappearance. The "new animal condition" of my title can thus be heard in the medical sense, viewing the living as subject to new forms of conditioning: their inevitable but deferrable death disposed them to new protocols of care, supervision, and amelioration. The term *condition* signals that the animal is not a taxonomic or ontological category but (like Man) a biopolitical concept, whose historical contingency becomes manifest through a genealogical foray into its conditions of emergence.

Biopolitics, which in principle addresses "life itself," has until recently proved relatively inhospitable to nonhuman lives.[63] Its enduring indifference toward nonhuman animals suggests that its "frame" cannot simply be stretched to accommodate animal life. Indeed, as Cary Wolfe shows, we must be critical of the framing mechanisms at work in biopolitics if we want to exploit the full potential of Foucault's analytic—one, for Wolfe, that can and does extend to nonhuman lives, pace a dominant European lineage of biopolitical thinkers.[64] In order to chart differentiated relations between different (human and nonhuman) life-forms, Wolfe invites us "to recalibrate our understanding of the biopolitical in terms of the *dispositifs* of biopower and their political articulation rather than the metaphysics of sovereignty."[65] Focusing on *dispositifs* or apparatuses—whose primary function, according to Giorgio Agamben, is precisely to "capture" living beings—demands that we analyze the operative and symbolic procedures that inform our relations to animals.[66] This book's focus on the strategies, protocols, and apparatuses that emerged to represent the animal in the nineteenth century allows me to examine what representation, as a biopolitical dispositif of capture, effectively does to animals.[67] If the animal enters the biopolitical stage as it disappears—indeed, by disappearing—then we must consider what stubbornly eludes biopolitics, what it is in principle incapable of representing.

I thus offer a genealogy of capture and the birth of its object, "the animal." The genealogy of the animal does not so much parallel as haunt Foucault's history of the human sciences and the epistemic creation of "Man"—the contours of which, tellingly, Foucault discerns in the study of animal bodies, turning not to philosophy or anthropology but zoology and paleontology.[68] Understanding how, in capture, animals appear in their disappearance helps us to see the paradoxical modernity of a character that otherwise appears timeless: the animal.[69] In fact, it is precisely the ahistorical or stock character of the animal that betrays its biopolitical modernity. Just as Man for

Foucault spuriously assumes a universal notion of humanity—stripped of any colonial, racial, and gendered specificity—so too does the animal imply something like a general animality. The animal, conceived as a technology of biopower, is an invention of recent date—and one interminably nearing its end, for it is construed as both imminently endangered and eminently reproducible.[70] Capture names the material and symbolic condition of the animal's emergence, but at stake is its sustained and sustainable disappearance. It is by disappearing, in other words, that animals appear for modern representation, as if nonpresence was a constitutive property of animality.[71]

ANIMALITY AS A TECHNOLOGY OF BIOPOWER

Animality, I propose, is the product of a historical rearrangement in the order of knowledge and power that was precipitated by the advent of the concept of life, which Foucault traces back to Cuvier's groundbreaking work in comparative anatomy and paleontology. These new disciplines, Foucault shows, hinge the appearance of life on the dissolution of living beings into their anatomical resemblances (classification) and semblances (fossils). Foucault famously writes that in the eighteenth century, "life itself did not exist. All that existed was living beings, which were viewed through a grid of knowledge constituted by natural history."[72] Natural history sought discrete living beings representative of their species; the new science of biology, by contrast, concerned itself with the invisible, transindividual current called life that is manifested through animals. Animals—which for Foucault constitute the paradigmatic objects for the emergent sciences of life—index the givenness of forces that they reveal as both hidden and ever-present: vitality, instinct, sexual reproduction.[73] Because life unfolds through species rather than individuals, death becomes something of a nonevent; the death of any one specimen does not negate the persistence of life across the species. Thus, death for animals becomes legible predominantly in terms of extinction, of species death—which paradoxically sanctions both conservation efforts and mass slaughter. (How else could we reconcile the growing concern for species endangerment with the lack of mainstream political consideration for the endless mass killing that takes place in factory farms, which Derrida aptly characterizes as the animal's "interminable survival"?)[74]

The new logic of life does not uniquely concern nonhuman animals. Humans also index the invisible powers of life; their health and vitality also become increasingly monitored and regulated; they also come to be conceived as a species, examined from the vantage of their anticipated extinction. This particular conception of humanity as a species is attested by the contemporary anxiety surrounding the Anthropocene, the "age of Man"; today, this anxiety is exacerbated by the undeniability of anthropogenic species extinction and climate change, and by extension by the looming shadow of humanity's disappearance, but its roots are traceable to the invention of life. From the outset, the modern concept of life has implied the recognition of the finitude of the living, and thus the finitude of Man as a living being.[75] The classical episteme forbade that Man be simultaneously subject and object of knowledge, and so Foucault asserts that in the seventeenth and eighteenth centuries, "man did not exist (any more than life)."[76] Man only emerges as positively knowable—and controllable at the biological level—at the threshold of biopolitical modernity, when he takes his own animality in charge.[77] His self-knowledge, however, hinges on the recognition of his programmed disappearance—a recognition that allows him to hoist himself (precariously, thus heroically) above the transience of the living.[78]

There, the hierarchies of power embedded in knowledge practices become apparent: Who has the authority to know? What ontological partitions does the modern episteme engender, and what do these partitions authorize in turn? When animality emerges from the ruins of classical thought's neatly tabulated taxonomies, Man is exposed as a historically contingent stabilizing dispositif.[79] Sylvia Wynter shows that the scientific and political distinctions precipitated by the emergence of life are inextricably enmeshed with the development of the European colonial project. According to Wynter, the "invention of Man" described by Foucault grows out of the nineteenth-century biologization and economization of the living, which themselves inherit the secularized view of humanity promoted by European Renaissance humanists. This transformation, she contends, was "made possible only on the basis of the dynamics of a colonizer/colonized relation that the West was to discursively constitute and empirically institutionalize on the islands of the Caribbean and, later, on the mainlands of the Americas."[80] By centering the colonial context, Wynter profoundly "unsettles" Foucault's periodization and provincializes his analysis. Wynter, moreover, prioritizes "the idea of race," which Foucault viewed primarily through the prism of sex.[81] Accounting for empire's rigid (if strategically mutable) racial taxonomies, she challenges majoritarian interpretations of biopower by introducing a racial counterpoint to Foucault's focus on sex, not to reject the premise of *The Order of Things* so much as to reveal its implicit condition in colonization and racialization.[82] Just as race and sexuality emerge as coconstitutive dispositifs, so too does species, I argue, become legible as a distinct technology of biopower. Species as a heuristic instrument wielded to domesticate the "untamed ontology" of life—to partition and organize what is imagined as biological continuum into subgroups made manageable through technologies of sex (breeding, sterilizing, etc.) yet presented as natural entities (thereby eliding the partitioning that constituted them in the first place)—cannot be thought outside of the development of the European colonial project and the institution of transatlantic slavery.

Nicole Shukin's remarkable *Animal Capital* paved the way for my study of the obfuscated or disavowed continuities in the biopolitical practices, technologies, and strategies that constrain and condition animal and animalized subjects. Shukin reminds us, for example, that Muybridge's motion-capture experiments on racehorses fed straight into Frederick Taylor's *Principles of Scientific Management.*[83] Earlier examples abound, however, in the context of U.S. chattel slavery, from the widespread (and constitutional) practice of manhunting reaffirmed by the Fugitive Slave Act of 1850, which authorized any white citizen to assume the role of the police and "return" fugitive slaves to their rightful owners, to the use of biology to determine the ontology of race via an antebellum law derived from animal husbandry, which established the child's status as inherited from the mother and treated enslaved populations not like but *as* livestock.[84] Attending to these "entangled forms of oppression," Bénédicte Boisseron warns, does not mean equating the historical exploitation, subjugation, and extermination of animals and racialized people.[85] Likewise, it would be simplistic to suggest that various material, legal, and conceptual models inherited from hunting, husbandry, and zoology merely prefigured, or were the precondition for, the racial governance of human populations in the nineteenth century. More promising are the possibilities opened up by a theory of animality capable of accounting for the transferability of operations of power and knowledge across the species line.

Animalization was a common strategy for justifying the subduction and suppression of enslaved and indigenous populations, but it had different effects and worked to different ends. In his 1829 autobiography, for instance, Pequot author and activist William Apess observes that Indians were "hunted like wild beasts" to sanction and enforce their displacement and genocide: "It has been the lot of the unfortunate aborigines of this country," Apess continues (quoting Washington Irving), "to be doubly wronged by the white man—first, driven from their native soil by the sword of the invader, and then darkly slandered by the pen of the historian. The former has treated them like beasts of the forest; the latter has written volumes to justify him in his outrages."[86] In her 1861 narrative of captivity and escape from slavery, Harriet Jacobs writes that enslaved women are "put on a par with animals" insofar as they are "considered of no value, unless they continually increase their owner's stock."[87] Without disputing the many commonalities in the treatment of Native American and black populations in the nineteenth century, these two examples illustrate the different functions performed by animalization, as well as the role of gender and sexuality in the constitution of the animalized subject.[88] What these examples reveal is that while animalization serves to naturalize racist hierarchies, it is not a straightforward strategy because "animal" is not a stable category (in Apess's narrative, it refers to a vermin to be eliminated; in Jacobs's, to an investment to grow and multiply). Animalization, crucially, does not hinge on an a priori ontological caesura between humans and animals; rather, as Zakiyyah Iman Jackson argues, we must understand how "the categories of *race* and *species* have coevolved and are actually *mutually reinforcing* terms."[89] Animality and humanity are thus by no means incompatible, nor do they operate binaristically. New World Slavery did not imply a process of dehumanization of African subjects so much as an animalization of their humanity; animalization, here, is not a simple denial of humanity but a biopolitical "technology for producing a *kind* of human" for whom "humanization and captivity go hand in hand."[90]

Instead of petitioning for the integration of excluded subjects into a normative concept of humanity inherited from Enlightenment thought, Jackson, like Wynter, proposes to attend to the alternative forms of humanity invented and performed by black communities. Glen Sean Coulthard likewise warns against "liberal politics of recognition" and inclusion that "promises to reproduce the very configurations of colonialist, racist, patriarchal state power that Indigenous peoples' demands for recognition have historically sought to transcend."[91] Because I understand capture to be, at its core, continuous with the projects of white settler colonialism and of the biopolitical management, regulation, and subjugation of racialized populations, I find invaluable resources in the tactics and stories of indigenous "survivance" deployed by Gerald Vizenor and elaborated by Jodi Byrd,[92] as well as in the counterpolitics and epistemologies of fugitivity advanced by critical race scholars such as Stephen Best, Saidiya Hartman, and Britt Rusert.[93] Survivance, for Vizenor, is irreducible to the narratives of survival in which dominant U.S. culture "trapped" Native populations in the first half of the century (e.g., the trope of the "vanishing American"). Likewise, fugitivity names more than a mere escape from confinement or a preliminary stage leading to a normative ideal of "liberation"; it is an active and creative modality of resistance forged from within and against the terms imposed by captivity and enslavement.

Minoritarian and shadow accounts like those of Jacobs and Apess openly or covertly contested the master narrative of capture that was being developed and disseminated at the time, laying bare the violence and hierarchies that capture actively disavows. Not only did these accounts counter the hegemony of this new regime of knowing and seeing, but they also produced counternarratives and fugitive epistemologies that diverted its tenets to practical, critical, and creative ends, rendering manifest the resistive potential immanent in capture.[94] This book, however, primarily focuses on how representations of the animal—as elusive, precarious, ungraspable—emerged and came to circulate widely through the influential works of figures who had the cultural, racial, and gender capital to popularize a particular way of seeing and understanding animal life. While these iconic figures of nineteenth-century American culture—these all too obvious "representatives of modernity"—registered and prototyped capture, they also wrestled with capture's imperatives and limitations. All entertained ambivalent relations with what the period recognized as scientific objectivity; all registered, more or less critically, the seismic shifts that shook up the life sciences over the century; all expressed anxiety about the epistemic vocation and generic identity of their works.

Although it situates the emergence of capture in the wake of the hunt, this book argues that capture is already immanent in hunting insofar as it expresses the will to know and apprehend animals. Capture emerges both within and after hunting, tracing a genealogy of control through the modern contours of biopolitical regulation in aggregate—a term that harbors a forgotten pastoral inheritance from herding practices (*ad-* ["toward"] and *grex* ["a flock"]).[95] Capture is not an exact science, however, but a continually perfectible and perfected set of technologies and discourses. Subsumed as it may be under stabilizing cognitive structures, strict regulations, and automatized material procedures, the animal is never perfectly seized. The pursuit of the animal, therefore, does not end with capture, hence the need to attend to the logic of the hunt that subtends the regime of capture.

Capture charts a shift in the nineteenth century from animals as potentially knowable to the animal as fundamentally unknowable and examines the representational technologies that propelled this transition. The book is organized into two parts and proceeds chronologically, examining through various figurations of animal containment the critical phases in the installment and intensification of forms of biopower over the nineteenth century. Part I, "Last Vestiges of the Hunt," examines the implications of the hunt's adoption as an epistemic frame in iconic early American cultural production. The first part thus investigates forms of knowledge and representation that are predicated on the possibility of immediate contact with animals just as they are being challenged by and subordinated to new epistemological formations. Part II, "New Genres of Capture," explores what happens when the animal encounter comes to be understood as necessarily mediated. I show that this loss of immediacy was not always perceived as tragic but was productive of literary and visual forms that attempted to apprehend and know the animal at a remove.

Each chapter attends to techniques of knowledge and control prototyped through visual and scientific experiments bent on understanding and ordering animal life, emphasizing one particular dimension, operation, or effect of capture. Chapter 1, "Still Lifes," examines Audubon's creation of an early census of birds through experiments in vision; Audubon, who epitomizes the last vestiges of the regime of hunting, equates seeing with knowing, though he despairs over the tacit equation of knowing and killing. Chapter 2, "Land Speculations," lifts into view the common logic behind land speculation and modern taxonomy in Cooper's *The Prairie,* which enlists a myopic naturalist as the new model of knowing and organizing the natural world; Cooper probes (and derides) the new order of things that conflates knowing with not seeing. Chapter 3, "The Fugitive Animal," explores the rise of early forms of biometric profiling and racial surveillance in Poe's tales of detection, where the animalized is known because it is *unseen*, surmised only through the traces of its passing—a premise that is prefigured by the ways in which Poe eludes the conventions of both knowledge and genre. Chapter 4, "Fabulous Taxonomy," considers the adaptation of anatomic profiling to emergent evolutionary discourses in Hawthorne's *The Marble Faun,* which responds to the changes marked in Poe not by restoring visibility but by developing a poetics and an ethics of unseeing: the refusal to see too much is, in Hawthorne, not a refusal to know but a desire to know differently.

Chapter 5, "The Stock Image," turns to protocinematic experiments to account for the grammar of biocapitalist modernity. It examines how in Muybridge, not seeing opens an alternative modality of knowing that can be used to desubjectify, to break down what is otherwise incomprehensibly continuous—that is, life as the force secretly animating living beings—into discrete, endlessly recombinable elements. This new mode of visual capture does not automatically lead to the destruction of the observed subject, I argue, but can help us rethink the concept of subjectivity. The Conclusion, "Life in Capture," imagines the relationship to animals that is still possible—indeed, that is newly compelled—by an age in which they appear, whether encaged or enframed, always at a remove. It outlines the terms of an ethics of capture—the responsibility toward subjects whose lifeworlds one shares but cannot fully comprehend—by considering what kind of life Martha, the "last passenger pigeon," who outlived her species by four years and tragically embodies the move from animals to "the animal," can be thought to have lived in captivity.

By offering a critical genealogy of the representation of animals as elusive, precarious, and endangered that came to circulate widely in the United States in the nineteenth century, I show that the new animal condition it indexes is deeply continuous with the projects of white settler colonialism and the biocapitalist management of nonhuman and human populations. Indeed, the desire to capture live animals in representation responded to and normalized the systemic disappearance of animals effected by unprecedented changes in the land, the new awareness of species extinction, and the automation of mass slaughter and the mass reproduction of farm animals. Capture names the paradoxical regime of vision by which animals came to be seen as at once unknowable yet understood in advance—a frame by which we continue to encounter animals today.

PART I

LAST VESTIGES OF THE HUNT

— 1 —

STILL LIFES

(AUDUBON)

> I wished to possess all the productions of Nature, but I wished life with them. This was impossible.
> —John James Audubon, *Ornithological Biography*

At the beginning of the nineteenth century in North America, one hunt ended and another began. Even as it was rapidly falling out of common practice, hunting did not disappear. A mode of pursuit that had long been associated with the acquisition of knowledge, hunting became all the more prevalent as a cultural and epistemological logic when new technologies of capture made it less urgent to gain or defend territory against animals and secure the dominance of Man—a category whose self-evidence will be one of this chapter's driving questions. Less of an immediate threat, animals came to be subjected to increasingly more invasive and furtive forms of knowledge and control.

If we believe *The Order of Things,* the nineteenth century discovered the "fantastic new powers" of the animal after its "great threat or radical strangeness had been left suspended or as it were disarmed at the end of the Middle Ages, or at least at the end of the Renaissance."[1] The relative "peace" gained in the aftermath of this disarmament and secured during the classical period constitutes for Foucault the implicit condition for the emergence of the modern animal and its counterpart, Man. While convincing in the Western European context, Foucault's chronology demands to be revised when one turns to North America, where the "great threat" of nature was hardly "left suspended" at the turn of the nineteenth century. It is not until the late 1830s, according to historian Roderick Nash, that the hostile and sublime wilderness—etymologically, "the place of wild beasts"—was converted in the American imaginary into a fragile wildness in need of protection. Nash makes John James Audubon the harbinger of this cultural transformation.[2] And indeed Audubon's *Birds of America* constitutes a fascinating document in which to track the epistemic shift charted in *The Order of Things* while attending to the continuities, sublimations, and residualities specific to the settler-colonial and frontier-oriented context of the nineteenth-century United States.

The hunt offers a compelling paradigm for reading this transformation in its colonial and transatlantic dimension. In the mid-eighteenth century, hunting was still commonly described as a form of war—a relatively equal contest between two opposing sides.[3] A certain epistemophilia that emerged during this period—evidenced in Europe by Buffon's colossal *Histoire naturelle,* Cuvier's epic enterprise of classification, and Darwin's 1831 zoological expedition on the *Beagle* (named after a hunting dog), and in the United States by the monumental collections of naturalists such as John Bartram, Charles Willson Peale, and Alexander Wilson—can be seen as the continuation of the hunt by other means. The shifting valence of hunting from martial to epistemological finds a burgeoning archive in the new prominence of natural history museums and science institutions, which depended on the products of the hunt—and on the elided labor of female, indigenous, and African American subjects—for their specimen collections.[4] Yet this shift did not occur at the same time on both sides of the Atlantic, and the United States, which in the first decades of the nineteenth century did not have much institutional infrastructure to support scientific endeavors (with the notable exception of the Peale Museum in Philadelphia, founded in 1786), often relied on the expertise of European taxonomists.[5] This transatlantic "lag" fostered a different breed of naturalists in America—men who scorned the derivative knowledge of "closet naturalists" and the abstraction of Cuvierian systematics, while at the same time seeking recognition from the European elite who patronized their work. No individual is more representative of this ambivalence than Audubon.

Born in Saint-Domingue in 1785, Audubon emigrated to France in 1791 to flee the Haitian revolution, then to the United States in 1803 to escape conscription into the Napoleonic Wars, taking up the management of his father's estates in Pennsylvania. He began making a name for himself as a producer of scientific documents and works of art at a moment when the United States was eager to uphold and promulgate its intellectual identity. The famed naturalist and artist was—and purposefully fashioned himself as—a hunter (Plate 1). Elisa New notes that he was embedded in a culture "whose 'views' were . . . frequently composed through gun sights,"[6] and his journal entries, observes Daniel Patterson, reveal "the symbiotic relationship between his gun and his paintbrush."[7] Audubon "engaged birds with the intensity (and sometimes the ferocity) of a hunter because hunting was the cultural frame out of which his encounter with birds emerged," writes his biographer Richard Rhodes. "In early nineteenth-century America, when wild game was still extensively harvested for food, observation for hunting had not yet disconnected from observation for scientific knowledge."[8] Hunting thus composed the "cultural frame" of Audubon's artistic and scientific practice, and the gaze of the artist-scientist was inextricable from that of the hunter. The haphazard, hands-on nature of his practice, however, was at odds with the systematic, objective, hands-off ethos of modern science,[9] and it would rapidly become at odds with modern sensibilities.[10] Just a few decades later, Henry David Thoreau would justify giving up hunting on ethical and epistemological grounds. "I sold my gun before I went to the woods," Thoreau declares; "during the last years that I carried a gun my excuse was that I was studying ornithology, and sought only new or rare birds. But I confess that I am now inclined to think that there is a finer way of studying ornithology than this."[11] Unlike Thoreau, who glorifies the experience of losing one's self in the woods, putting himself on the level of the animals he studies, Audubon went to find his specimens in "nature" with the express ambition to bring them back.[12] His practice is thus exemplary of what I call the hunt regime, in which animals appear fundamentally knowable. Whereas Thoreau actively sought to blur the frontier between culture and nature, Audubon extracted animals from their native haunts, a process that was synonymous with knowing them (as suggested by Audubon's signature pun "drawn from nature," which accompanied all his sketches).[13] Yet his art also manifests an attention to something that necessarily eludes the hunter: Audubon despaired of not being able to endow his models with life. "The moment a bird was dead," he laments in his 1831 *Ornithological Biography,* "however beautiful it had been when in life, the pleasure arising from the possession became blunted."[14] A journal entry recounts the epiphany that led him to invent a new drawing technique to animate his paintings: "One day while watching the habits of a paire of Pewees . . . a thought struck my Mind like a flash of light, that nothing after all could ever answer my Anthusiastic desires to represent nature, than to attempt to Copy her in her own Way, alive and Moving!"[15]

It is this irrepressible urge to instill his sketches with life that makes Audubon the pivot between the hunt regime and the capture regime, for while he highlights the labor (as an artist, hunter, and scientist) needed to produce his object, he desperately yearns to render an objective and lifelike image of the bird. On the one hand, he valorizes the hunt as offering a degree of intimacy and proximity with animals that makes his knowledge more authentic; on the other, this same hands-on approach disqualifies him as a scientist during a period when detachment was becoming the guarantor of scientificity. This ostensible delinking of the labor of the hunter from knowledgeable pursuits, I propose, signals an epistemic shift, which has epistemological and ontological consequences for both the object of knowledge and the knowing subject. Yet I argue that observation for hunting and observation for knowledge were not fully disconnected by the pressures of scientific standardization and specialization; instead, at the moment when science is said to have become objective, hunting simply receded from overt consciousness, instead lodging itself within the period's epistemological unconscious.

LIFELIKE

In the foreground of Audubon's *Golden Eagle,* a bird soars into the air, almost too large to be contained by the painting, holding a dead or dying rabbit in its clenched talon (Plate 2) and threatening to exceed the limits of the canvas. In the background, almost imperceptible on the immaculate coat of snow, the hunter (said to be a portrait of Audubon himself) is dwarfed by the majesty of the surrounding massifs. *Golden Eagle* (1833) is part of a series of works intended by Audubon to offer a reliable census and exhaustive representation of the then-exotic feathered fauna of the United States. "My ardent Wish to Compleat a collection of drawings of the *Birds* of our Country, from *Nature* all of Natural *Size,* begun about 15 Years since," he writes to the governor of Arkansas in 1820, "and to Acquire by *occular,* or reliable observations of others the knowledge of their Habits, & residence; makes me wish to travel as far at Least as the Osage Nations on the Arkansas as also along the whole of our Frontiers."[16] While Audubon's depiction of the golden eagle is informed by his careful scrutiny of the animal, the scene is imbued with a distinctively "unnatural" quality. Certainly, Audubon valued the golden eagle for its ornithological singularity, but the allegorical dimension of the scene is undeniable. The impeccable whiteness of the prey amplifies the fierceness of the eagle, which seems to have been recruited as a mascot for the American colonial project.[17] In Audubon's painting, the bird, "a permanent resident in the United States," is soaring westward—like Audubon himself, seeking to travel as far as the Osage Nations—charting the course of the empire's Manifest Destiny.[18]

As art historian Theodore Stebbins notes, *Golden Eagle* was likely modeled after Jacques-Louis David's painting, *Bonaparte Crossing the Alps at Grand-Saint-Bernard* (1800, Plate 3).[19] Richard Rhodes details the commonalities between the two, namely their mirroring color schemes, the pointing gesture of Bonaparte's hand that is reproduced in the eagle's beak, and the upward trajectory of their nearly identical landscapes:

> Light flooding into both pictures from the upper left illuminates the eagle and its white prey as it illuminates Napoleon and his white horse. The drop of blood sweating from the hare's torn eye duplicates a red touch of embroidery at Napoleon's waist. But the conqueror and his rearing white horse combine in the eagle into one magnificent raptor, urging upward: the eagle's beating wings duplicate Napoleon's golden, wind-swirled cape, while the eagle's open-beaked cry is the horse's open-mouthed whinny and the eagle's glare of defiance is the horse's bulging wild eye.[20]

The eagle occupies the position of Napoleon (and his horse), and Audubon positions himself as a simple, horseless soldier. Despite this seeming modesty, Rhodes observes, the two paintings are crucially different in one element of their representation: unlike David's heroic model, the fictional Audubon has already climbed the mountain and is represented "shinnying down the chasm with his prize."[21] If Napoleon is the eagle, then what are we to make of the dead eagle on the hunter's shoulder?

If we read this picture as a parodic rewriting of the Louisiana Purchase, it hails the naturalist in buckskins as victorious over the emperor adorned with all the attributes of sovereignty. Conquering the New Continent through hard work and firsthand observation, the humble hunter of French descent succeeds where the great Napoleon had failed; the hunter-naturalist affirms his new identity as an American by substituting for Napoleon's elaborate semiotics of power the uncontrived natural aura of the bird of prey. Audubon's painted triumph also has the flavor of personal revenge, for in 1803 (the year of the Louisiana Purchase), Audubon's father had enjoined his son to flee France to avoid being drafted into Napoleon's army. In an autobiographical sketch titled "Myself," Audubon recalls that his father had frequently traveled to "that portion of our Southern States called . . .

FIGURE 5. Film still from *John James Audubon: Drawn from Nature,* 2007. Artist Walton Ford demonstrates Audubon's technique of posing the dead animal on a grid in order to draw it. The cage-like grid was then obliterated by the landscape painted over it.

Louisiana, then owned by the French Government."[22] When Audubon landed in the United States, he forged his passport, changed his name from Jean-Jacques to John James, and indicated that he had been born in Louisiana. The *Golden Eagle* is all at once a scientific document, a work of art, a political pamphlet, a declaration of America's artistic and scientific independence, and a self-mythology.

This emblematic reading of the painting invites a closer examination of the place occupied by Audubon's oeuvre in representing and disseminating the U.S. imperial project.[23] Replacing the figure of Napoleon with that of the fierce raptor enlists the motif of the hunt to naturalize colonial conquest and even perhaps to change its nature: the hunter-colonizer appears to be not a foreign power imposing itself by means of arbitrary and external violence but a modest huntsman whose conquest is sanctioned by the unstoppable violence of a boundless Nature of which he is but a part.[24] The naturalization and, as we will see in the next chapter, indigenization of the hunter is characteristic of the insidious logic of settler colonialism.

The symbolic reading that Audubon's painting invites underlines its unnaturalness, its patent lack of realism—a lack that is strongly conveyed by the rigid quality of the animals portrayed: the eagle and the hare appear to have just escaped from a taxidermist's workshop. Although Audubon is known for the eidetic quality of his paintings, here he presents us with something more closely resembling a *nature morte,* or still life. And as it happens, it was indeed a still life. "My drawings have all been made after individuals fresh killed, mostly by myself," Audubon explains, "and put before me by means of wires, &c. in the precise attitude represented, and copied with a closeness of *measurement* that I hope will always correspond with *nature* when brought into contact. The many foreshortenings unavoidable . . . have been rendered attainable by means of square of equal dimensions affixed both on my paper and immediately behind the subjects before me."[25] Though this method is reminiscent of long-established techniques for drawing real life models (Figure 5), Audubon does not use the grid to "allow for shifts in scale," art historian Jennifer L. Roberts argues, but rather "to map out the precise details and contours for transfer from the bird to the page."[26] Less icons than indexes, Audubon's drawings dreamed to present the thing itself.[27] What Roberts calls Audubon's "pictorial preservation" is a last-resort strategy—one premised, ironically, on the death of his models; Audubon killed his models in order to fix them, to stave off their disappearance.[28]

Despite its indexical fidelity—in fact, because of it—Audubon's technique explains the pictorial rigor mortis of his productions. The paintings' vivid colors and action-packed dramaturgy do not offset what Branka Arsić calls Audubon's "mortification of nature," which makes "his famous bird drawings appear as faces of death, with thick, continuous lines forever imprisoning the birds in their forms, as if those lines were thus themselves an immutable category enabling the setting of taxonomies."[29] Indeed, the violence that underpins Audubon's attempt to capture and fix animals upon his canvas is played up by the contemporary American artist Walton Ford. In his 2004 *Delirium,* Ford (who specializes in large-scale animal watercolors) painted a kind of satire of Audubon's *Golden Eagle* that foregrounds the destructive methods that Audubon's paintings hide (Plate 4). With its smoking beak, its claw caught in a leghold trap, and a small metal dart piercing its heart, Ford's raptor seems at first glance to have been taken from a book of fables. And yet, as we will see, *Delirium* is more historically accurate than Audubon's original.

One needs to read the promotional text that accompanied *The Birds of America* to know the backstory of Audubon's acquisition of his model for *Golden Eagle.* We learn from his *Ornithological Biography* that Audubon did not hunt the bird, as the painting suggests. He bought it from the proprietor of Boston's Columbian Museum, Ethan Allen Greenwood, who had asked him to identify a live eagle purchased from a New Hampshire fox hunter who accidentally caught the bird in his spring-traps. Audubon, having brought his new acquisition home, confesses to his fascination with the bird, introducing it to his readers as his "captive" and "royal prisoner"—a regal descriptor that supports the insurgent reading of Audubon's repudiation of French Empire and allegiance to American democracy:

> The bird was produced [by Greenwood], and as I directed my eye towards its own deep, bold, and stern one, . . . I determined to obtain possession of it. The Eagle was immediately conveyed to my place of residence, covered by a blanket, to save him, in his adversity, from the gaze of the people. I placed the cage so as to afford me a good view of the captive, and I must acknowledge that as I watched his eye, and observed his looks of proud disdain, I felt towards him not so generously as I ought to have done. At times I was half inclined to restore to him his freedom, that he might return to his native mountains; nay, I several times thought how pleasing it would be to see him spread out his broad wings and sail away towards the rocks of his wild haunts; but then, reader, some one seemed to whisper that I ought to take the portrait of the magnificent bird; and I abandoned the more generous design of setting him at liberty, for the express purpose of shewing you his semblance.[30]

The "little voice" that tells him to execute the animal, which he attributes to his scientific instinct, may also be a product of Audubon's uneasiness with the gaze of the animal, who defiantly returns the naturalist's observing gaze. Unlike Ford, Audubon renders the eagle's face as distinctly anthropomorphic, and in this passage, the pronouns he uses to describe the bird tellingly shift from "it" to "him."[31] Audubon genders the bird male—a decision that seems not the outcome of a careful anatomic examination (in his notes, he describes the specimen as an adult female) but of an irrepressible rivalry between humans and animals, one that Audubon often dramatized in his paintings.[32]

Resolved to "take the portrait of the magnificent bird," Audubon found the specimen too challenging to draw from life. He first considered electrocuting the eagle but decided instead on asphyxiation, deeming this method "the easiest for ourselves, and the least painful to him." He shut the bird in a small room with a pot of burning charcoal. "I waited, expecting every moment to hear him fall down from his perch," he writes, "but after listening for hours, I opened the door, raised the blankets, and peeped under them amidst a mass of suffocating fumes. There stood the Eagle on his perch, with his bright unflinching eye turned towards me, and as lively and vigorous as ever!" He repeated the operation several times, but the animal refused to die:

> We were nearly driven from our home in a few hours by the stifling vapours, while the noble bird continued to stand erect, and to look defiance [*sic*] at us whenever we approached his post of martyrdom. His fierce demeanour precluded all internal application, and at last I was compelled to resort to a method always used as the last expedient, and a most effectual one. I thrust a long pointed piece of steel through his heart, when my proud prisoner instantly fell dead, without even ruffling a feather.[33]

This violence that lies behind the image is what Ford brings to the fore in his satire of Audubon's composition. Yet Ford does not simply capitalize on the irony that made Audubon kill the animal in order to reintroduce it pictorially, as if alive, in its natural habitat; he also satirizes Audubon's self-mythology and revisionist tendencies. Indeed, it is not just the material event of the bird's putting to death that Ford's painting exposes but rather the specific (transactional) form of violence that Audubon's painting artfully conceals by presenting himself as a hunter. In *Golden Eagle,* the naturalist dressed in hunting gear proudly carries a dead eagle on his back, although we remember that Audubon purchased the bird from the director of a museum, who himself had bought it from a poacher who accidentally caught the bird in a trap set for foxes.

The mise en abyme is all the more remarkable because *Golden Eagle* is the only painting of Audubon's to include a human character, and all the more intriguing because Audubon is not usually regarded as a particularly self-reflexive painter. In Ford's watercolor, the figure of a hunter lies in the snow, as if dead. In *Golden Eagle,* the hunter is very much alive and active. He appears comically small, almost irrelevant, yet the whole scene is depicted from his perspective. Audubon's hunter sees the world from below, but Audubon-the-painter adopts a God's-eye (or bird's-eye) view—an omniscient perspective. The painting literalizes the problem that representation poses to objective knowledge, which posits an irreducible distance between the knowing subject and the object known. If the hunter depicted in the margin of Audubon's painting is intended to represent the painter himself, then the scene that he observes both from above and below exposes the irreconcilable dualism of the modern observer. This dualism is also seen in the image of the eagle itself, the object of the painting. Audubon renders two versions of what appears to be the exact same eagle, simultaneously captured (on the hunter's shoulder) and free (as a bird). The fact that the eagle is at once dead and alive in the picture, like Schrödinger's cat in his box, implicitly correlates the killing of the empirical animal and its transformation into a representative specimen. In *Golden Eagle,* Audubon is simultaneously the naturalist fascinated with apprehending the live creature and the painter who must sacrifice the object for the sake of his own artistic execution: "I wished to possess all the productions of nature," he confesses in his biography, "but I wished life with them. This was impossible."[34]

THE EXECUTION OF THE SUBJECT

How are we to understand what Audubon experiences as a representational aporia? How are we to read his confessional impulse in *Ornithological Biography* (a title that binds life-writing with the study of birds) and his autobiopictorial impulse in *Golden Eagle*? What is the relationship between subject formation, animal death, and representation? This section is an implicit engagement with Derrida's claim that the "calculation of the subject"—who in Western modernity is traditionally male, adult, white, and carnivorous—rests on a foundational "sacrifice" of animal and animalized others.[35]

In his own animal biography, *The Animal That Therefore I Am (Following),* Derrida borrows the motif of the hunt to expose the disavowed violence that founds the Man/animal dyad and to challenge the right "men have given themselves" to say "I." Derrida exploits a semantic ambiguity in the French language in order to challenge the grounds of an anthropological ontology—surreptitiously sustained by a hunting logic that, elsewhere, I have called "huntology"—that frames an untold multiplicity of living beings in the homogenizing concept "the animal." Western thought, Derrida asserts, has from its inception sought to secure an ontological difference between Man and animal by peremptorily annexing the right to say "je suis" and systematically depriving animals of the capacity to respond. The title of his essay, "L'Animal que donc je suis," plays on the double meaning of this "je suis," which can mean both "I am" and "I follow." Derrida tricks language and forces his reader into identifying with the animal ("I am the animal") while simultaneously recognizing the distance maintained by the one who chases or goes after the animal ("I am following the animal"). The phrase "l'animal que je suis" maddeningly collapses the assumed atemporality of the utterance "I am" with the sequentiality of "I follow." The conceit lays out how the animal pursuit tacitly shapes Man himself. Derrida thus allows us to apprehend anthropogenesis—the making of Man—as a relational economy that disavows its relationality and rationalizes or naturalizes its predatory constitution. He dramatizes the elision of relation, the erasure of the animal's exclusion, which conditions the emergence of "the human"—and a fortiori modern Western Man, this figure that arrogates to itself the right to "call[] itself human."[36] Derrida's formulation strongly echoes Wynter's critique of European Man's overrepresentation of itself "as if it were the human itself."[37] And while Derrida does not explicitly engage racism and colonialism in his work on the animal, Zakiyyah Iman Jackson notes that his project remains useful for theorizing the animalization of racialized subjects insofar as it seeks to unsettle "Man's exceptionalism and epistemological grounding, his own claim to dominance and legitimation."[38] Bringing his analysis of sacrificial violence to bear on "the American racial scene," Jackson argues that the "heteropatriarchal manhood that Derrida questions *arises out of and is consolidated under the conditions of antiblack slavery* and its afterlife, such that blackness itself qualifies one for sacrifice."[39] This added dimension is all the more compelling in Audubon's case given recent speculations about the painter's own biracialism (Audubon was officially the natural child of his father's chambermaid Jeanne Rabin, but some speculate that his mother might have been Sanitte Bouffard, who was mixed race).[40]

I do not dispute the thesis that a general "noncriminal putting to death" (Derrida's definition of sacrifice) underwrites the erection of the Western subject and underlies the right to say "I," but I wish to pause on Derrida's use of the word *sacrifice,* which in principle implies a minimal degree of ritualization.[41] What kind of subject is produced when putting-to-death becomes systematized, deritualized, and concealed (as is the case in Western secularized societies, where the consumption of animal products has never been higher but where the slaughtering of animals takes place out of sight)? What do we glimpse when we read Audubon's image for what it cannot or will not show when it comes to animal death, and what do these elisions reveal about the making of its maker? In modern criticism, it is now commonplace to denounce the murderous practices that underwrite Audubon's oeuvre, pointing out that it is only historical amnesia that today makes his name synonymous with conservation and species protection.[42] Of course, Audubon belonged to a time before the notion of species extinction became widely accepted as a scientific reality, although he

FIGURE 6. Walton Ford, *Sensations of an Infant Heart*, 1999. Watercolor, gouache, pencil, and ink on paper, 59 ½ × 40 ½ inches (151.1 × 102.9 cm). Courtesy of the artist and Paul Kasmin Gallery.

(rather belatedly) came to realize—and publicize—the fact that his dear birds were becoming endangered, in part because of overhunting.[43] My interest here is not to adjudicate his hypocrisy or culpability; instead, I wish to reflect on the exceptional position occupied by the observing subject in his work, which, I argue, is the source of the seeming contradiction between violence and conservation, between his proclaimed intention to render his subjects "with life" and the fact that his "birds are rendered at the moment of the kill."[44]

To account for the predatory character of Audubon's ornithological pursuits, many have turned to a passage from Audubon's journals. In this autobiographical meditation, titled "Myself," Audubon recalls an incident from his youth in Saint-Domingue "that perhaps did lead [him] to love birds, and finally to study them with pleasure infinite":[45]

> My mother had several beautiful parrots and some monkeys, one of the latter was a full-grown male of a very large species. One morning, while the servants were engaged in arranging the room I was in, "Pretty Polly" asking for her breakfast as usual, "Du pain au lait pour le perroquet Migonne [*sic*]," the man of the woods probably thought the bird presuming upon his rights in the scale of nature; be this as it may, he certainly showed his supremacy in strength over the denizen of the air, for, walking deliberately and uprightly toward the poor bird, he at once killed it, with unnatural composure. The sensations of my infant heart at this cruel sight were agony to me. I prayed the servant to beat the monkey, but he, who for some reason preferred the monkey to the parrot, refused. I uttered long and piercing cries, my mother rushed into the room, I was tranquillized, the monkey was forever afterward chained, and Migonne [*sic*] was buried with all the pomp of a cherished lost one.[46]

This excerpt stages a competition between two archetypally anthropomorphic animals, representing the two "sides" of man: the talking parrot—on the side of logos, ethereal grace, innocence, freedom—versus the ape—on the side of mimicry, brute force, criminality, captivity. Between its erotic and Oedipal subtexts, and the racial, gender, and social tensions that animate it, this scene—which is uncannily redolent of Poe's "Murders in the Rue Morgue"—is ripe for all kinds of allegorical interpretations.[47] Indeed, Walton Ford gives at least five different pictorial renditions of the episode (Figure 6). According to Christopher Iannini, who attends to Audubon's anxiety about uncertainties surrounding his birth and racial identity, this episode is an emblematic "recasting of the Haitian revolution";[48] along similar lines, Nicholas Mirzoeff sees it as "a primal scene of the white supremacist imagination;"[49] and Christoph Irmscher and Michael Ziser interpret it as a veiled confession of Audubon's deep-seated ambivalence, asking whether the painter kills to represent or represents to kill.[50] All, however, concur that this scene, in which the autobiographical and the historical collide and interanimate one another, is key to understanding Audubon as a representative subject of his time.

The self-cogitations articulated in this autobiographical vignette are also on display in *Golden Eagle.* The painting replays the same racial paranoia: a dark, wild beast swoops on a defenseless white hare, and the hunter heroically intervenes to right this wrong. If Audubon represents himself as a bird killer, however, his beautiful rendition of the eagle distinguishes him from the uncouth hunter, and from the simian "man of the woods" (a phrase that curiously invokes Audubon himself, who sometimes went by Jean-Jacques La Forêt), who violently ends the bird's life.[51] In the painter's hands, death is rendered beautiful; it appears continuous with nature—and, paradoxically, with life itself.

In fact, it is precisely this representation of death-in-life (or life-in-death) that enables the painter's strange omniscient subject position. According to Ziser, in Audubon's work, death "is present not as a hidden, vitiating subtext of historical violence but rather as an emphatically present point of reference from which the condition of mortality, shared by bird and man, as enabling subjective perception is acknowledged."[52] The dynamic of the hunt engages the life not just of the hunted but also, dialectically, of the hunter. Their destinies are deeply entwined. Indeed, one may go so far as to perceive the hunter as himself "becoming bird," perched as he is on a fallen tree—a dangerously precarious position, balanced over a precipice. Yet if death is everywhere present in Audubon—if, in fact, it is the condition for representation itself—the putting-to-death in Audubon's journals is not as explicit as it may seem. Ziser, for instance, detects a subtle concealment of violence in Audubon's journals: "It is more than a curious fact that, even though he did a fair amount of his own hunting, Audubon rarely used the pronoun 'I' with the verbs 'killed' or 'shot' in his journal. . . . This is true, at least, when the animal killed is an insectivore or herbivore. When a raptor or carrion feeder is involved, however,

Audubon does tend to use the 'I.'"[53] The subject is more likely to assert its (grammatical) sovereignty when opposed to a worthy challenger.

Audubon's selective dissimulation of violence is perhaps less curious when we approach his work through the lens of what I have in the introduction called the "biopolitics of vision." What tends to disappear in biopolitical modernity, we recall, is not death itself so much as the deliberate and conspicuous action of putting to death; it is not the fact of death but the sovereign right to kill—what Achille Mbembe calls "necropower"—that is repressed, rationalized, or naturalized.[54] This does not mean that sovereignty's old right "to take life or let live" suddenly ceased to be exercised, only that it came to be supplemented by a new type of "power" that "does not erase the old right but which does penetrate it, permeate it."[55] Foucault traces the emergence of this new power to transformations in the "theory of right"—though he carefully distinguishes it from the legal lexicon of "rights," which construes its subject as citizen. According to Foucault, these transformations originate in the seventeenth-century theories of contract insofar as they postulate subjects that enter into a contract "in order to protect their lives." Perpetually anxious, always under threat, the contractual subject abandons his right to kill in order to stay alive. Taking the example of Hobbes, Foucault explains that the Leviathan's power can no longer be a power to take life because the sovereign's mission is precisely to guarantee that its subjects will not kill one another. Insofar as the sovereign is constituted—Hobbes writes "authorized"—by subjects who give up their individual sovereignty, life must "remain outside the contract to the extent that it was the first, initial, and foundational reason for the contract itself."[56] Henceforth emancipated from sovereignty, power addresses not just a citizen (a subject of right), nor even just "man-as-individual," as it does with disciplinary apparatuses, but "man-as-living-being," or "man-as-species," through "a 'biopolitics' of the human race."[57]

Audubon's enterprise can be read within the terms of this transformation insofar as his bird census is a requisite for registering the decline or extinction of certain avian species. Audubon is a biographer of birds, but he is also a demographer reporting on their "habits" (mating rituals, migration patterns) and providing information about the milieu in which they thrive. Even though we remain far from the precise technologies measuring fertility and mortality rates that Foucault describes, we can see how *The Birds of America* participated in this development. What interests me here, however, is Audubon's persistent trouble with the question of "life," which he consistently frames as a representational problem. If the act of representation is equal to the act of killing, it raises the question of how the painter should represent himself to his readers. I suggested above that fashioning himself as a hunter did not merely gratify Audubon's European patrons' stereotypes of the U.S. frontiersman (although it did). It also served to authenticate Audubon's scientific enterprise: contrary to the myopic view of European scientists (from whom he actively dissociated himself while courting their approval and patronage), the hunter-naturalist could claim a more intimate and situated knowledge of his object. Posing as a hunter also enabled him to justify the violences he committed in the name of scientific progress. A true man of nature, the hunter naturalizes his right to kill—in the case of *Golden Eagle,* he converts it into self-defense, a right to protect his own life (in the painting, the miniature hunter appears as a potential prey for the gigantic raptor). If he occupies the sovereign position of knower, this position is strategically made to appear precarious, unstable, contingent, and thus legitimately earned.

We can also understand Audubon's selective effacement of the predatory "I" in the terms of Foucault's analysis of the inception of the modern subject of biopolitics. Foucault's study of Diego Velázquez's 1656 painting, *Las Meninas,* which opens *The Order of Things,* offers a reading of classical perspectivalism, which is founded on an irreducible invisibility. Of the epistemic model presented by Velázquez, Foucault observes that "the profound invisibility of what one sees is inseparable from the invisibility of the person seeing—despite all mirrors, reflections, imitations, and portraits." Something—the author, the beholder, the viewing subject—is necessarily left out of the frame: "the function of that reflection is to draw into the interior of the picture what is intimately foreign to it: the gaze which has organized it and the gaze for which it is displayed."[58] If the entire world were captured in the representation, it would not be a representation but the world itself—or the world would be pure representation. This impossible coincidence between the subject and its representation heralds the modern excision of the human observer from the world it represents precisely so that the world can present itself, without human intervention—in other words, objectively. Velázquez insists upon this representational divide, but, as Foucault suggests, the separation is also an elision of the subject, which cannot know itself (or for which self-knowledge is not a question). This subject will only be fully emancipated from its object, Foucault claims, in the nineteenth century. This emancipation underlies the birth of the modern subject, who comes to be simultaneously subject and object of knowledge. What happens in modernity could be characterized as the elision of the classical elision, a second-degree invisibilization, a naturalization of the unrepresentable sovereign position that is occupied by the knowing/representing subject. As life becomes this "sovereign vanishing-point, infinitely distant but constituent," modern Man appears by disappearing; Man, quite fundamentally, creates himself by abstracting himself from the world he seeks to describe—just as he creates "the animal" by capturing it.

In her critical reading of *The Order of Things,* Sylvia Wynter insists that Man composes only a small fraction of humanity—a white, male, bourgeois "ethnoclass" that passes for "the human species as a whole."[59] If Man is indeed a recent invention, as Foucault claims, this invention is but a "mutation" that perpetuates the co-option of the status of "full human" for a dominant minority.[60] The discontinuities registered by Foucault's archaeology of the human sciences, Wynter claims, are subtended by the unquestioned continuity of a "cultural field" that maintains a racist "order of existence."[61] Foucault's Man is little more than the biologized and economized iteration of the Enlightened subject of rights, who itself is a rationalized and secularized avatar of the Judeo-Christian subject. Not only has Man consistently erected itself in contradistinction with non-Western and nonwhite others, but it has actively foreclosed the emergence of other "genres of the human" by "overrepresent[ing] itself as if it were the human itself."[62]

At issue is thus the colonization of truth itself by and through representation: the truth once believed to be "supernaturally ordained" has been secularized into an ostensibly supracultural "objective" truth.[63] One "cannot 'unsettle' the 'coloniality of power,'" Wynter asserts, "without a redescription of the human outside the terms of our present descriptive statement of the human, Man, and its overrepresentation."[64] We must take "overrepresentation" literally, as it names a problem of self-presentation: the problem, namely, of a representation that does not offer itself as representation but seeks to pass for the thing itself.

Audubon worked on *The Birds of America* during the transition to the new relationship between observing subject and the world that Foucault describes. Thus, his work reflects the classical episteme just as it was being challenged by the modern episteme—the logic of the hunt precisely as it was shifting into the logic of capture. Lorraine Daston and Peter Galison firmly situate Audubon in a time before "mechanical objectivity" became the predominant epistemic virtue, noting that his "bird drawings were printed on double elephant folio paper in order to approximate life size as closely as possible" but "did not preclude mannered compositions . . . or anthropomorphic stances."[65] They remind us that Audubon's paintings were "criticized by some contemporary naturalists as falsifications of nature" (although a similar artistic method had won English naturalist George Edwards the Royal Society of London's Copley Medal in 1750).[66] Ann Shelby Blum also contends that the "ethos of objectivity, expressed in the technical language of systematic description of generic and specific types, was deeply at odds with Audubon's celebration of the observer as participant and his recording of singular events whose actors were individual creatures."[67] Branka Arsić likewise compares Audubon's epistemological orientation with that of his collaborator, English zoologist Thomas Nuttall, positioning Audubon within the classical episteme, in a time when "life itself didn't exist":

> Even though Audubon and Nuttall collaborated for many years and on many projects, their approaches to ornithology are different, indeed

> so much so that one can claim their methodologies belong to different centuries. Audubon's is from the eighteenth century. Following eighteenth-century models of natural history—the classicist belief in allotting to each creature its proper category, trusting that the world can be exhausted through extensive descriptions—Audubon seeks to distribute life into fixed tiers or, as he puts it, to organize specimens "according to [his] notions." Since the specimens are more likely to fit notions when dead, Audubon contrives and ideates method of representing birds, rendering them as programmable automatons.[68]

Audubon's drawings, which (in the words of Arsić) forever imprison his birds in "immutable categor[ies] enabling the setting of taxonomies,"[69] reveal that he represents the epistemic regime that Daston and Galison call "truth-to-nature," whose ambition is to reveal "the one and only ur-form of a plant, animal, or crystal."[70] While I do not contest this categorization, I wish to mark how painfully aware Audubon was of the changing demands of a discipline that he "had entered as an inexperienced, if enthusiastic, autodidact."[71]

While Audubon willfully emphasized his firsthand observations of animals, he also questioned the reliability of the naked eye as an instrument of knowledge. Jennifer Roberts argues that his adamant commitment to actual-size representation stems from a deep-seated distrust in "eyeballing." For Roberts, this distrust—which he shares with a character in Cooper's *The Prairie* whom we will meet in the next chapter—was primarily meant to safeguard the American landscape and wildlife against the logics of abstraction and exchange to which they were increasingly subjected in the first decades of the century.[72] Yet Audubon's "near-indexical" method, his proto-photographic technique of direct "transfer from body to page,"[73] also betrays his wariness toward the naked eye's susceptibility to deception, a wariness characteristic of the representational regime Daston and Galison call "mechanical objectivity."[74] The classical "truth-to-nature" model, in which Daston and Galison situate Audubon, relies on the selective observation of the experienced artist-naturalist, who aims to represent the fundamental "type" of the species; conversely, the "mechanical

FIGURE 7. John James Audubon, *Golden Eagle, Aquila chrysaetos.* Collection of the New-York Historical Society. Digital image created by Oppenheimer Editions.

objective" paradigm wishes to completely disarticulate the knowing subject from the known object, for in the mechanical objectivity model, the self qua subject is identified as the source of error and thus must be eliminated.[75] The emergence of the new ethos of objectivity may explain why, when *The Birds of America* was published, the hunter in the original *Golden Eagle* painting had disappeared from the background (Figure 7).

"Whether on his own or on Audubon's instruction," Rhodes notes, the printer "Robert Havell removed the little woodsman from the plate he made of the *Golden Eagle,* . . . removing along with it a level of meaning that only the original watercolor has sustained."[76] Something is lost, as Rhodes laments, but the elision itself is meaningful. We can only speculate as to why the figure of the hunter was excised from the painting's background. It could be, as Irmscher surmises, that Havell eliminated it "for reasons of consistency: in *The Birds of America,* humans are only represented metonymically through buildings in the backgrounds of plates featuring, as a rule, waterfowl or shorebirds."[77] Or we could read this erasure of the toiling self, as I have suggested, as a retroactive disavowal of the violent extraction on which the self is unavowably premised and as a negative guarantee of the painting's objectivity.[78] Audubon's self-erasure would literalize the effacement that constitutes the figure Foucault identifies as modern Man—which in the eighteenth century, Foucault writes, "did not exist (any more than life)."[79] Unlike *Las Meninas,* whose ingenious composition is always chasing its subject out of the frame, forbidding it from being at one with the world it represents, Audubon's elision surreptitiously reconciles the observer and the observed.[80] Whereas Velázquez insists on the dilemma of the spectator/subject, exposing their impossible coincidence, Audubon—in the published version of *Golden Eagle*—negates the creative gap between the self and the world; the observer born out of this elision is left to proudly contemplate its own image in the representation of the animal.

LAND SPECULATIONS

(COOPER)

> Now the hunter steps aside . . . and the naturalist comes forward.
>
> —Richard Rhodes, *John James Audubon*

The erasure of the figure of the hunter from Audubon's *Golden Eagle* that closes chapter 1 finds an echo in the disappearance of one of the nineteenth-century United States' most popular fictional heroes, Natty Bumppo, whom James Fenimore Cooper introduces from the outset as the representative of a species destined for extinction. *The Pioneers,* the first installment of the *Leatherstocking* chronicle, opens with the transformation of Cooper's iconic huntsman into a poacher. The very first scene of *The Pioneers* (1823) recounts a dispute between Judge Temple and Natty Bumppo (and his companion Oliver Effingham) over whether a buck slain on Temple's land belongs to the hunter who killed the deer or to the settler who owns the land. The hunter wins the argument, but Temple brings the buck home, demonstrating that land ownership trumps hunting as a mode of acquisition, despite the undisputed merits of the latter (more noble and manly, less wasteful). The dispute replays early nineteenth-century legal debates over the "rule of capture" that underwrites the privatization of resources perceived as unowned, or "naturally fugitive."[1] "The basic conflict," Cooper scholar Kay Seymour House argues, "is between two guardians of the land, and the basic realignment of forces comes when young Oliver Effingham abandons Natty's idea of land use (hunt it as the Indians did) and joins Judge Temple in cultivating it."[2] Although this reading is accurate from a narrative point of view, House's framing symptomatically excludes the Native Americans from the dispute, or rather includes them as mere analogies ("hunt it as the Indians did"). Just as Temple's daughter Bess and his black slave Agamemnon are not invited to weigh in on the debate—"Aggy . . . can't vote, being a slave; and Bess is a minor"—the indigenous people remain without an active voice and, unlike the other two, without a presence.[3] This invisible silencing replays the historical exclusion of Native Americans from land treaties and more broadly sheds light on the process of "enclosure" that worked to dispossess them of their territories.[4]

The expropriation and privatization of Indian ground encapsulated in this foundational scene is the tacit condition for the "settling" of a capitalist system of exchange and circulation, an economic arrangement that is initiated and made secure by a process of deterritorialization—the violent conversion of territories into an isonomized land infinitely divisible into salable parcels. To understand the conceptual "origin" of this deterritorialization, Eric Cheyfitz turns to John Locke, who famously chooses the untenured "wastes" of the Americas—on which lives "the wild Indian, who knows no Inclosure, and is still a Tenant in common"—as his example of choice to theorize an economy of private property.[5] Locke models this economy after the ancestral practice of the hunt. According to this "original law of nature," Locke explains, wild animals become the property of whoever "labors" to acquire them. The labor of pursuit, in other words, legitimizes acquisition (as a corollary, the fallacious notion that indigenous people did not cultivate the land justified its spoliation by the European colonizers). Yet when the hunt is turned into a "law," the physical event of capture is preempted by an epistemological conversion, which turns the pursued object into property even before it is acquired. In Locke's model, the hunted prey need not be captured in order to be property; instead, his model reconfigures the prey as essentially unowned and therefore always "ripe for the taking." From this perspective, Russ Castronovo concludes, the prey "is always already property."[6] Since, as Locke has it, the pursuit of the hunt is said to "begin" property, the antagonism between the white hunter Bumppo and the settler Judge Temple is less profound than it seems. The people who are truly excluded from the debate are those who have no stake in capitalism's drive to acquire property: women and slaves, who do not own themselves,[7] and indigenous people, for whom the State does not recognize any "notion of property" (as the Supreme Court decreed in the 1823 *Johnson v. Mcintosh*).[8]

Although Locke uses the hunt as a paradigm for the "beginning" of property, he quickly adds that positive rules supersede this primitive or "uncivilized" law of nature: the land and its resources ultimately belong to those who enclose and cultivate them. Similarly, in *The Pioneers,* although Judge Temple did not kill the deer, he takes it home, and Bumppo—accused of committing "offenses against private rights"—is in the end banished from Temple's land.[9] Once indispensable to "taming" the wilderness, the hunter must disappear for the colonial project to appear complete. This dynamic (which should be recognizable as the dynamic of capture) is most evident in the third installment of the *Leatherstocking* saga, *The Prairie* (1827), which stages Bumppo's death at the dawn of the nineteenth century. The hunter's demise, which Cooper's romance situates in the context of the Louisiana Purchase, marks a critical transition in modes of colonial conquest and land management. It also accounts for the systemic "disappearance of animals" from the American landscape. *The Prairie* makes these transitions explicit by pairing Bumppo's erasure with the rise of an unassuming character, the shortsighted taxonomist Obed Bat. By replacing his perspicacious hunter with a myopic naturalist, Cooper presents the disappearance of the hunter as effected less by an empirical than by an epistemological transformation, a transformation in regimes of vision. Cooper openly laments the loss of a more embodied and immediate relationship to nature by making the pitiful figure of the naturalist emblematic of newly prominent types of vision—namely, scientific and economic speculation. Yet he also calls attention to discreet but significant continuities between the forms of vision epitomized by the white hunter and the naturalist. In so doing, the romance recognizes the hand of capture in the predatory operations of land expropriation and speculation and their consequences for both animals and animalized populations.

From the outset, *The Prairie* depicts the new nation's prosperity and security as predicated on the systematic "taming" of land and human and animal populations. As a romance, it exemplifies the temporality of capture, for romance was already a dying genre at the moment of *The Prairie*'s publication; like the unsettled prairie itself, like the hunt and the hunter, the romance was passing away. Cooper's elegiac celebration of things past seems in retrospect an attempt to lay claim to the American past itself. Romance as a genre, then, is a form appropriate to Cooper's subject, the operations of settler colonialism: it not only represents but performs the strange temporality of the subjugation of land and indigeneity. This subjugation was ongoing, indeed accelerating, at the moment Cooper writes *The Prairie,* but the work depicts it as already accomplished, as belonging to a romantic, quasi-mythological, and resolutely bygone age:[10]

> Most of those who witnessed the *purchase of the empty empire,* have lived to see already a populous and sovereign state, parcelled from its inhabitants, and received into the bosom of the national Union, on terms of political equality. The incidents and scenes which are connected with this legend, occurred in the earliest periods of the enterprises which have led to so great and so speedy a result.[11]

As indicated in the *Oxford English Dictionary,* the verb *purchase,* which has since become synonymous with "to buy," denotes the acquisition of land by means other than inheritance.[12] From the Middle French *pourchasser,* to "chase" or "hunt down," the term encrypts in its etymology the violent pursuit inherent in the idea of property (which Locke associates with the labor of the hunt) but ultimately distances itself from this originary violence by signaling a rupture. Defining *purchase* in opposition to inheritance breaks the connection between current and previous owners, effectively erasing the land's past and making it appear pristine and "empty." And indeed, the despoliation of Native tribes' land is depicted by Cooper (himself a land speculator) as a peaceable transition and equitable transaction, an inevitable outcome of Manifest Destiny—in a sense, as already having happened.[13] This sense of predestination serves as an act of "legitimation," which, Achille Mbembe argues, always accompanies the "founding violence" of colonial conquest and universalizes the new colonial order.[14] The colonial state posits as "preaccomplished" the violence that founds and sanctions its authority—a "magical" operation that Deleuze and Guattari name "capture."[15]

This chapter reads *The Prairie* to argue that the prospective and preemptive logic of capture it displays hinges on a form of taxonomy, broadly defined as a method (*nomos*) for ordering (*taxis*) the sensible.[16] I show that modern taxonomy—a paradigm whose standardizing logic subtends the gridding and mapping of the United States imposed by the 1785 Land Ordinance and generalized by the Northwest Ordinance of 1787—rests on an operation of vision that is blind to its own limitations. I outline capture as a way of seeing in order to show not only what capture makes visible but also what it obscures, and how the animal and the animalized appear and disappear under capture.

"THE PURCHASE OF EMPTY EMPIRE"

Set in 1805, just two years after the Louisiana Purchase that doubled the country's size, *The Prairie* is fraught with the tensions of U.S. territorial expansion, for it remained to be seen how the young nation would be changed by the acquisition of the vast expanse of land west of the Mississippi River. The titles of Cooper's four other installments of *The Leatherstocking Tales* are based on human characters, but *The Prairie* is titled after its setting, which is strikingly different than the dense woodlands of upstate New York where the first two installments (*The Pioneers* and *The Last of the Mohicans*) had been set. As Cooper describes it, the titular prairie is the last retreat for "the barbarous and savage occupants of the country" and a provisional refuge for those who, like Bumppo, wish to escape the law. Its arid swaths, undulating like a moderately agitated ocean, seem to repel vision, as "the eye [is] fatigued with the sameness and chilling dreariness of the landscape" (13). This monocular, wearied eye cannot read the prairie; indeed, as the narrator observes, only a "practiced reader" will not be deceived by the seeming interminableness and sterility of the landscape (14). How, Cooper asks, does the land both resist and lend itself to representation? How can one navigate the prairie, which the settler's eye perceives as an asemiotic "no man's land"? How does one read and write—"code," "decode," and "overcode," to borrow Deleuze and Guattari's terminology—the blank page of the Louisiana territory?[17]

In the preface to the 1832 edition of *The Prairie,* Cooper presents the as-yet-undomesticated tract of land as a natural frontier blocking further western expansion: "the broad belt, of comparative desert, which is the scene of this tale, appear[s] to interpose a barrier to the progress of the American people westward."[18] But in the American imaginary, the frontier is not simply a demarcation line separating the wild from the civilized; it is also the mythical soil in which the American dream is rooted, the phantasmatic and utopian "elsewhere" that serves as the breeding ground for the creature whom Leslie Fiedler dubs the "New Man, the American *tertium quid.*"[19] Insofar as it traces the perimeter beyond which myth and imagination come to supplant and supplement knowledge, the frontier constitutes at the same time a threat and a promise, both for the emerging nation and for its poet-historian Cooper.[20] As the romance opens, Cooper announces that the challenge for the now-doubled nation will be to tame and supervise its new inhospitable territories and assimilate the animalized "swarms" of nomadic, "restless people . . . hovering on the skirts of American society" (9). What the narrator calls the "empty empire" of Louisiana was, of course, anything but: it was home to many indigenous peoples and an untold number of plants and animals. This paronomastic turn of phrase uses the discourse of the colonizer, whose "eye," as Mary Louise Pratt observes, "produces subsistence habitats as 'empty' landscapes, meaningful only in terms of a capitalist future."[21] This strategic production of emptiness is, as Pratt suggests, not just a rhetorical trick but also a visual one.

"Vision" is an equivocal notion in *The Leatherstocking Tales.* It denotes both the distinctive perceptual faculties of the American eye (emblematized by the hero of the saga, the hunter Natty Bumppo, also known as "Hawkeye") and, at the same time, the typological or "visionary" rhetoric intended to justify and exonerate the white settlers' plunder. Recent scholarship has tended to cast Cooper as "the scapegoat for the national myopia"—to reduce the *Leatherstocking* franchise to an apology for expansionism. However, Elisa New observes that Cooper is anything but myopic. In fact, he devotes "uncommon concentration to verbal transpositions of retinal impressions and much space—proportionally—to lamenting the failures of sight."[22] New concedes that the impressionistic character of Natty's vision (like that of America itself) can function "to accommodate facts to his own projections," seeing in "unsettled American ranges" "bourgeois homes-as-found." Yet, New says, Cooper (and Bumppo) also deploys another type of vision, less rapacious and ignorant, more pragmatic and environmentally respectful—the vision of the hunter: while he "passes into archaism, the range-finding he practices outlives him."[23] Playing empiricism against imperialism (two positions that are by no means incompatible), she detects the survival of the hunter's point of view in the poetry of experience of Dickinson, Moore, and Williams, as well as in the pragmatic philosophy of Thoreau and James, among others. While I find New's corrective valuable, I would nuance her characterization of Cooper's condemnation of U.S. "visionary" expansionism as being the result of "bad visual practices."[24] Cooper does not simply take issue with the settlers' "national myopia" as a mere "failure of sight" or the result of inadequate attention; he also theorizes this myopia in its positivity, asking not just what sight myopia impedes but also what sight it enables and what the specific powers of myopia are. How can we characterize this capacious-yet-blurry regime of vision, which appears undeserving of or indifferent to the phenomenal specificities of America's landscapes? Let us call it speculation.

"Speculation" aptly describes the work of vision in *The Prairie,* if only because Cooper, who was living in Paris at the time he wrote the romance, never set foot on the territory he pictures so vividly. As for his other romances, he drew his inspiration from books, in this case from geologist and botanist Edwin James's *Account of an Expedition from Pittsburgh to the Rocky Mountains* and Nicholas Biddle's edition of Lewis and Clark's notebooks. Moreover, the verb *speculate* is apt because it conjugates seeing in the conditional. To speculate—from *specere,* to look—assumes a form of precognition, or foresight, and it carries a sense of contingency, of imagination, of betting on events to come. In speculation, one perceives objects and subjects as potential investments—a form of seeing that environmental law scholar Jedediah Purdy calls the "providential vision" of the natural world, a perspective that "turned early Americans into an army of settlers . . . even to the point of making settlers blind to the inconvenient facts of weather and geography."[25] "Blindness" here has nothing to do with a lack of eyesight; it is a metaphor for the calculated act of ignoring possible loss—in fact, it names the margin of loss that is built into the venture capital model of settler colonialism.[26]

The Prairie dramatizes this speculative tendency—which Audubon wished to exorcize with his paintings—by contrasting Bumppo's keen and focused eyesight with the large-scale, low-resolution, preemptive mode of vision that Cooper associates with the work of the myopic taxonomist Bat. Taxonomy, in the romance, is introduced as a highly speculative science insofar as it precodes details as significant solely from the vantage of an imagined but intangible whole (*e pluribus unum*). Taxonomic speculation apprehends objects that are meaningless on their own: bodily organs "matter" primarily in terms of the function they perform within a given organism, just as actual individual locations in America were meaningful primarily as topographic "nodes" in Jefferson's grid system.[27] Taxonomy, for Cooper, is a holistic form of vision that sees beyond the detail of the thing itself, that strategically *over*sees or *super*vises. Taxonomy is not only a mode of vision; above all, it is a mode of *di*-vision—of sorting out, splitting up, packaging and parceling into conceptual buckets things that had previously seemed incommensurable and thus undifferentiable.

IMPERIAL PROJECTIONS, IMAGINARY SPECIMENS

In *The Prairie,* the aging Natty Bumppo, once a mighty frontiersman and hunter and now but a "miserable trapper," seems likely to be supplanted as protagonist by his naturalist foil, Dr. Obed Bat (115). We first encounter Dr. Bat (or Battius, as he prefers to be called) in the semidarkness of early dawn, returning from one of his scientific expeditions. Bat is a cartoonish, easily spooked wildlife expert, a poor man's Audubon, with something of a habit of improvising the genus and species of the flora and fauna he encounters. Driven by what we are told is his "thirst for natural history," Dr. Bat has attached himself to the caravan of the Bush family, a nomadic tribe of squatters with whom he is roaming the "virgin territory" of Louisiana in search of untapped natural treasures.

Losing his path back to camp one day, Bat accidentally "discovers" a new species. In retelling the encounter, he boasts of having risked his life "in behalf of mankind" in the hopes of documenting his find. While the hunter Natty Bumppo is inseparable from his gun (his nickname is "la longue carabine"), Bat aligns himself not with the gun but with the pen: he ultimately confesses that his pistol was merely "adapted to the destruction of the larger insects and reptiles" and therefore of too small a caliber to shoot the specimen. Facing down the terrible beast, the man of science fumbles for his notebook. "I did better than to attempt waging a war, in which I could not be the victor," he later says, "I recorded the event" (70). Bat's action (which anticipates the gun camera by a few decades) binds together nonpower and knowledge production, and his rhetoric makes it clear that the martial approach is being replaced—or, more precisely, prolonged, as the comparative "better" suggests—by an epistemological survey.[28] His entry about his discovery, a delectable pastiche of Linnaean taxonomy, discusses how he himself first encountered the animal, which he names *Vespertilio Horribilis Americanus.* He offers a detailed description of the beast's terrifying dimensions (eleven feet long, six feet high) and anatomic characteristics: "*Head,* erect, *nostrils,* expansive, *eyes,* expressive and fierce, *teeth,* serrated and abundant. *Tail,* horizontal, waving and slightly feline. *Feet,* large and hairy. *Talons,* long, arquated, dangerous. *Ears,* inconspicuous. *Horns,* elongated, diverging and formidable. *Colour,* plumbeous-ashy, with fiery spots. *Voice,* sonorous, martial and appalling." After recounting his observations of the animal, Bat sententiously exclaims: "There, . . . there is an animal, which will be likely to dispute with the Lion, his title to be called the King of the Beasts!" (71).

Shortly after, Bat is suddenly terrified at the sight of a dark form running toward him once more. He is convinced that he is again confronted with his newly discovered specimen, only to realize that the form is in fact his faithful donkey, Asinus (whose name is his taxonomic descriptor). It becomes undeniable that it was his own ass that the naturalist was contemplating all along. But Bat blames his mistake on an optical phenomenon known as persistence of vision, in which an image endures after the object seen is no longer present (persistence of vision is how the nineteenth century explained the visual phenomenon of the thaumatrope, whose two faces, when twirled, magically appear to be a single image). "The image of the Vespertilio was *on the retina,*" he explains, "and I was silly enough to mistake my own faithful beast for the monster" (73). Bat prides himself on seeing not "with the organs of sight" but with what he claims are "much more infallible instruments of vision: the conclusion of reason, and the deductions of scientific premises" (105). As a consequence, the good doctor (whose surname teases his lack of clear vision) does not *see* but *oversees* the animal and thus overlooks the particularities of his specimen. "Blinded by hubris," as William Kelly observes, "he extends the ideals of the Enlightenment to a ludicrous extreme," attempting to "impose absolute order on nature through scientific classification."[29] Refusing anatomical coherence, the improbable assemblage he describes proves a chimera, a figment of his own positivist imagination. Bat's monster is quite literally the creature of taxonomy, an index for how his knowledge summons into being what it sets out to describe.[30] Yet if Bat creates a "monster," it is not because he relies too much on his senses or imagination, as Descartes warns, but ironically because he proves to be overly methodical. Part feline, part bovine, part avian, his animal does not elude taxonomy. On the contrary, it lends itself all too easily to the procedures of classification: it is excessively prone to being itemized and captured. Desperate to make the "phenomenal" appearance coincide with a set of preestablished criteria, Dr. Bat is guilty of what Derrida calls a bêtise, a term that David Wills (appropriately for us) translates in the English as an asininity.[31] The naturalist's retina (like his "reason" and his "scientific premises") is a trap in which the animal, even before it exists, is already caught. *Retina* comes from the Latin *rete,* meaning "net," a reference to the retina's fibrous texture. But as the Vespertilio anecdote suggests, this net does not just capture the animal as it is; it operates as a grid through which the animal becomes legible. To a large extent, the encounter between the man of science and the animal was pre-scripted. Trapped in his own system of representation, Dr. Bat sees nothing but a projection of his self (indeed, he literally makes the captured animal in his own image, *vespertilio* being the Latin for "bat").

Bat is an exemplary specimen of the "formulaic, effete, and implicitly feminine European naturalists" despised by American journalist and author of the romance *The Hunter-Naturalist* (1854), Charles Wilkins Webber. Unlike his personal hero Audubon, Webber laments, these "'scientific pedants in silk stockings' and 'pur-blind Professors,' . . . had 'technicalised' the study of nature 'into what may almost be called a perfect whalebone state of sapless system . . . so heavily overlaid by the dry bones of Linnaean nomenclature as to become a veritable Golgotha of Science.'"[32] The rivalry between buckskinned naturalists and the scientific elite reveals another logic at work in the Vespertilio episode. Bat's stated desire to encounter a beast that might prove a match for the lion is a reference to the famous historical contest between French naturalist Georges-Louis Leclerc, Count of Buffon, and Thomas Jefferson. At the time when Cooper situates *The Prairie,* this "arms race" still raged on. When Jefferson appointed Lewis and Clark for their 1804 expedition, he still held out hope that the explorers might find a living mammoth that could compete with the African elephant. Buffon had declared this impossible, for he saw all animals native to the Americas as smaller and weaker than their counterparts in the Old World. In his *Histoire Naturelle,* Buffon famously pondered at length over the assumed absence of large animals in the Americas, ultimately laying the blame on the New World's humid climates. He noted that the elephant, which roamed the Old Continent, was nowhere to be found on the new. The only animal that remotely resembled the elephant was the Brazilian tapir, but this "elephant of the New World," Buffon derided, was but "the size of a six-month-old calf, or a very small mule."[33] According to Buffon, American animals were not essentially different from their Old World cousins—only degraded. The argument went something like this: you in America have the tapir, we have the elephant; you the puma, we the lion; you the llama, we the camel; and so on. Buffon conceded, however, that insects and reptiles flourished in the New World, but only because they were "impure" and "swollen by the humid heat." (Similarly, Buffon noted that the only American domestic animal that grew as large as its Old World counterpart was the pig, but he immediately added that the pig was doomed by birth to a lowly status.) Because of the New World's geotaxonomic inferiority, the "degeneracy" of the New Continent, Buffon argued, all nature was condemned to wither in America's "unripe soil."[34] In so doing, Buffon presented the exploitation of the New World as a moral imperative.

Buffon's theory sparked far-reaching controversy, but it infuriated no one more than Jefferson, who famously devoted a large portion of his *Notes on the State of Virginia* (1785) to documenting how America's animals more than measured up to European (indeed, all Old World) fauna.[35] And soon after his rejoinder was published, Jefferson exhorted Harvard University president Joseph Willard to encourage the study of America's natural history. Yet these refutations came from neither a mere desire to establish the United States' intellectual independence nor a will to correct a scientific wrong, nor were they simply the byproduct of a battle of male egos. Jefferson's ambition was, above all, an economic strategy. His *Notes* were initially written as "an application for a loan" in response to a questionnaire sent by French diplomat François Barbé-Marbois, who, as Napoleon's secretary of the treasury, would later play a crucial role in brokering the Louisiana Purchase.[36] The stakes of Jefferson's game of taxonomic one-upmanship was to convince potential investors of America's economic viability, and animals served as metonyms for the health of the young nation.

I mention this well-known taxonomic controversy not just because the Vespertilio episode alludes to it but because it illustrates how selectively Buffon (like Dr. Bat) relied on empirical observation. In order to appreciate the logic at work in the dispute, one must attend not only to what Buffon saw but also to what he could not or would not see. Buffon's theory required that he overlook the presence (and actual characteristics) of certain animals in order to reconcile two seemingly contradictory phenomena: the supposed absence of large animals, on the one hand, and the attested exuberance of insects and reptiles, on the other. If all of nature was governed by a unique principle, as he posited, how could he account for such different responses to the New World's climate? Buffon's answer was to disregard smaller and lower species as morally degraded. If insects and reptiles prospered outside of Europe, it was because they were constitutionally degenerate, but if they were degenerate, paradoxically, it was because they were small. Antonello Gerbi argues that Buffon's disdain for small animals "was reinforced by [a] particular physiological characteristic of his, namely his shortsightedness, so serious as to prevent him from even using the microscope."[37] To be clear, I am not suggesting that Buffon's taxonomic myopia is merely a matter of his not looking hard or closely enough at America's fauna, as the American naturalist Alexander Wilson asserts, nor am I suggesting that his scientific epoch is characterized by a generalized indifference to empirical fact, for this would imply that increased attentiveness to detail could compensate for the failures of taxonomic vision.[38] It is not just that taxonomy is a problem of vision but that taxonomic vision, in both its classical and modern iterations, appears to be haunted by an irreducible blindness. So one mode or era of scientific knowledge does not see *better* than another, but within each scientific era we find distinctive blind spots—blind spots that must be understood not as impairing vision but as constituting it.[39]

THE PHENOMENOLOGY OF CAPTURE

Cooper's own naturalist suffers from a different type of myopia. He embodies the paradox of the New World, whose novelty remained largely defined and conditioned by the Old World, and personifies the expansionist logic that enlisted natural history in the American imperialist project, in the process taking animals and other beings hostage in a coercive system of classification. But at stake in Cooper's portrayal of Bat is neither merely the Oedipal drama unfolding between the Old and New Worlds nor still the complicity between natural history and empire apparent in the doctor's martial rhetoric. Bat's *libido sciendi* is also symptomatic and emblematic of a transition between two distinct epistemological models, introduced by Cooper's romance as the transition from hunt to capture. Bringing into focus the differences and similarities in the ways Bumppo and Battius approach animals can help us account differently for the precipitous "disappearance of animals" that has characterized the last two centuries. Tellingly, in Bat's confrontation with the Vespertilio there is no "encounter" to speak of, since the sudden appearance (or rather, apparition) of the animal—a dark form emerging from an open field—is immediately caught and replaced with a preposterous taxonomic profile of the scientist's making.

By contrast, when French phenomenologist Maurice Merleau-Ponty chances upon animal life, it is the animal, not the observer, that "invents the visible." The observer receives a disorderly "impression" that surges unexpectedly and wrinkles the smooth veil of invisibility in which the animal (here defined as "a living matter that moves") was hiding:[40]

> We see the protoplasm move, a living matter that moves; to the right is the head of the animal, the left its tail. From this moment on, the future comes before the present. A field of space-time has been opened: there is the beast there [*Un champ d'espace temps a été ouvert: il y a là une bête*]. The perceived crawling is, in sum, the total meaning of the partial movements figured in the three phases, which make action as words make a sentence. There is a perception of continuity between cause and effect. Michotte questions those who doubt this causality: they have what Nietzsche calls "scientific myopia."[41]

According to Merleau-Ponty, animal life is not graspable and isolatable as such—is not comprehensible in any of the "partial movements" carried out over three separate phrases—but as "a fold, the reality of a process . . . unobservable up close."[42] Here Merleau-Ponty refers to an experiment conducted by Albert Michotte in *La perception de la causalité* (1946), a "duck test" of sorts in which moving traits projected on a screen give "the characteristic impression of life, whatever the familiarity of the spectator with animals." The partial movements of the animal "*make* action" just as "words make a sentence." In other words, the impression of unbroken causality (which Merleau-Ponty compares to the sense of continuity conveyed by grammatical predication) is the implicit condition for the "appearance" of the animal that becomes "visible only globally and escap[es] from attentive perception."[43] Yet if the living being remains "unobservable up close" (as it does in Foucault's analysis of life as a principle of animation), Merleau-Ponty nonetheless endows it with a singular power of expression. It is the animal, not the scientist, who is granted the "power to invent the visible." The animal/animate, for Merleau-Ponty, is something like a haecceity, an absolutely singular mode of individuation, irreducible to any transcendental law like the law of causal succession.

Causality, indeed, is for Merleau-Ponty not an a priori principle that organizes life but the name of the global "perception of continuity" whereby meaning is given to and by the sudden appearance of a living being. Animal behavior is not "meaningful" solely from an external, objective point of view, which is capable of reconstructing a significant sequence of events out of the animal's instinctive and sometimes (apparently) objectless gesticulations. Rather than explaining animal behaviors in terms of objects and ends, Merleau-Ponty characterizes them as "styles."[44] From the phenomenologist's point of view, then, "scientific myopia" stems from the mistrust of one's impressions, not from a defective vision that demands to be enhanced.[45] For Dr. Bat, however, the phenomenal "*il y a là*" of animality, the "ecce" that conditions its visibility, is immediately suppressed and contained by a caption: "there . . . there is an animal, which will be likely to dispute with the Lion, his title to be called the

King of the Beasts!" (71). There are two "theres" there. It is tempting to hear the doctor's stuttering as a suturing, as if the second "there" signaled the reassertion of control and mastery over the first "there," which is a marker of surprise, a pointer that is not yet attached to an intelligible object.[46]

Battius admits that he made a mistake in taking his donkey for a new species, but in his own defense, he claims entrapment: the fault is not his but his retinas'. It is his eye that induced him to commit the epistemic crime. Bat's invocation of persistence of vision as an alibi is revealing. For him, the problem comes from a flaw intrinsic to the human eye, which proves insufficiently competent to capture the animal, requiring the assistance of mechanized apparatuses (but the opposite is also true: Bat's taxonomic vision is so good at capture that it produces a king of beasts with which nature is incapable of keeping up).[47] The naturalist appears as a harbinger of the new age of "mechanical objectivity," which Lorraine Daston and Peter Galison define as "blind sight," as the "attempt to capture nature with as little human intervention as possible."[48] In objectivity, taxonomic representation becomes an idealized form of capture. The transition I locate occurs at the moment when the human hand—the labor of the hunter, the craft of the painter, the observing subject—recedes from view as the source of knowledge. This does not mean that the hand no longer constitutes the distinguishing mark of humanity, only that the labor of prehension/predation is obliterated or sublimated. This emancipation of the hand not only defines the ethos of mechanical objectivity, which Daston and Galison describe as a "hands-off epistemology,"[49] but more generally it subtends the idea of the "invisible hand" that ideally presides over the free-market economy and the nation's Manifest Destiny.

ENDGAME: THE TRAPPER

In *The Prairie,* Cooper dramatizes this sublimation in his portrayal of how the hunter is replaced by the trapper.[50] In the other installments of the *Leatherstocking* series, Bumppo is presented as an uncompromising hunter. The word *trapper* is not used once in either *The Last of the Mohicans* or *The Pioneers,* in which Bumppo is already seventy years old. Indeed, Bumppo explicitly scorns trapping; in the flashback to Bumppo's youth in *The Deerslayer* (1841), the twenty-one-year-old huntsman exclaims: "I am no trapper. . . . I live by the rifle. . . . I never offer a skin that has not a hole in its head besides them which natur' made to see with, or to breathe through."[51] But in *The Prairie,* the protagonist is introduced as an eighty-some-year-old frontiersman too old to catch anything except through the trickery of traps. The woodsman would remain anonymous if not for his tendency to reminisce about his former exploits. The erosion of his identity as a hunter is figured by his new insistence on being called a trapper; a shadow of his former self, Bumppo no longer feels worthy of his famous aliases, Hawkeye and La Longue Carabine, which celebrate his once-great hunting skills. Despite his decline, however, Bumppo still plays a critical role in domesticating the hostile landscape of the prairie. But since he is too weak to go after animals, he lets the animals come to him. The impotence that characterizes the trapper illuminates a troubling affinity between the aging Bumppo and his myopic foil, Dr. Bat. Cooper hints at their unlikely kinship when he has the old hunter blame his failing eyesight for his transformation: "It is no cause of wonder," Bumppo exclaims, "that a man whose strength and eyes have failed him as a hunter, should be seen nigh the haunts of the beaver, using a trap instead of a rifle" (117). The naturalist, Cooper seems to suggest, is the consummate trapper. Bat himself tries to convince Bumppo that they may not be as different as the latter would like to think. Both are, in Bat's words, "lovers of the same pursuit" (98), although Bat has consolidated the hunter's pursuit into a system. The shift from hunt to capture that is illustrated by Bumppo's metamorphosis into a trapper and Bat's usurpation of his place is thus less a rupture than a form of sublimation, in the Nietzschean sense.[52]

Another scene of animal encounter—or lack thereof—makes apparent the differences and similarities between the aging hunter and the naturalist. Shortly after rescuing the young Inez de Certavallos from her abductors, Bumppo and his friends find themselves threatened by the "sudden exhibition of animal life which changed the scene, as it were by magic":

> A few enormous Bison bulls were first observed scouring along the most distant roll of the prairie, and then succeeded long files of single beasts, which in their turns were followed by a dark mass of bodies. . . . The herd, as the column spread and thickened, was like the endless flock of the smaller birds, whose extended flanks are so often seen to heave up out of the abyss of the heavens, until they appear as countless and as interminable as the leaves in those forests over which they wing their endless flight. Clouds of dust shot up in little columns from the centre of the mass, as some animal more furious than the rest ploughed the plain with his horns and from time to time a deep hollow bellowing was borne along on the wind, as if a thousand throats vented their plaints in a discordant murmuring. (198)

Endless, interminable, countless: the herd is a living swarm uncannily reminiscent of Audubon's depiction of flocks of passenger pigeons:

> Like a torrent, and with a noise like thunder, they rushed into a compact mass, pressing upon each other towards the centre. In these almost solid masses, they darted forward in undulated and angular lines, descended and swept close over the earth with inconceivable velocity, mounted perpendicularly so as to resemble a vast column, and when high, were seen wheeling and twisting within their continued lines, which resembled the coils of a gigantic serpent.[53]

When he attempts to parse this impenetrable "mass" of life, Audubon approaches the phenomenon like a math problem, calculating "one billion, one hundred and fifteen million, one hundred and thirty-six pigeons in one flock."[54] The numbers are precise, but their function is mythical. The scene illustrates Kant's experience of the "mathematical sublime," in which a subject becomes aware of the superiority of her power of reason over a phenomenon overwhelming for her senses. The pigeon, Audubon muses, can only be conjugated in the plural: "When an individual is seen gliding through the woods and close to the observer, it passes like a thought, and on trying to see it again, the eye searches in vain; the bird is gone."[55]

Likewise, Cooper's bison are introduced as a superorganism that is approachable only by analogy (*like, as if*). The group is utterly paralyzed, captivated by the sight of this terrible manifestation, until the silence of the bewildered spectators is broken by the trapper, who, "having been long accustomed to similar sights felt less of its influence, or rather felt it in a less thrilling and absorbing manner." Bumppo, immunized by virtue of exposure against the aura of the spectacle (already on the side of mechanical reproduction), throws down his rifle and "advance[s] from the cover with naked hands, directly toward the rushing columns of the beasts" (198). Like Moses parting the Red Sea, Bumppo splits in two the torrent of life rushing toward them: "The head of the column . . . divided, the immovable form of the trapper cutting it, as it were, into two gliding streams of life" (201). Cooper's description of how Bumppo divides the flow of wild animals uses terms strikingly close to those used by Deleuze and Guattari in *A Thousand Plateaus.* Not quite the unmoved prime mover, Bumppo is the "immovable form" that (like the taxonomist) interrupts, parcels out and organizes life, the arithmetic force that breaks the one into two. If no longer a hunter—a fact made explicit by his throwing down his rifle and advancing untooled, "with naked hands"—Bumppo is not a trapper either so much as the trap itself.

Bumppo's metamorphosis into a trapper (and a trap, as in the bison scene) cannot simply be attributed to the character's senescence. For most critics, the trapper's lost youth "sounds an elegiac note not only for a way of life and a wilderness that is vanishing beneath the settlers' axes but for the passing of the frontiersman as a type."[56] But the hunter's decline and eventual death also herald a transformation in the way the animal came to be perceived in modern America. The hunter's transformation into the trapper signals a stricter distribution of the sensible between Man and "the inferior animals of the creation," and as a corollary between the people who have supposedly outgrown their drive to hunt and those who have not. This does not mean that settlers stopped hunting—quite the contrary. Hunting increased exponentially with the proliferation of railroad networks and the improvement of gun technology: on average, a white hide hunter killed one hundred buffalo a day in the 1870s, a death rate that (with the help of cattle-borne disease and changes in the land) brought the species to the brink of extinction in the 1890s. But by then the nature of the hunt had changed: settlers were no longer hunting buffalos, they were hunting *the buffalo.* The hunt had become pure slaughter, a systematic, large-scale meat grinder that was actively encouraged by the U.S. Army, for the death of the bison would weaken or even exterminate those Native tribes whose livelihood and cultures relied on the buffalo, or at least make them dependent on governmental aid to survive.[57] Yet even as the settlers were prompted to overhunt the buffalo, indigenous hunting cultures were actively "discouraged" by the government, which sought to promote farming.[58] In the same way humanity was commonly deemed to have "evolved" from hunter-gatherer to agricultural societies, hunting was frequently presented in the young republic as a temporary expedient supposed to yield to a more civilized and "humane" set of practices.

At the end of *The Prairie,* it has become clear that the hunter—too liminal, too literal, too animal—must disappear.[59] In contrast to the arc typical of early American captivity narratives, which are generally premised on the possibility and desirability of returning to "civilization," there is no going back for Bumppo, who demands to be buried far from the din of the settlements.[60] "I am without kith or kin in the wide world," the old hunter confides in his last breath. "When I am gone, there will be an end of my race" (383). With the benefit of hindsight, we can see that this is true. When the old trapper tries to pass on his legacy to the Pawnee Hard-Heart, whom Bumppo names his only son, this does not allow his legacy to live on; instead, it symbolically condemns Hard-Heart to survive spectrally in a time that is no longer his—a time that is neither for Indians nor for hunters.[61] Both the Indian's spectral survival and his disappearance as both programmed and interminable are enshrined in what White Earth Ojibwe scholar Gerald Vizenor calls the "manifest manners" of hegemonic narratives—an erasure that is effected by silencing those who survived but also by representing, as Cooper did, an Indian that never was.[62] For Cooper—a master of manifest manners, on a par with a Thomas Jefferson or a

George Bancroft—"language did the capturing, binding Indian society to a future of certain extinction."[63] By casting the Pawnee warrior as incommensurably superior to the prodigal white settler and thus unfit to survive in a corrupted modern world, Cooper's fiction effectively sanctuarizes the Indian.[64] Considered from the perspective of what Dana Luciano terms "chronobiopolitics," the Indian appears as an essential precondition that is continually abjected even as it is valorized, included by way of exclusion—or, as Agamben would say, "captured" as "bare life," a life continuously exposed to death, whose originary exclusion from the political paradoxically founds politics.[65] "Presenting Indians as bare life—as dying 'remnants,'" Mark Rifkin elaborates, "addresses their status within the regime of US policy as if it were a function of natural facts, pre-political or apolitical conditions to which US institutions respond, but the biopolitical figure of dependence presumes a vision of geopolitical incorporation that precedes it, the latter appearing as merely background for the former."[66] In other words, Rifkin shows that biopolitics cannot be thought without a geopolitics of land occupancy, the "bare life" of indigenous peoples without the "bare habitance" exemplified by the making "empty" of the empire in Cooper's romance.[67] To challenge this imperialist view, bareness must be recognized as a product or effect of the work of biopolitics, not its precondition.

Tellingly, in *The Pioneers,* which is set twelve years before the events of *The Prairie,* Bumppo describes the death of his friend Chingachgook as "natur' giving out in a chase that's run too long."[68] The life of the Mohican is entirely subsumed under the motif of the hunt. The end of the chase for the Native American (and for "natur'" itself) metonymically marks a historical transition in the rights and modes of occupation of the land. Indeed, the figure of the Native American, whom the author sees fading before his eyes, emblematizes the precarious openness of the land:

> The Great Prairies appear to be the final gathering place of the red men. The remnants of the Mohicans, and the Delawares, of the Creeks, Choctaws, and Cherokees, are destined to fulfil their time on

> these vast plains. The entire number of the Indians, within the Union, is differently computed, at between one and three hundred thousand souls. Most of them inhabit the country west of the Mississippi. At the period of the tale, they dwelt in open hostility; national feuds passing from generation to generation. The power of the republic has done much to restore peace to these wild scenes, and it is now possible to travel in security, where civilised man did not dare to pass unprotected five-and-twenty years ago.[69]

The binding of the Union's peacemaking to the "extinction" of the previous occupants of the land lays bare the settler-colonial logic of the passage.[70] Cooper wrote this preface two years after Andrew Jackson signed the Indian Removal Act, a moment when the land of the Great Plains had been for the most part "secured" and peace "restored." In a recognizably Hobbesian gesture, Cooper equates pacification with the process of civilizing the ageless and natural belligerence of the "savages." Yet, in the same breath, the idea that peace has been "restored" (rather than imposed) implies that the pacification of the land is in effect a return to normal.

Of course, Cooper's (and the U.S. government's) erasure of the violence that produced this "peace" was only invisible to those who had a vested interest in not looking. Writing at the same time as Cooper, the Pequot preacher William Apess derides the hollow moral pretexts on which colonial conquests are predicated, exposing the murderous agenda that belies the peaceful rhetoric of the settlers. Quoting the Scottish historian William Robertson (Apess frequently enlists white authors to denounce the brutality of white imperialism), Apess writes that the first colonists of Virginia "hunted the Indians like wild beasts, rather than enemies" (the simile ambiguously leaving it to the reader to determine whether "wild beast" applies to hunted or hunter). He continues:

> And as the pursuit of them to their places of retreat in the woods was both difficult and dangerous, they endeavored to allure them from their inaccessible fastnesses, by offers of peace and promises of

> oblivion, made with such an artful appearance of sincerity as deceived the crafty Indian chief, and induced the Indians to return in the year 1623 to their former settlements and resume their usual peaceful occupations. . . . On the approach of harvest, . . . the English fell suddenly on all the Indian plantations, and murdered every person on whom they could lay hold, and drove the rest to the woods.[71]

Apess does not simply reverse the roles that historiography and literature have typically attributed to settlers and Natives—civilized/barbarian, peaceful/belligerent, human/animal—he also shows how this rhetoric works to naturalize the "extirpation" of the Indians and exculpate the republic's genocidal politics, which is presented as following a preordained agenda.[72]

This strategy would only intensify in the so-called Age of Democracy epitomized by Jackson's presidency.[73] "Whereas white supremacy had been the working rationalization for British theft of Indigenous lands and for European enslavement," historian Roxanne Dunbar-Ortiz observes, this was less useful in the United States, for "democracy, equality, and equal rights do not fit well with dominance by one race, much less with genocide, settler colonialism, and empire."[74] It was at this time that the United States developed a new "origin myth" in the figure of the hunter, with Cooper as its most famous scribe. "Cooper devised a fictional counterpoint of celebration to the dark underbelly of the new American nation," writes Dunbar-Ortiz: "the birth of something new and wondrous, literally, the U.S. American race, a new people born of the merger of the best of both worlds, the Native and the European, not a biological merger but something more ephemeral, involving the dissolving of the Indian."[75] The term *dissolving* hints at the ostensible attenuation of the violence visited on indigenous people in the "Age of Democracy." This new technology of conquest is the development of the myth of the hunter, but the hunt and the hunter must always be conjugated in the past tense. The hunt must belong to the infancy of the nation (or, under Roosevelt, as something one episodically returns to as a prophylactic measure). This explains why in 1827, the hunter of *The Prairie* must disappear as the nineteenth century dawns, yet Cooper can write two more installments portraying Bumppo in the prime of life: *The Pathfinder* (1840) and *The Deerslayer* (1841), set squarely in the eighteenth century. The hunter fully and manifestly becomes himself and a fixture of American mythology when and because his historical prototype is deemed or has been made extinct.

The hunter as a technology of conquest was needed for taming and charting unknown territories. Once these territories became preknown and preowned (as with the Land Ordinance), the hunter no longer has a raison d'être. Or rather, it must vanish in order to conceal the ongoing violence that underlies the subsumption of difference under speculative topographies, epistemologies, and economies. Here we glimpse how colonialism, in its "democratic" phase, is wedded to capitalism. Glen Sean Coulthard explicitly connects these two, enlisting Marx's concept of "primitive accumulation" (with which Marx theorizes how land grabs conditioned the emergence of capitalism) to explain how "formative acts of violent *dispossession* set the stage for the emergence of capitalist accumulation and the reproduction of capitalist relations of production by tearing Indigenous societies, peasants, and other small-scale, self-sufficient agricultural producers from the source of their livelihood—*the land.*"[76] For Coulthard, as for Patrick Wolfe, the land is the "primary motive" of settler colonialism; we can thus account for Dunbar-Ortiz's discussion of the invisibilization of violence by theorizing different relations to the land and its human and animal occupants under the regimes of hunt and of capture.

FROM SURVEY TO SURVEILLANCE

For the frontispiece of their section on the "apparatus of capture," Deleuze and Guattari borrow from French agronomist Noël Chomel's 1732 *Dictionnaire œconomique* the image of a bird trap (Figure 8). According to David Gissen, "such traps illustrated a larger 'apparatus of capture' that . . . took the form of stockpiling nature to impose economic control over the productivity of the earth and convert open territories into saleable land."[77] In Chomel's encyclopedia, the drawing of the trap is accompanied by very detailed instructions on how to capture partridges: after carefully spanning the net, the trapper is to hide behind a blind, made to look like a cow, in order to lure the birds, who have learned to be afraid of the figure of man but not of a placid bovine. Once the partridges are sufficiently close to the entrance of the circular net (*tonnelle*), the trapper can spring from behind his Trojan cow to collect the prey.[78] Everything is meticulously represented in the illustration except for the human trapper, as though the trap was capable of working of its own accord. Even more intriguing is the background of the picture: the parallel lines of the furrows of the field display the homogenizing force imposed by the State apparatus on the land as well as on the birds herded into the tonnelle, which is itself parallel to the furrows. Chomel's drawing suggests that the discontinuity between hunting and capture (in this case, the capture of the land as agriculture) revolves around issues of presence and absence, or, more precisely, visibility and invisibility (here, the trapper is doubly invisible, hidden behind the luring cow and absent from the picture).

To account for this invisibilization, Deleuze and Guattari develop the concept of the threshold, which they oppose to the concept of the limit. Whereas the limit marks the last item of a series and supposes the exploitation of a finite territory, the threshold marks the beginning of stock or reserve and supposes the exploitation of a land. What distinguishes the territory from the land is that the exploitation of the former is "governed by the law of temporal succession," while what governs the latter is "the law of spatial coexistence." The hunt takes place on a territory that is not fully mappable; capture, however, demands an isonomized, striated land (think of the railroad as condition for the slaughter of the buffalo). Once the threshold is crossed, "the force of serial iteration is superseded by a power of symmetry, reflection, and global comparison" (a shift similar to that traced in this chapter, from the hunter's violent encounter with individuated animals to their generic taxonomization by the naturalist, or their shooting en masse, as in the famous pigeon massacre in *The Pioneers*). Deleuze and Guattari continue: "We therefore distinguish between serial, itinerant, or territorial assemblages (which operate by codes) and sedentary, global, or Land assemblages (which operate by

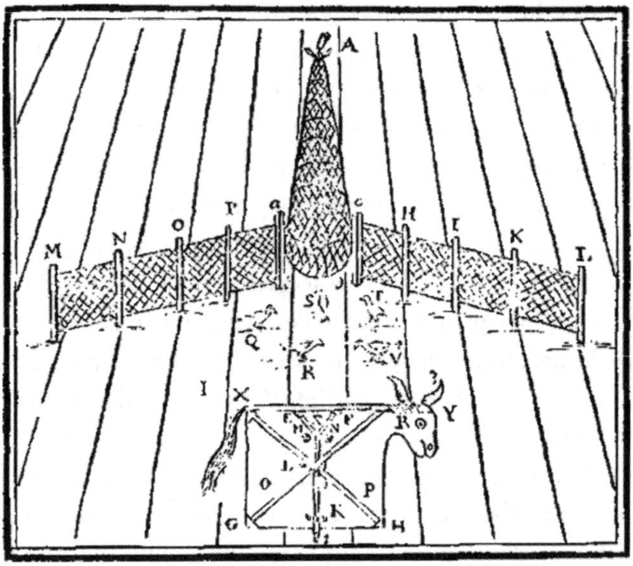

FIGURE 8. *Tonnelle*: Entry for "Perdrix," Chomel's *Dictionnaire œconomique,* 1732. Frontispiece to "Apparatus of Capture," in Deleuze and Guattari, *A Thousand Plateaus.*

overcoding)."[79] In these two models, the earth appears respectively as territory and land, and animals (as I note in Figure 3) appear respectively as prey and livestock.

Chomel's image of the trap illustrates well the radicality with which capital deterritorializes the land and the flows of labor. The "capitalist decoding" depicted in the image, however, is less a deterritorialization proper than the systematic destruction of territory and the structural foreclosure of reterritorialization. The standardized parceling out of the land forbids certain modes of occupation, tending to dispossess both human and animal populations of a territory.[80] This deterritorialization—the United States' expropriation of land with the settlement of the frontier and the Indian Removal Act—is precisely the process encoded in Cooper's works. This process leaves territories "empty" and up for grabs while at the same time preparing a mobile (deterritorialized) class of workers made dependent on capitalist modes of production and consumption (the Natives made dependent on government aid rather than subsistence hunting).[81] When territory becomes land, nonproductive or counterproductive forms of mobility (such as itinerancy or nomadism) become criminalized, and precisely by being criminalized, they are made to appear threatening or violent, tautologically reinforcing the mandate of security and control.[82] The causality is flipped; the State seems within its right to punish the "primitives." Its violence is not only legitimized but naturalized.

Or rather, it is biologized. We recall that the shift from natural history to biology analyzed in *The Order of Things* occurs when historicity is injected into the timeless tabulations of classical taxonomies. To the extent that a biological continuum is assumed, the variety of living beings indexes a more fundamental variability of form. From the standpoint of biology, in other words, taxonomic difference becomes a function of time.[83] Species no longer marks a different place in the order of things—a different "case" in the taxonomic table—so much as a different time (Darwin's theory of evolution would soon consecrate the scientificity of this intuition). Likewise, what Foucault calls biopower implies a biological continuity that exists below the threshold of phenotypical and organic differentiation. Race, then, which becomes an explicit technology wielded to fragment "the field of the biological that power controls," operates genealogically (in the Darwinian sense): it ascribes differences of degree (rather than of kind) according to a "transcendental" principle of descent. Foucault expressly links a general notion of "evolutionism" with the racism that developed alongside "colonizing genocide."[84]

From this perspective, we understand how deeply biological reason informs modern racial politics and, as Scott Lauria Morgensen shows, how deeply the logic of settler colonialism informs modern biopolitics. The white settlers' politics of eradication and replacement works alongside efforts to exterminate indigenous lifestyles by absorbing them into the hegemonic culture. The very idea of assimilation suggests that any form of coexistence across difference is by definition temporary. The marking of some behaviors as "primitive" fits a strategy of conquest that does not eradicate populations outright but marks them with an expiration date: they will either perish or be assimilated.[85] This explains how the elimination of indigenous peoples, which is still ongoing today, can be construed as "perpetual" and how this framing elides the ways that people, languages, and cultures persist despite this project. Morgensen suggests that the Indian reservation, which produces this "state of exception" by effectively bracketing surviving Native American tribes as existing both inside and outside of America's narrative of progress, is a prototype for the concentration camp, identified by Foucault and Agamben as a paradigmatic site of modern biopolitics.[86] The point is not to "compare" the atrocities of the Final Solution with those of the U.S. Indian policy, as Mark Rifkin notes, but rather to suggest that the genocidal biopolitics of the twentieth century is continuous with, and indeed subtended by, "the geopolitics of statehood and thus the dynamics of settler-state imperialism."[87] As Morgensen claims, "Scholars must not interpret modern state biopolitics or its extrapolations in global governance as recent rather than deeply historical phenomena. Nor should we let the preeminent role of any settler state in those processes appear to be the action of 'the West,' without specifying how settler colonialism acts as the West's leading edge by establishing *grounds* for the globalisation and universalisation of its governance."[88]

One of the ambitions of this chapter has been to sketch a critical history of settler colonialism through Cooper's fictional account of changing technologies of conquest and management. I have examined colonialism particularly as it relates to nonhuman animals but without losing sight of the material, ecological, and political consequences of this project for human populations. Also at stake is the larger question of how universalist principles like "the West," with their attendant rationalities and dispositifs, can be historicized and effectively criticized. Precisely because they pose as universals, these principles seem impervious to historicization.[89] Deleuze and Guattari's "Apparatus of Capture," an elaboration on Marx's notion of primitive accumulation, asks what mechanisms preside over the enigmatic transition from "precapitalist" to capitalist society—that is, from a so-called primitive economy of relative exchange (like the potlatch) to a capitalist system of absolute exchangeability. To account for capitalism's muddy origins, Marx lists various exemplary sites of expropriation, from the "emancipation" of the English peasants—"free to exchange [their] labor" when "free of material resources," Saidiya Hartman ironizes[90]—to the looting of the West Indies and North America, made possible by the "enslavement and entombment in mines of the aboriginal population" and "the commercial hunting of black skins."[91] At stake is the rendering as prehistorical—indeed, "primitive" or "aboriginal"—of the violent exploitation that is underway. This frames that expropriative violence as anomalous, positioning violence's end (in truth, its simple occlusion) as a return to "normal."

Those who find themselves exploited or dispossessed are thereby also rendered "primitive" (although Marx does not articulate this connection). Deleuze and Guattari insist, first, that the societies designated as primitive are never without, nor are they before, but are always *against* capitalism; it is not that they have not yet discovered or developed this economic system, in other words, but they actively refuse to engage in it. Second, they explain the sleight of hand by which the violent expropriation that underpins the "emergence" of capitalism "posits itself as preaccomplished." The question, they ask, is: How does this violence justify itself? Their answer: By organizing a police state.

> *State policing or lawful violence* . . . consists in capturing while simultaneously constituting a right to capture. It is an incorporated, structural violence distinct from every kind of direct violence. . . . State overcoding is precisely this structural violence that defines the law, "police" violence and not the violence of war. There is lawful violence wherever violence contributes to the creation of that which it is used against, or as Marx says, wherever capture contributes to the creation of that which it captures. This is very different from criminal violence. It is also why, *in contradistinction to* primitive violence, State or lawful violence always seems to presuppose itself, for it preexists its own use: the State can in this way say that violence is "primal," that it is simply a natural phenomenon the responsibility for which does not lie with the State, which uses violence only against the violent, against

> "criminals"—against primitives, against nomads—in order that peace may reign.[92]

Our task is now to understand how this form of pacific violence functions not just rhetorically as Manifest Destiny but biopolitically. This same pacific violence operates in the conception of its object—the human and nonhuman populations it seeks to monitor and control. I have contended that over the course of the nineteenth century, the explicit violence of hunting is folded into a form of pursuit that is less acquisitive than regulatory (just as territorial conquest is folded into land management). This contention expands on Foucault's insight that the emergence of the police state is an expression of liberal government's mission to keep peace (instead of making war) and his analyses of "security" as the modern form of pastoral governance.[93] In principle, security has renounced the direct violence of the hunt, which targets individuals. Instead, it seeks to affect a "population" indirectly, by intervening in the milieu that conditions its existence. But hunting does not vanish; instead, it is integrated as a technology of regulation, as an immunitary mechanism (moving from end to means).

In an interview, Foucault explains that for a long time the practice of "hunting down vagrants, beggars . . . remained outside the field of the judicial, legal practice. . . . And then, at the beginning of the nineteenth century, the police enforcement of social selection was integrated in the judicial practice because, in the Napoleonic State, police, justice, and penitential institutions were linked to each other."[94] In other words, the police became trappers of human beings, targeting primarily marginalized, primitivized, animalized men. Perhaps because he focuses mainly on the European context, Foucault tends to underplay the centrality of what Grégoire Chamayou calls the police's "cynegetic power," the power to hunt down.[95] This new system is not simply repressive but proactive, and it is concerned not only with the physical but also the visual apprehension of those who might present a risk. If, as I have suggested, capture is a specific way of seeing and knowing, then we have to investigate the paradox that makes its objects both preknown and unknowable at the same time, and as such subject to endless scrutiny and investigation. No author better than Edgar Allan Poe theorizes the office performed by the police, whose historical function is to criminalize and apprehend—or chase and capture—those who reject work or engage in economies unsanctioned by the state.[96] In Poe, capture appears precisely as this system that naturalizes and presupposes the crime, thereby literally bringing the criminal *into being*. It is a strategy of knowledge and management that sanctions in the same gesture the criminalization of the "primitives" and the animalization of those accused of a crime. The next chapter explores how animality becomes weaponized by this system of control.

PART II

NEW GENRES OF CAPTURE

— 3 —

THE FUGITIVE ANIMAL

(POE)

> But cynegetic violence does not occur only at the time of the first acquisition, but also later on, as a means of governing. The hunt continues after the capture.
> —Grégoire Chamayou, *Manhunts*

> Nothing . . . prevents the police system from undergoing in its turn an evolution along the line of the application of scientific principles. . . . Have not hunters in all ages been incited by information connected with natural history, and, inversely, do not naturalists have something of the hunter's instinct?
> —Alphonse Bertillon, *Signaletic Instructions*

This chapter leaves the open expanses of Cooper's prairie for the reticular topology of the modern city, and the capacious genre of the romance for the more constrained format of the detective story. While the vast swaths covered by Cooper's hero demand a long saga, a serialized epic spanning almost a century, Poe's urban settings formally call for a very different textual space: compact, dense, and jumbled—a topology reflected in Poe's polysemous and labyrinthine language, in which it seems that there is not enough room for ideas to deploy and characters to develop. What we witness in the shift from prairie to city can be characterized as the transition from territory to milieu—a transition not fully coterminous but complementary with the conversion of territory into land analyzed at the end of the previous chapter. Whereas the land apprehends space as essentially workable, enclosing and standardizing it to maximize economic productivity, the milieu apprehends space as a habitat, as a material environment more or less favorable to the health and stability of a given population. The land supervises laboring bodies and subjects them to disciplinary mechanisms, while the milieu exercises protocols of security over a population.[1]

Foucault recalls that "milieu" was a biological concept developed by Lamarck (whose momentous influence on the nineteenth-century United States, Kyla Schuller shows, was later eclipsed by the discredit of his theories after Darwin).[2] The milieu construes space as the medium through which a government can affect populations; in a milieu, inhabitants are treated not as legal subjects or as a people (as under sovereignty), not as individuated bodies capable of specific tasks (as under discipline), but as "a multiplicity of individuals who are and fundamentally and essentially only exist *biologically bound to the materiality within which they live.*"[3] Tracing the concept to its biological origin, as Foucault does, invites us to take the terms *territory* and *milieu* more literally than Foucault did—to return them to the animal figure from which they were derived.[4] The previous chapter examined a literal (capitalist, colonialist) case of deterritorialization and the imposition of the new visual logic by which certain phenomena were disappeared. This chapter asks what happens to animals when we move (and move them) from the wilderness to the city. Foucault's sovereignty (for me, the sovereignty of the hunt) is attached to territory, and security (for me, the logistic of capture) implies a milieu. In a territory, the question was one of navigation and conquest—of how to apprehend what is unpredicted because it is as yet unknown (but knowable); now the question is flipped, becoming one of how to manage the aleatory emergence of something that is assumed (yet unknowable when taken in isolation).

Foucault understands the question of milieu as primarily a problem of circulation: how do we ensure safety without inhibiting the circulation of people and merchandise? Poe, in contrast, often dreams of closed spaces—spaces where nothing circulates between outside and inside—but at the same time shows that no perfect immunity can ever be achieved, especially not from the animal. As in viral immunization, Poe suggests that a foreign agent must be introduced to work as antibody; this antibody is the detective, whom Poe cryptically portrays as a hunter, as we will see. For Walter Benjamin, the hunter and the detective have in common an ability to decipher signs that elude most observers, and he finds in Cooper's hunter the prototype of Poe's detective: "Owing to the influence of Cooper," Benjamin writes, "it becomes possible for the novelist in an urban setting to give scope to the experience of the hunter. This has a bearing on the rise of the detective story."[5] Thus turning to detective fiction offers a conceptual frame for understanding the afterlives of hunting in the material and symbolic economies of urban modernity—for understanding how, in the words of Chamayou, the "hunt continues after the capture."[6] How does the modern city, with its attendant challenges (such as overpopulation, crime, and public health), compel new apparatuses of capture? How do technologies of tracking and surveillance incorporate and sublimate the hunt, and what role is the animal made to play in this new hunt? Capture, I argued in the introduction, assumes fugitivity not as a faculty but as a property of its object. Hence, under capture the animal is conceived as essentially elusive. This chapter reads Poe's tales of detection, to which scholars of animal studies have frequently turned to theorize the modern animal condition, to examine how capture models a biopolitical mode of racialized management and control.[7] It moves from the assimilative logic of settler colonialism to the immunitary logic of the Middle Passage, which aims to subdue nonnative populations who have been forcibly imported and to stave off the specter of their acculturation—to maintain them quite literally "out of place."[8]

Heeding Toni Morrison's claim that "no early American writer is more important to the concept of American Africanism than Poe" helps us to understand how ascribing illegibility and illogicity to the animal presented a powerful discursive resource for the policing of black subjects.[9] Building on Morrison's insight, Lindon Barrett analyzes the correlation between detection and racialization in Poe's crime fiction, reading "The Murders in the Rue Morgue" as a "monument to Reason" that sought to delegitimize nonwhite subjects' "presence" in the United States by portraying them as essentially unreasonable and animated by an uncontrollable form of bestiality.[10] Poe's tale does not merely repeat the stereotype of non-Westerners as lacking reason, however; it also shows that a subterraneous and ambiguous operator is required to do the "purifying" work of Reason. Portrayed as a hunter, the detective is charged with capturing what Reason, in principle, cannot know—what must escape the bounds of Reason for Reason to know and remain itself.

RACE, ANIMALITY, CRIMINALITY

Although the figure of the detective is arguably an American invention, since "The Murders in the Rue Morgue" (1841) is typically credited with inaugurating the genre of detective fiction, Poe sets his tales of detection in the context of the mid-nineteenth century European city. Detective fiction would only cross the Atlantic a decade after Poe published "The Murders in the Rue Morgue" (1841) with the publication of George Thompson's popular *City Crimes; or, Life in New York and Boston.* Why did Poe choose European cities? It is as if he had to deterritorialize his own fiction in order to reflect on the effects of market-driven urban deterritorialization. The cities he chooses (Paris and London) are paradigmatic sites for the deployment of modern governmentality: the rise of a police force, the bureaucratization of life, and the increasing reliance on statistics and population-level thinking. At the time Poe wrote, both cities were undergoing intensifying urban standardization. As Benjamin observes, since the French Revolution, and especially during Napoléon Bonaparte's administration, Paris was increasingly submitted to "a multifarious web of registrations—a means of *compensating for the elimination of traces* that takes place when people disappear into the masses of the big cities."[11] This process would soon be aided by a vast number of biometric technologies like fingerprinting and photography, which equipped law enforcement agents and criminologists with a more precise and mechanically assisted "objective" method of identification.[12] This proliferation of surveillance apparatuses laid the foundations for the rise of the detective story, which "came into being when this most decisive of all conquests of a person's incognito [photography] had been accomplished." "Since that time," Benjamin asserts, "there has been no end to the efforts to capture [*dingfest machen*] a man in his speech and actions."[13]

Capture knows no end because what Benjamin describes as the "conquest of incognito" does not render a person "cognized," in the sense of making them positively known; rather, it captures the incognito as such by preserving "permanent and unmistakable traces [*Spuren*] of a human being."[14] Biological details are assumed to be the most personal and inimitable features of a subject's identity, but they appear as traces, as clues of a person who, in principle, remains irreducible to biometric data. In cities, Benjamin suggests, people disappear *as animals.* The city privileges a semantic form of understanding over a somatic one; symbolic identificatory markers offset the evanescence of bodily traces; street names do not index physical places but are referential nodes in an abstract network meant to ensure the circulation of goods and persons. Because the modern city is overcoded with textuality, it is easy not to find one's way and yet almost impossible to lose it: "Not to find one's way around a city does not mean much. But to lose one's way in a city, as one loses one's way in a forest, requires some schooling. Street names must speak to the urban wanderer like the snapping of dry twigs."[15] Like the hunter heeds in the wild seemingly insignificant clues like the breaking of a twig,[16] the detective makes sense of (the animal) signs and sounds that the city has obscured or rendered irrelevant (odors, for instance, are methodically eliminated to avoid offending the nostrils of urban consumers).[17] The detective alone can read between the lines of the new "web of registrations" that ensnares the modern subject. An inheritor of an age-old venatic knowledge, the detective is a reassuring character insofar as he "compensates" for the modern erasure of somatic traces. Yet he is also an immunological technology that works to tighten the city's surveillance network by catching what necessarily escapes the vigilance of the police.[18] The detective is a furtive agent who supplements the regulatory apparatus of the police, which in turn relies on an atavistic "cynegetic power," a power to hunt down and chase away those who do not conform to the standards of modern life.[19] Thus the detective is not just another name for the flaneur, that emblem of modernity celebrated for eluding the coercive structure of early commodity culture by strolling aimlessly and losing himself (as opposed to being lost) in the city.[20] The detective is a hunter.

As such, the detective can be seen as the American counterpart to the more European figure of the flaneur. Not that hunting is a uniquely American activity, but the hunt for human beings was closely associated with the United States in the nineteenth century, where it was practiced openly and routinely under chattel slavery.[21] In the aftermath of the Fugitive Slave Act of 1850, Frederick Douglass notes that the "power to hold, hunt, and sell men, women and children" has become "coextensive with the star-spangled banner and American Christianity," under which man is but "a bird for the sportsman's gun."[22] Officially abolished by the Thirteenth Amendment, legal forms of manhunting perdured after Emancipation, just as slavery remained legal for those convicted of a crime.[23] As this chapter examines how the hunter metamorphoses into the detective in Poe's fiction, it enables us to reflect on what Saidiya Hartman calls the "afterlives of slavery" and the technologies that accompanied the correlative "metamorphosis of 'chattel into man.'"[24] Overt subjugation belongs to the hunt regime, as it is predicated on physical captivity; the covert forensic subjection of populations belongs to the regime of capture. The infamous scene of Eliza crossing the Ohio River in *Uncle Tom's Cabin* epitomizes the former, while the attic space in which Harriet Jacobs is held in *Incidents in the Life of a Slave Girl* represents the latter. Eliza crosses a spatial border to shake off her pursuer, who is "after her like a hound after a deer," but Jacobs manages to escape her captivity by thwarting her captor's calculations: instead of moving north, she moves up, hiding in a space she calls her "loophole of retreat" that confuses the expected coordinates of flight.[25] Stowe's and Jacobs's narratives limn two topologies of escape, which correspond to two different conceptions of the slave's fugitivity: in the former, fugitivity is a faculty of the slave; in the latter, it has been commuted into the slave's "property," to borrow from Stephen Best.[26] Hidden in the "nonspace" that is her attic, Jacobs is not directly exposed to the violence of her captor, but neither is she fully emancipated from his threat; her loophole literalizes her being caught in a liminal state, between freedom and captivity. It would take a different kind of logic to detect her presence—a different kind of hunter.[27] Poe's detective, I argue, is a harbinger of this new type of hunt. Recovering the detective's predatory function is thus an invitation to consider what debt the modern societies of control owe to the history of transatlantic slavery and the extent to which modern surveillance technologies were specifically designed to target racialized populations.[28]

Conceptually, characterizing the detective as a hunter has two immediate implications. First, it reveals how criminality became explicitly aligned with animality as racial science and the new discipline of criminology emerged. Foucault summarizes this transition at the beginning of *The Birth of Biopolitics* as the moment when the penal system no longer asks the accused "What have you done?" but "Who are you?" The object is no longer to punish the acts of an individual but to capture the hidden "truth" of his being and to reform his conduct. The question "Who are you?" is paradoxically not addressed to a fully volitional, rational subject but to an individual understood as the byproduct of his milieu and instincts. Second, it brings to light the new place and function assigned to animality in the modern imaginary. What the genre of the detective story invents is a new hermeneutic frame that posits the animal as literally ungraspable, as essentially fugitive, which tautologically justifies its continuous surveillance. The problem of the animal—which cannot write, and thus cannot be read—poses the task of detecting it as one of decryption. Borrowing from Benjamin, I call decryption the act of "reading what was never written" (animal traces rather than human writing); but decrypting is also, as Poe helps us see, the subversive act of seeing writing as traces.[29] Insofar as it supposes the discovery of something that eludes the grasp of logos, decryption is a form of biopolitical reading. It does not take signs at face value, for what they denote, but observes what they betray about the signatory: a mysterious disposition or drive that can be monitored, tracked, rechanneled, but never positively known. It is the animal's presumed unintelligibility, Poe shows us, that subjects it to endless capture.

OFF THE GRID

The antihermeneutic I call decryption is a faculty that Benjamin ascribes to the flaneur, who masters the difficult art of losing himself in an urban setting. *Not to find one's way* is the suspension, or rather the indefinite protraction, of a telic movement that envisions an endpoint toward which one is progressing. *Losing one's way,* however, is an end in itself (or a pure means). The flaneur must willfully give himself over to the city. This immersion calls for a different kind of attention, which, Benjamin asserts, was "fixed for the first time and forever afterward by Poe in his story 'The Man of the Crowd.'"[30] In "The Man of the Crowd" (1840), Poe's narrator prides himself on being able to "read" the history of each anonymous passerby. He describes the movements of the London mob:

> The wild effects of the light enchained me to an examination of individual faces; and although the rapidity with which the world of light flitted before the window prevented me from casting more than a glance upon each visage, still it seemed that, in my then peculiar mental state, I could frequently read, even in that brief interval of a glance, the history of long years.[31]

His scanning gaze is suddenly "arrested and absorbed" by an old man's countenance because of "the account of the absolute idiosyncrasy of its expression": "How wild a history," the narrator says to himself, "is written within that bosom!" He proceeds to shadow the stranger through the crowd but finally gives up after a frenzied day spent following him, recognizing that the old man cannot be read: "It will be in vain to follow; for I shall learn no more of him, nor of his deeds. The worst heart of the world is a grosser book than the

'Hortulus Animae,' and perhaps it is but one of the great mercies of God that '*er lasst* [*sic*] *sich nicht lesen* [he will not let himself be read]'" (396). While ordinary men are open books for the narrator, the old man's idiosyncrasy, his absolute secrecy or privacy (*idios*), forces him to relinquish his pursuit.

Poe draws the portrait of the chased man as an escape artist, an elusive creature persistently evading the perspicacity of the narrator.[32] Not *in* but wholly *of* the crowd, the old man pulsates in time with the movements of the masses. He hardly seems human; unable to return the gaze of the narrator (which would reassure the narrator of his humanity), the old man raises the specter of Descartes's automaton, as Kevin McLaughlin observes.[33] But when we recall that the Cartesian animal is but a machine, and when we heed the clues disseminated in Poe's text (the emphasis placed on the character's "wildness," the uncanny "shriek" he emits, his "stalk[ing] backward and forward, without apparent object"), we begin to wonder if the man of the crowd is not, after all, something of an animal.[34] The narrator however, too bent on "reading" the man of the crowd, fails to catch him because he is not enough of a hunter—a hunter of men, a detective. For Benjamin, "Poe's famous tale 'The Man of the Crowd' is something like an X-ray of a detective story. It does away with all the drapery that a crime represents. Only the armature remains: the pursuer, the crowd, and an unknown man who manages to walk through London in such a way that he always remains in the middle of the crowd."[35] Nearly all the ingredients for a detective story are here gathered: the busy metropolis, the eerie throng, a breathless pursuit. The only things missing are a crime (although the narrator catches a glimpse of what he believes is a dagger) and a detective.

Poe's subsequent tale, "The Murders in the Rue Morgue," remedies these absences. In this story, Poe's unnamed narrator and his friend C. Auguste Dupin roam the streets of Paris until they are suddenly gripped by a headline in the *Gazette des tribunaux*: "Extraordinary Murders." The newspaper account describes how a dozen neighbors and two policemen, alarmed by a succession of "terrific shrieks" issuing from the fourth story of a house in the rue Morgue, had broken open the doors of a house to discover Madame and Mademoiselle L'Espanaye's apartment "in the wildest disorder." The police find the body of Mademoiselle L'Espanaye forced up the narrow aperture of the chimney, with bruises around her throat indicating that she had been throttled to death. The body of her mother is discovered lying in a small yard in the rear of the building with her head entirely cut off by a razor found in the apartment. While the belongings of the wealthy widow are scattered across the floor, nothing has been taken. The investigation will later note that "if we are to suppose gold the motive of this outrage, we must also imagine the perpetrator so vacillating an *idiot* as to have abandoned his gold and his motive together" (422; emphasis added). To be sure, financial gain hardly seems a plausible motive for such gruesome deeds.

The neighbors report having heard two voices, one gruff and one shrill. The gruff voice is described without hesitation as that of a Frenchman, while the source of the shrill voice stubbornly evades consensus among the witnesses (the Dutch witness supposes it the voice of a Frenchman, the French that of a Spaniard, the Spaniard that of an Englishman, and so on). What is more, the door of the apartment is locked from the inside with no other possible points of exit, the two windows appearing to be securely fastened by a stout nail. "To this horrible mystery," the *Gazette* reads, "there is not as yet, we believe, the slightest clew" (405–6). Drawing on this seemingly incoherent tangle of evidence, Dupin, an amateur sleuth who takes it upon himself to solve the case, investigates the mysterious killings through a process of elimination—deductive reasoning based on negation. First, he reminds the narrator that the voice of the perpetrator remained positively unassignable despite a gaggle of witnesses representing nationalities from across Europe. With decidedly loose and xenophobic logic, Dupin disregards—without entirely ruling out—the possibility that the voice may be that of a non-European (because "neither Asiatics nor Africans abound in Paris" [416]) or of a madman (because even madmen "are of some nation" [423]). Second, assuming that "Madame and Mademoiselle L'Espanaye were not destroyed by spirits," he speculates that the perpetrator must have had near-preternatural agility (417). He asserts that logically, one of the two windows must have served as the means of egress, then displays for his audience the mechanism by which the windows "have the powers of fastening themselves" (418). There "*must* be something wrong . . . about the nail," he concludes. And as if his words possessed incantatory powers, the nail reveals itself to be fractured (although "the fissure was invisible"). The nature of the crime is "altogether irreconcilable with our common notions of human action," and the fingerprints left behind bear "the mark of no human hand" (422–24). Most of these "clews" (the archaic spelling Poe uses for *clues*) suggest the work of a nonhuman actor. After reading a passage from *Le règne animal* (1797) in which Cuvier profiles the animal, Dupin ultimately identifies the perpetrator as an "Ourang-Outang" (Poe's spelling), recently escaped from the guardianship of a French sailor who brought the animal back from his journey to Borneo. This at last renders the animal legible.[36]

Poe's tale raises the question of whether the Ourang-Outang qualifies as a juridical actor, subject to the law and thus a potential "murderer" (a legal rather than a moral category).[37] The reader is misled by the title of the short story into expecting a murderer, a human actor endowed with reason and intention; this mirrors the misreading of police, whose perceptions, as Dupin teases, are no less "hermetically sealed" than the crime scene (423). Although Poe situates the ape's guilt outside of the realm of the reasonable, he does not disculpate the animal; he simply displaces the locus of culpability.[38] "Conscious of having deserved punishment" (429), the ape is unambiguously marked as guilty. However, his guilt derives not from malicious intents but from uncontrollable instincts. The creature's initially "pacific purposes" of shaving Madame L'Espanaye only turned into "wrath," "anger," and "frenzy" when the poor woman started screaming. The ape is shown to be deeply "impressionable"—Kyla Schuller's term for subjects' variable susceptibility to emotions—but lacks "the sentimental capacity of self-regulation."[39] The ape is literally moved by emotions over which he has but little control.

In its alignment of animality with criminality, the story exposes the racial underpinnings of the new mode of governing that it depicts:

the system recognizes culpability while denying intentionality—it enables punishment while denying the rationality (even full humanness) of the actor. This system was prototyped in the criminalization of enslaved subjects, whose intentionality, Hartman observes, came to be "acknowledged only as it assumed the form of criminality."[40] Only by committing a crime—often the crime of "stealing" themselves from their captor by attempting to escape—were slaves recognizable by the law as subjects and not just as properties. For Colin Dayan, this negative access to subjecthood through criminality is one of the "legal fictions" that inspire Poe's brand of gothic, which relentlessly diagnoses the "redefinition of civil life in the nineteenth-century US," and specifically how the law could turn people into property by dissociating physical and legal personhood. Slaves, she explains, "can be declared human only insofar as they err. . . . The accretion of positive or human qualities, yoked as it is to the fact of property, outfits slaves for one thing only: crime. Their only possible act, recognized by society, is a negative one."[41]

Christopher Peterson's astute reading of "Murders in the Rue Morgue" argues that Poe's ape is the evolutionary ancestor of all the criminals in the detective fictions that follow it. In making this claim, Peterson leans on Foucault's analysis of how punishment evolved when the penal apparatus began to routinely seek assistance from science and medicine; modern law, Peterson argues, focuses less on crimes than on criminals (less on *what* than *who*), which suggests that the motivation for crime is a question not of free will but of instinct, of having surrendered to something that is already within one. Ironically, the modern criminal is not "the origin of his or her actions," Peterson explains. "Rather, human criminals recapitulate the animalistic impulses of their progenitors in a deterministic fashion."[42] Peterson reads Poe's story against the grain of interpretations that see the ape as an "allegory" for the black subject, for this reading depends on a strict opposition between animality and humanity, with black people placed firmly in the animal category. According to Peterson, animality must instead be construed as a new technology of control that, even as it disproportionally targets racialized people by portraying them as dominated by their impulses, requires that all humans be recognized as animals (if differentially so, some being deemed more animal than others).[43] Inherent in this new formation, however, is the risk of dissolving the very accountability that the penal system seeks to enforce. The figure Poe chooses to walk this tightrope—to identify figures subject to criminal impulses yet accountable for punishment—is the detective. Because the detective is external to the legal system, his work gives justice (or punishment) the appearance of objectivity and disinterestedness. The police outsource the labor of decrypting animality to the detective, who alone can (and alone must) "read, in the silent, nearly imperceptible tracks left by his prey, a coherent sequence of events."[44]

Indeed, Dupin alone is capable of "reading the entire riddle" that the police could not, despite their methodical examination of the scene (414). It is, in fact, because of their very meticulousness that they cannot fathom what happened: they look too closely and thus (like Dr. Bat of the previous chapter) cannot see the larger story to which the "clews" belong. Dupin derides their efforts as excessively profound, asserting that truth is "invariably superficial" and never "where we seek her":

> The depth lies in the valleys where we seek [truth], and not upon the mountain-tops where she is found. The modes and sources of this kind of error are well typified in the contemplation of the heavenly bodies. To look at a star by glances—to view it in a side-long way, by turning toward it the exterior portions of the *retina* (more susceptible of feeble impressions of light than the interior), is to behold the star distinctly—is to have the best appreciation of its lustre—a lustre which grows dim just in proportion as we turn our vision *fully* upon it. A greater number of rays actually fall upon the eye in the latter case, but, in the former, there is the more refined capacity for comprehension. By undue profundity we perplex and enfeeble thought; and it is possible to make even Venus herself vanish from the firmament by a scrutiny too sustained, too concentrated, or too direct. (412)[45]

The lie of truth, the detective observes, is the belief that access to it is granted by in-depth scrutiny.[46] Truth is visible to those who are able to look sideways, to divert their attention from its object so as to see it with more clarity. In criticizing the police's shortsightedness, the detective pays tribute to the nebulousness that is indispensable to understanding phenomena as complex and dynamic—an idea Poe goes on to develop extensively in "Eureka," where he discusses at great length the "nebular theory" of Laplace and its refutation by Dr. Nichol.[47]

The amateur detective is already in a marginal position, and from this position he does not look directly at the crime but rather at the milieu in which the crime takes place; he apprehends the case through the slant of police reports and newspaper accounts. He reads between the lines, focusing on what is not seen:

> The wild disorder of the room; the corpse thrust, with the head downward, up the chimney; the frightful mutilation of the body of the old lady; these considerations with those just mentioned, and others which I need not mention, have sufficed to paralyze the powers, by putting completely *at fault* the boasted acumen, of the government agents. They have fallen into the gross but common error of confounding the unusual with the abstruse. But it is by these deviations from the plane of the ordinary, that *reason feels its way,* if at all, *in its search for the true*. . . . In fact, the facility with which I shall arrive, or have arrived, at the solution of this mystery, is in the direct ratio of its apparent insolubility in the eyes of the police. (414; emphasis added)

Ironically, the police are at a loss to find the murderer precisely because they are desperately looking for *a murderer.* The first hint at the possibility that the crime might be of "another nature" is given by the *Gazette des tribunaux*:

> A murder so mysterious, and so perplexing in all its particulars, was never before committed in Paris—if indeed a murder has been committed at all. The police are entirely *at fault*—an unusual occurrence in affairs of this nature. There is not, however, the shadow of a clew apparent. (411)

The qualification expressed here ("if indeed a murder has been committed at all") mimics a corrective rereading that is at work in Dupin's investigation: the solving of the murder requires that its very premises be called into question.[48] In Poe's story, the murderer does not premeditate, indeed does not even precede, the murder; the status "murderer" is retrospectively postulated as its a priori condition. By calling attention to the limitations of the deductive model underpinning the police's methods, "The Murders in the Rue Morgue" can be approached not just as an allegory of black animality but more broadly as an allegory of reading.[49] Instead of being "confounded by the seeming absence of motive," Dupin is able to read in this absence the very signature (though a signature is perhaps never read but only authenticated) of the animal whose murderous "style" is farcically described as "*excessively outré*" (422).

Dupin is introduced from the outset as a reader. He operates "from his armchair," first learning of the murders in the *Gazette* and resolving the case by posting an ad in the newspapers. Crucially, he has access to the same details as any ordinary reader of the sensational press that developed with the rise of metropolises, but he reads these details differently.[50] Foucault refers to Dupin's same *Gazette des tribunaux* in his explanation of the difference between the gutter press and the detective novel: the *faits divers* of the former gave readers the impression that delinquents were "everywhere to be feared," while the detective novel, born around the same time and often printed in the same journals, identified criminals as anomalies that "belonged to an entirely different world, unrelated to familiar, everyday life."[51] The *faits divers* and the detective novel apparently play opposite roles, but Foucault insists that they are complementary, for in these "crime stories," "delinquency appears both as very close and quite alien, a perpetual threat to everyday life, but extremely distant in its origin and motives, both everyday and exotic in the *milieu* in which it takes place."[52] What could be closer and yet more exotic than the ape—that cousin to humanity—who committed the first murder of the first modern crime story? The ape, not indigenous to France, is evidently "out of place" in Paris; he was brought there by the same colonial and capitalist order that connected distant parts of the world and developed the metropolis. This particular animal, we are told, was first captured on the island of Borneo by a French sailor who smuggled him into the country with the intention to sell him. The ape is introduced in Paris as a commodity—a trajectory that evokes the forcible displacement of African subjects and their conversion into chattel during the Middle Passage. While the sailor's confession at the end of the story provides a rational explanation for the ape's presence in Paris, the police's blindness indicates that the animal should not, and thus cannot, be there—that it has no place in the capital. In the ape's aporetic position, we glimpse the impossible ontology and legal status of the enslaved subject, simultaneously dead and alive (Orlando Patterson), thing and person (Colin Dayan), captive and fugitive (Stephen Best).

Ironically, it is the gridded space of the city and the probabilistic interpretive grid of the police, aimed at surveilling, identifying, and locating its subjects, that make it possible for the animal to "get away with murder." Because in this anthropic environment its presence is deemed improbable—though, curiously, more probable than the presence of "Asiatics" or "Africans"—the beast evades the purview of the police entirely.[53] The ape is untraceable because it is unlooked-for; it cannot be tracked because its presence cannot be fathomed in the first place. Though he will reveal that the supposed hermeticism of the apartment is but a trompe l'oeil, at first Dupin looks like a prestidigitator pulling an orangutan out of his sleeve. Because the animal's improbability has been hardened into an impossibility, its appearance has been converted into an apparition. "The Murders in the Rue Morgue" is not a gothic tale, but it alludes repeatedly to the "preternatural" character of the events. And after all, the detective story is but an extension of the gothic, the difference being that the supernatural is eventually explained away by the detective.[54] In Poe's more explicitly gothic texts, animals are often equated with spectral presences threatening the peace of domestic spaces (the black cat coming back from the dead, the raven tapping on the poet's window, the sphinx beetle ominously crawling on a spider thread along the window sash of a Hudson Valley country house, etc.). The appearance of animals in human habitats, it seems, has grown to exceed the bounds of plausibility. Regardless, animals doggedly return to haunt the humans as if they have not been properly killed or banished but simply encrypted, like the titular beast in "The Black Cat," returning from the dead to be discovered within the liminal space of the cellar wall. The animal in Poe occupies a möbian topology, simultaneously inside and outside (the space of) the human.[55]

THE MORGUE

The morgue is, like a crypt, a place for storing dead bodies; the term *morgue* originally designated a building in Paris where corpses were kept until identified. The unidentified body in Poe's morgue is not that of the dead victim but that of the fugitive perpetrator. Not only is the identity of the murderer not yet known (the premise of all whodunits), but Poe also suggests that it is ultimately unknowable. He challenges the very notion that there is a fully volitional and rational "who" at all behind the murders. This is less a dehumanization than an animalization of the criminal: uncontained animality is posited as the secret cause of criminality.[56] Poe's tale, Akira Mizuta Lippit observes, "brings to the surface a characteristically modern catastrophe": "[The] domicile of mankind has been assailed from the outside, indeed *by* the outside."[57] But this "outside," Poe suggests, is always with us—even in a bourgeois apartment on the fourth floor of a Parisian building—and indeed, always already within us (hence the need of an immunological agent to contain it). Hermetic seclusion cannot protect against the animal's invasion, as the L'Espanayes' lot shows. Yet if the animal is always with us, it is nowhere to be found, neither here nor there, but trapped in an altogether unlocalizable place. It has been encrypted.

Encryption, for Lippit, is the lot of the animal in modernity, this "crucial moment in the consolidation of metaphysics during which the superiority of humanity is achieved from the lowest ranks of being."[58] Lippit writes:

> According to the dialectic of humanism, an a priori animality (thesis) is subsumed by a competing humanity (antithesis): as a result,

> animality ceases to occupy a proper space apart from the humanity that succeeds, appropriates, and enframes it. The animal, according to that historical rendering, no longer remains in the realm of ontology; it has been effaced. . . . In this manner, the animal becomes an active phantom in what might be termed the crypt of modernity.[59]

The animal for Lippit remains a foreign body lodged in the very foundations of modernity: "Because modern philosophy fails to *eliminate* entirely the residues of the animal, its texts continue to inscribe the secret history of the animal as phantom."[60] Construed as "undying" by a dominant lineage of Western thinkers from Leibniz to Heidegger—deprived of a life of its own, yet endlessly "destined to survive"—the animal has a troubling tendency to endure without ever being fully present.[61] The animal thus poses an insoluble problem to modern thought because, in Lippit's dialectical rendering, it must be sublated for human subjectivity to be complete, yet it stubbornly resists this sublation.

It is not surprising that Lippit would engage Hegel in his explanation of how animality is configured in Western modernity; as Derrida shows in *Glas* (which he claims to have written "in the depths of an absolute crypt"), the Hegelian hermeneutic works very much like a digestive tract, aspiring to transubstantiate foreign phenomena into the wholeness of Spirit.[62] "Everything shall be incorporated into the great digestive system" that is Spirit, Derrida explains, "nothing is inedible in Hegel's infinite metabolism."[63] Almost nothing, that is. In his lectures on the *Philosophy of History,* Hegel notes that zoolatry, the worship of animals, is predicated upon the belief that the animal is, and has always been, "truly Incomprehensible":

> We also, when we contemplate the life and action of brutes, are astonished at their instinct—the adaptation of their movements to the object intended—their restlessness, excitability, and liveliness; for they are exceedingly quick and discerning in pursuing the ends of their existence, while they are at the same time silent and shut up within themselves. We cannot make out what it is that "possesses" these

> creatures, and cannot rely on them. A black tom-cat, with its glowing eyes and its now gliding, now quick and darting movement, has been deemed the presence of a malignant being—a mysterious reserved specter. . . . The lower animals are the truly Incomprehensible.[64]

This incomprehensibility is also encountered in Spirit, says Hegel, but Spirit has the capacity to comprehend itself, whereas animals remain utterly unsublatable. The only way to "comprehend"—or better, "apprehend"—animals is to name them. "According to Hegel," Lippit explains, "the act of naming transforms animals from independent beings into idealized beings: language, in essence, nullifies animal life. In disappearing, the animal leaves only its cry."[65]

It is precisely this contrived sublation—this sublimation—that is at work in the discursive economy of a modernity that encrypts that which it cannot overtly process.[66] The problem is thus not that the animal cannot speak (like Poe's ape, whose cry was deemed unintelligible by the witnesses) but rather that it cannot be heard. Because its shrill cry is deemed inarticulate, it becomes utterly inaudible. Instrumentalized as handy philosophical concept and yet resistant to conceptualization, the animal occupies an untenable position: it is simultaneously close at hand and at a safe distance, unknowable yet understood in advance. Within the Hegelian frame, any attempt at imagining or conceiving the nature of animals is seen as fallacious sympathizing or naïve anthropomorphism. In order to prevent the animal from interfering with our human affairs, it must be "framed" or allegorized as "truly Incomprehensible," locked up in an artificial niche—or, in Derridean terms, buried alive in a crypt.[67] To account for the unaccountable incarceration of the animal in modernity, it has been necessary to devise new structures that could accommodate its "undying" nature. Lippit finds these structures mainly in the Freudian theory of the unconscious but also in the cinematic apparatus and in modern genetics (as I elaborate in chapter 5).[68] In these unlocalizable recesses of modernity, the animal is kept, to quote Derrida, "alive, but as dead" (a phrase whose self-corrective structure performs the nonlogical topology of the crypt). The edifice of modern thought thus depends upon the adverb "as" that enforces the belief in a hermetic partition between the human (which is both alive and *as* alive) and the nonhuman. In order for the animal to disappear entirely, the crypt cannot be just another place but must be a nonplace. Hence the shock when animals resurface in a supposedly secured place, hence the impression that one has been attacked not *from* but *by* the outside.

In Hegel's skittish black tomcat, we glimpse a prototype of Poe's feline protagonist in "The Black Cat" (1843). The narrator recounts this "most wild, yet most homely narrative" from behind the bars of a prison cell. Formerly an avowed "pet lover," he explains how he repeatedly dreamed of killing, then actually killed, his black cat Pluto (597). After returning home one night, the intoxicated narrator gouges one of the cat's eyes out of its socket with a penknife before hanging the animal in his garden. Shortly after this macabre event, his house inexplicably burns to the ground except for one wall, on which appears, "as if graven in *bas relief* upon the white surface, the figure of a gigantic *cat*" (600). The narrator immediately rationalizes this protophotographic "apparition," forgetting Pluto and his guilt, until one night he chances upon another black cat, who is in all respects similar to his old pet except for an indefinite white splotch on its chest.[69] The animal follows the narrator to his new house and "domesticate[s] it self at once" (601). Soon, the narrator finds himself resenting his new pet. A "certain sense of shame, and the remembrance of [his] former deed of cruelty," prevent him from abusing it until one day when the cat makes him stumble on his way to the cellar. Losing his temper, the narrator attempts to kill it; instead, he accidentally buries the axe intended for the cat in his wife's skull. In order to conceal his deed, he immures the body of his murdered wife in his cellar:

> Upon the fourth day of the assassination, a party of the police came, very unexpectedly, into the house, and proceeded again to make rigorous investigation of the premises. Secure, however, in the inscrutability of my place of concealment, I felt no embarrassment whatever. The officers bade me accompany them in their search. They left no nook or corner unexplored. (605)

Just as the police are about to vacate the cellar, leaving the corpse undetected and the deed unpunished, a strange noise is heard, "a voice from within the tomb!" This voice, exclaims the narrator, was "a cry, at first muffled and broken, like the sobbing of a child, and then quickly swelling into one long, loud, and continuous scream, utterly anomalous and inhuman—a howl—a wailing shriek. . . . I had walled up the monster up within the tomb!" (606). The story invites not only a reading about crypts and disappearing/reappearing dead/alive animals but also an economic reading. This reading is elicited because the narrator's fortune is intimately bound to the cat's (cats') pathetic lot and by the question of who or what is invited to circulate in and out of the house (just as for Foucault, the problem of the modern city is who or what is allowed to circulate in or out of it). Whereas the ape in "The Murders in the Rue Morgue" is never "present" (though it lurks in every aperture), the cat ultimately betrays where it has been hiding/hidden. It was held captive neither in nor out of the house but on its threshold, incorporated into the house's very walls—we might say "eaten" by the house, sublated within it. If "no eyes could detect anything suspicious," walls in Poe stories have ears (and a mouth), and the animal returns with a vengeance: "Upon [the head of my wife's corpse], with red extended mouth and solitary eye of fire, sat the hideous beast whose craft had seduced me into murder, and whose informing voice had consigned me to the hangman" (606).

The tale easily—perhaps too easily—lends itself to a psychological reading: the undying creature is the objective correlative of the narrator's unsuccessfully repressed murderous impulse and guilt. Poe's stories have often proven hospitable to symbolic interpretations—psychoanalytic hermeneutics in particular—that, under the pretense of illuminating the truth underlying the story, have buried certain details under a critical apparatus at once ingenious and smothering.[70] The best example may be Marie Bonaparte's identification of the black cat with Poe's mother: "Though a tom and named Pluto, we should not be misled, for the Black Cat, as it were, is a totem of Poe's mother, conjured up by [Poe's cat] Catterina's presence round the house and bed of his consumptive mother-figure, Virginia."[71] One of the (many) problems of this reading is its outright conflation of the empirical figure of the author with the fictional narrator (Bonaparte's thesis is that Poe's entire oeuvre becomes intelligible when viewed through the prism of infantile trauma caused by the death of the author's mother).[72] The animal in her interpretation is glossed over, readily purloined, put at a safe distance (*pur-loign*) to facilitate the conversion of signs into symptoms. Even when Bonaparte underlines Poe's affection for his pet cat, she immediately converts the animal into a mere "cipher." She disregards the fact that Catterina's very name encrypts the animal, thereby disavowing the visual agency to which the cat owes its name (from *cattare,* "to see").[73]

Is it possible, in Poe, to recognize the cat in its own right? Can the animal be seen, and can it see for itself? Can the animal signify without being transfigured into an empty signifier? An earlier story by Poe, "Instinct vs Reason: A Black Cat" (1840), suggests that he was actively preoccupied by these questions. In this essay-like tale, which is yet another story about an animal escaping a space designed by and for humans, the narrator gives a detailed account of the stratagems used by his pet to open the kitchen door, which muddies the "line which demarcates the instinct of the brute creation from the boasted reason of man—a boundary line far more difficult to settle than even the North-Eastern or the Oregon" (371). The animal appears as an untraceable frontier. The cat in the story is a plausible blueprint for "The Black Cat," and the minute description of the door's complex mechanism also anticipates the intricate technical explanations of the self-fastening window that Dupin will elaborate in "The Murders in the Rue Morgue." These careful forms of phenomenological attention displayed in "A Black Cat" offer one path that Poe follows in order to consider the animal as animal—one that harks back to Montaigne's playful interaction with his cat and anticipates Derrida's insistence that the cat seeing him naked in his bathroom is a "real cat . . . [not] *the figure* of a cat."[74] But "*A* Black Cat" does not become "*The* Black Cat" until Poe incorporates it into his fiction. There is thus another path to seeing the animal—the path that, following Poe's and Benjamin's cues, I have called decryption. One does not decrypt an animal sign like one decodes a cipher.

Decryption is not about heightened or enhanced attention, and it has little to do with "cryptography," for cryptography remains at bottom a form of writing (*graphein*) that can always, in principle, be decoded.[75]

The crime scene in "The Murders in the Rue Morgue" is not a cipher and thus cannot be decoded; it makes no sense, from a logical point of view, since it seems that nothing has been premeditated. It resists the kind of observation associated with the police, who are portrayed as being excessively methodical, as proceeding too much "by 'the book'" (398). Yet Dupin claims that this very absence—the lack of signs of premeditation that would allow the police to decode the narrative—are precisely what lead him to unravel the puzzle of the killer's species. From this perspective, the ape's attempts at signifying are but a vain and grotesque pantomime, an "empty gesture" that does not point toward a coherent subject or rational actor. The ape means nothing, signifies nothing, as French scholar Bruno Monfort contends: the razor with which it slits Madame L'Espanaye's throat is but a hollow semiophore because it is not wielded by a human hand—or, as Monfort sees it, by no hand at all (the title of Monfort's essay is "Sans les mains," meaning "hands-free" or "without hands").[76] Yet the text indicates that the ape does have hands, only not "human hands." The Ourang-Outang is thus a senseless, "pure mimetic force,"[77] only from a certain anatomical view that chooses to see difference instead of similarity.[78] By granting the ape hands, Poe's text portrays the primate as a rebellious animal unwilling to recognize the place to which it has been consigned (in the Western city and in the taxonomic order).

The ape's crossing of borders exemplifies a central concern of Poe's animal tales: debunking the fantasized hermeticism of human spaces and scripts. These stories evidence, invite, and perform different modalities of writing and reading sustained by an altogether different kind of reason. Although Dupin presents himself as a hyperrational figure who approaches the animal as a logical problem—he claims to recover the lost ape because of the animal's assumed illogicity—he concedes that it takes the skills of a hunter to ferret the animal out of its crypt. Just before inspecting the nail upon which the mystery's resolution depends, Dupin boasts of his analytical method:

> To use a *sporting phrase,* I had not been once "*at fault.*" The *scent* had never for an instant been lost. There was no flaw in any link of the chain. I had *traced* the secret to its ultimate result,—and that result was the nail. It had, I say, in every respect, the appearance of its fellow in the other window; but this fact was an absolute nullity (conclusive as it might seem to be) when compared with the consideration that here, at this point, *terminated the clew.* (419; emphasis added)

"At fault," emphasized here by Poe's quotes, does not imply that Dupin never committed a logical error, as Baudelaire's translation of the tale suggests, but that the detective was never thrown off the animal's scent. The "sporting phrase" in question stems from the French *en défaut,* which in the elaborate scenography of medieval hunts designated the process by which auxiliaries, often dogs or birds of prey, were misled by the quarry to pursue another animal in its stead.[79] Priding himself with never losing the scent of the animal—never allowing himself to be deflected to chasing a human being (understood as a rational creature)—the detective decrypts the signs of the animal escaped from its vault.

DECRYPTION

Let us follow Dupin one last time, picking up the trail where it went cold for the Parisian police. As I have suggested, Poe's tale can be approached as an allegory of reading. Many of the clues scattered throughout the story are explicitly intended for the reader and bear little diegetic significance. When the detective insists on the necessity of using a hunter's ear and nose to decrypt the maze of the modern city, he underlines the fact that the police do not have even "the slightest clew" (406). Sound and spelling matter: first, in this *clew* one hears the French for *nail* (*le clou*), whose invisible fissure Dupin discovers, the key to the locked-room mystery. This pun betrays a line of fracture in the *clew/clou,* a linguistic transgression in which the *clou* (the nail) phonetically encroaches upon the semantic clue given to the reader. But the modern spelling, *clue,* would also perform this punny work, for it, too, is a homophone of the French *clou.* Poe's use of the archaic variant thus has another function: it conjures the tale's indebtedness to the myth of Theseus and the Minotaur. Thus spelled, *clew* also evokes the ball of thread given by Ariadne to Theseus to mark his way out of the labyrinth.[80] This orthographic clue is another hint at the resolution of the story (the final encounter with a semihuman, homicidal creature).[81] Attention to the composition of the text at the level of the word (and especially the letter, with its phonetic and archeonymic entanglements with the semantic and semiotic levels of the text) makes this "reading" possible. The clue is literally in the clew.

The tale recounts not one but two of Dupin's investigations, which illustrate the extraordinary powers of the analytic mind. The first scene of the tale (which is almost as well known as the solving of the murders) depicts Dupin showcasing his deductive faculties. This scene offers suggestive clues about how animal signs may be decrypted in "The Murders in the Rue Morgue." The narrator provides a "case in point" to illustrate the truth of Dupin's boast that "most men, in respect to himself, wore windows in their bosoms" (401). In this exemplary anecdote, Dupin and the narrator are silently strolling down a Parisian street when suddenly the detective breaks the silence to agree with the narrator's unspoken thoughts (which center on the mediocre performance of Chantilly, a cobbler recently converted to acting, who he deems unqualified for playing the role of Xerxes in Crébillon's eponymous tragedy). The narrator is "amazed": how did the detective read his mind? Dupin retraces the steps of his analysis: "The larger links of the chain run thus—Chantilly, Orion, Dr. Nichol, Epicurus, Stereotomy, the street stones, the fruiterer" (403). In these "running links" we can glimpse Dupin's theory of reading, tracking his trail of thought back to its source by remembering the "primitive" knowledge of the hunter.

Dupin reminds his friend that as they had crossed the street, a fruiterer with a large basket of apples had thrust the narrator upon a pile of paving stones. This stumble, Dupin infers, caused the narrator to reflect on "stereotomy," the method by which the street is paved. This in turn led him "to think of atomies, and thus of the theories of Epicurus." Dupin had recently mentioned to the narrator that "the vague guesses of that noble Greek had met with confirmation in the late nebular cosmogony" (of Dr. Nichol, though this link is missing in Dupin's reconstruction). Upon hearing this, the narrator could not avoid casting his "eyes upward to the great *nebula* in Orion," a gesture that corroborated Dupin's speculations. Finally, the thought of Orion triggered the memory of the line about Chantilly in the newspaper the day before: "*Perdidit antiquum litera prima sonum.*" Dupin explains this rather cryptic *mot d'esprit*:

> I had told you that *this was in reference to Orion, formerly written Urion; and, from certain pungencies connected with this explanation,* I was aware that you could not have forgotten it. It was clear, therefore, that you would not fail to combine the two ideas of Orion and Chantilly. That you did combine them I saw by the character of the smile which passed over your lips. You thought of the poor cobbler's immolation. So far, you had been stooping in your gait; but now I saw you draw yourself up to your full height. I was then sure that you reflected upon the diminutive figure of Chantilly. (404; emphasis added)

Crucially, every step of the deductive chain had been produced or confirmed by the physical signs that index the narrator's thoughts: stumbling, stooping, smiling, etc. This episode also reminds us of Dupin's contention that stars are viewed more distinctly when contemplated "in a side-long way," for part of the confirmation is the narrator's glance up to the constellation—a reminder that eyes are never just seeing, but can be seen seeing—and as the observer is captivated by his surrounding, other eyes are upon him.

In this allusion to the nebula lies another clue, whose full luster appears if we look at it sideways. In Greek mythology, Orion is the great hunter, a figure who is at times assimilated to the giant Nimrod, "the great Hunter before God" who originated the project of the Tower of Babel. Orion is not a fortuitous link in Dupin's chain but a surrogate for himself as the detective-hunter. In certain versions of the myth, Orion is blinded by Artemis (the goddess of the hunt) because he threatens to surpass her, but he continues to hunt using his other senses until his sight is restored by the god of the sun, Helios (the name Muybridge adopted as a photographer, incidentally). Orion is thus the one who does not see, or who sees with new eyes. He is the arch-hunter, never "at fault," who never loses the scent of his animal prey. But ironically, Dupin hints that the hunter himself has a scent, making himself liable to being hunted.[82] The giant owes his original name, Urion, to his birth from the urine of Jupiter, Neptune, and Mercury.[83] Over time, Dupin recalls, his name was corrupted (*perdidit*), concealing the "pungencies" associated with it (hiding ignoble origins behind a new name, just as the cobbler Chantilly sought to climb the social ladder by playing the role of a king, just as the ape's shaving could be interpreted as a sign of its attempt to pass as human).[84] The transformation of Orion's name performs a literal sublimation—a sublimation at the level of the letter. About this alteration, Ovid writes: "*Perdidit antiquum litera prima sonum,*" meaning "the first letter has lost its original sound." Dupin quotes the Latin poet who laments the counterintuitive degeneracy of language (wherein decay gives way to purification, as the obscene letter no longer smells). This sanitization marks the shift from soma to semiosis, from hunt to capture. The hunter-detective is the one who exhumes the stench of the animal from within the ostensible cleanliness of the letter, who decrypts the traces that unknowingly animate the human institution of written language. With his reference to Urion/Orion, Dupin thus acknowledges his dependence on his senses rather than mere logic. Not only does he track the scent of the animal encrypted in the letter, but he also shows that it takes an animal to smell it out (Orion is both the hunter and the hunted). "[Feeling] his way . . . in search of the true," Dupin is Nietzschean avant la lettre: "It is my fate," writes Nietzsche in *Ecce Homo,* "that I have to be the first *decent* human being; . . . I was first to experience lies as lies—smelling them out.—My genius is in my nostrils."[85]

In the beginning was the word *Urine* (with which animals mark their territories), but this pungent origin soon covered its own tracks—and the evolutionary tracks leading from the ape to the human. *Urion* is made *Orion*; the prefix *Ur* (denoting origin) became the conjunction *Or* (indicating equivalence).[86] Combined, these two fragments spell out the first syllable of *Ourang-Outang*. This may be the reason behind Poe's strange spelling. Or perhaps *Ourang-Outang* is spelled this way because, unlike the more traditional variants, there is but one single letter setting apart the two hyphenated words: *OuRang-OuTang* (from *orang*, "man," and *hutan*, "forest"). In *Le règne animal*, Cuvier notes that *Ourang*, meaning "reasonable" in Malay, applies to the human as well as to the Ourang-Outang and the elephant.[87] The only "thing" preventing the senseless repetition of the same—the only "thing" that stands between human reason (ourang) and animal instinct (outang)—is a single letter. The balance between reason and unreason, between body and mind (or head), between human and animal, rests upon the (dis)articulation of two letters. The letters become sigils of their animal descent. Specular chase: Edgar Allan Poe, whose imprimatur is EAP, encrypts his own signature: *APE*. Therein Poe acknowledges his debt to the animal language ghosting human language.[88]

CREATURES OF REASON

With the figure of the detective, the archaic knowledge of the hunt does not disappear but becomes subordinated—Foucault would say "subjugated"—to a form of knowledge that dons the white mantle of Reason.[89] For Lindon Barrett, Dupin is a direct descendent of that exemplary "figure of reason," French naturalist Georges Cuvier, both "in terms of intellectual notoriety and in assuming the co-implication of the bestial and the non-European."[90] Barrett makes Dupin the figurehead of an enlightened order of things that subjects nature to an inescapably rational and deeply hierarchized system of classification.[91] Barrett's reading is convincing, but I would qualify his claim that "Dupin and Poe share Cuvier." His claim rests on these three having a shared belief in pure rationality, a belief that rests on a strict partition between mind and body.[92] But this partition, for Dupin, is precisely the "reason" for the prefect's error, whom Dupin mocks for being "all head and no body" (431). Poe writes Dupin as a fundamentally ambiguous figure who displays not just logos but *mètis*, or "cunning," another form of intelligence that is typically associated with both the practical acumen of the hunter and the wiliness of the hunted animal.[93] In Poe's story, *mètis* has been subjugated to rational logic, as the ape, eventually, is made subject to the rational grid of surveillance in the city. The hunt only appears cryptically, between the lines; when the animal(ized) rises to the surface, it is as if by magic, because its traces have been deemed illegible and the technique for decrypting them has been delegitimized. So Barrett is right that non-Western subjects and unreasoned animals are affiliated with one another, and he is right that this is a story about keeping the unwelcome animalized and racialized others under control. Reason, however, is less the means than the alibi of this immunological operation.

Dupin undergoes a certain degree of animalization in order to "feel [his] way . . . in search for the true" and "scent" the traces of the lost animal, but he ultimately proves a relatively safe figure: he closes the mysterious case, restores order in the city, and reassures the good people of Paris that the borders delimiting their space and species remain strong. Yet the tale's denouement hinges on a troubling aporia. It is only when the detective postulates an unbridgeable threshold of difference between the human and the animal that the ape is allowed to make his entrance. Thus glimpsed from across an abyss of unknowability, the animal disappears just as it comes into being; he is presented as a purely negative being whose motivations cannot be fathomed, whose voice defies intelligibility, and whose actions occur on an absolutely incommensurable plane (symptomatically, the animal is never physically present in the diegesis but exists only through retrospective narration of his owner, the sailor). He exists only cryptically, as that which stubbornly eludes the ingenuity of the police, who are guilty of proceeding excessively "by 'the book.'" Yet for Dupin it is the police's form of reason, not the animal, that is essentially negative.

The epigraph of Poe's tale introduces Dupin as a modern-day Ulysses, an allusion that encrypts how he successfully solves the puzzle posed by the story's titular murders: "What song the Syrens sang, or what name Achilles assumed when he hid himself among women, although puzzling questions, are not beyond all conjecture" (397). The reference to the sirens anticipates the threat posed by the orangutan to the fantasized hermeticism of species difference: whether depicted as winged creatures or mythical beings with the trunk of a woman and the tail of a fish, sirens are hybrid creatures, part-human, part-animal. Their captivating melodies allure sailors onto rocky shores where they perish in shipwrecks or, in some versions, are eaten alive by the sirens. The challenge raised by Poe's epigraph thus lies less in hearing the sirens' song than in surviving their encounter to report what was heard. In the Homeric account of the myth, Ulysses orders his crew to chain him to the mast of his ship and to ignore his supplications to set him free. Although Ulysses probably hears the sirens sing—a probability challenged by Kafka in his rewriting of this episode of *The Odyssey*—his knowledge requires self-alienation.[94] The episode of the sirens is an allegory of the pursuit of knowledge (typically rendered as the masculine conquest of a feminized object); the story of Ulysses and the sirens posits knowing as both irreconcilable with and tragically dependent on aesthetic experience, on one's sensory contact with the world. Bondage and isolation are the price that Ulysses must pay to know what song the sirens sang (a knowledge he cannot directly share with his crew).

Poe's version of this tale differs significantly from the original Greek story. In Homer's version, Ulysses must chain himself to avoid being captivated by the sirens' hybrid of humanity and animality, but in Poe's tale it is the humanlike animal that ends up captured.[95] What the narratives share, though, is their construal of knowledge—a knowledge intimately tied to the issue of ontological difference—as fundamentally grounded in detachment and distinction. Indeed, once it has been identified as a nonhuman animal and locked up in the Jardin des Plantes (Cuvier's favorite haunt and workplace), excised from the anthropic milieu of the city, the murderous ape is no longer seen as a threat to the human community. The tale of detection invites a prophylactic interpretation of Dupin as a champion of human exceptionalism, but it also reflects on the types of knowledge that are overtly and covertly at work in the capture of the fugitive animal. What other genres does the new animal condition allow and invite when animals appear far gone? This is the question that will preoccupy us in the next chapter, which reads Nathaniel Hawthorne's last published romance as a poetic response to the hegemonic submission of knowledge and imagination to the new form of rationality that Cuvier emblematizes. Here I turn to Hawthorne's own attempt—and self-avowed failure—to pen an elusive creature. In Hawthorne's romance, it is no longer the place of the animal that is in question but its time: while Poe's beast emerges from some unmappable elsewhere, Hawthorne's instead comes out of the depths of a time before the human.

— 4 —

FABULOUS TAXONOMY

(HAWTHORNE)

> "Unfitness to pursue our research in the unfathomable waters." "Impenetrable veil covering our knowledge of the cetacea." "A field strewn with thorns." "All these incomplete indications but serve to torture us naturalists." Thus speak of the whale, the great Cuvier, and John Hunter, and Lesson, those lights of zoology and anatomy.
> —Herman Melville, *Moby-Dick; or, The Whale*

In a chapter titled "The Fossil Whale," the narrator of *Moby-Dick* turns to paleontology in hopes of once and for all capturing—fully understanding, completing his knowledge about—the animal after which the novel is named. After presenting his credentials as a geologist (his former employment as a stonemason and a ditchdigger), Ishmael speculates on the remains of a skull found in the middle of Paris in 1779, which the founder of comparative anatomy Georges Cuvier had pronounced "to have belonged to some utterly unknown Leviathanic species."[1] Ishmael then recounts the comical misidentification of a colossal skeleton exhumed in Alabama in 1842.[2] Initially diagnosed as the relic of a Tertiary marine reptile and thus christened Basilosaurus (the "king lizard"), the skeleton was shipped to England where, upon meticulous examination of the fossil's teeth, the famed paleontologist

Richard Owen, the "British Cuvier," declared it to belong to an extinct type of whale that had lived at the end of the Eocene epoch. Thus, the Basilosaurus descended into the inscrutable waters of cryptozoology, a pseudoscience involved in the search for animals whose existence or survival remains unfounded (the Loch Ness monster or Sasquatch being archetypal cryptids).

Curiously, however, Ishmael invokes Cuvier less to dispel the mystery enshrouding Moby Dick than to emphasize and extol the undecipherability of a beast said to be older than time itself. *Moby-Dick*'s venture into paleontology grants a properly mythic dimension to the "antechronical creature" that is the whale, whose skeleton furnishes "*but little clue* to the shape of his fully invested body" (498; emphasis added).[3] In contrast to Cuvier's method, for which a single fragment of bone provided an almost certain way of knowing the whole of the animal, Ishmael allows the immensity and undecipherability of the critter itself to contaminate his text. When he chooses to introduce the whale "in an archaeological, fossiliferous, and antediluvian point of view," he deliberately selects ostentatious and pompous adjectives (497): "Applied to any other creature than the Leviathan—to an ant or a flea—such portly terms might justly be deemed unwarrantably grandiloquent. But when Leviathan is the text, *the case is altered*" (496). We must read the altered "case" literally, as the very size and shape of the letters composing the book swell from minuscules to majuscules under the influence of its enormous subject: "Unconsciously my chirography expands into placard capitals. Give me a condor's quill! Give me the Vesuvius' crater for an inkstand!" (496). The whale, whose superlative magnitude demands that he be treated in an "imperial folio" and described with the "weightiest words of the dictionary," thus silently shapes the volume set out to contain it. If his "fully invested body" tends to vanish under the scalpel of modern science, the animal impresses itself into the figure of the novel to which it bequeaths his name.

This chapter pursues the possible correlation between literary form and the question of animal capture raised in the previous chapter. Following Ishmael's insight, it shows that different genres are more or less disposed to the apprehension of different animals, more or less suited to the specificity of their object. In "The Murders in the Rue Morgue," Poe's fugitive ape ultimately proved containable, with the help of Cuvier's taxonomic profile and by the frame of the detective story. But other "cryptic animals"—creatures that defy modern classification because of their supposed immortality (Melville's whale) or incoherent hybridity (Cooper's ass)—seem to constitute the end of modern fiction, in the double sense of its motivation and its ruin. In this chapter, I focus on Nathaniel Hawthorne's *The Marble Faun* (1860), which also invokes Cuvier in its attempt to apprehend an elusive creature, but unlike "The Murders in the Rue Morgue," theatrically rejects the authority of the naturalist. Hawthorne's romance can thus be read, I propose, as a response to Poe's detective story. Both "The Murders in the Rue Morgue" and *The Marble Faun* take place in Europe, both make their cryptic protagonists criminals, and both meditate on the animal's place (or lack thereof) in the urban spaces that make up the backdrop of their narratives and in the cultural imaginaries that predate the Darwinian revolution.[4] These works also constitute self-reflexive experiments in the evolving art of fiction writing, which responded to the pressures of and found itself shaped (at times invigorated, at times inhibited) by what we could call the modern anatomic reason epitomized by Cuvier, who devised a taxonomic hermeneutic that presumed knowledge about animality—a necessary principle for his science of comparative anatomy—while casting animals as unknowable in their singularity.

CASE IN POINT: HAWTHORNE'S PROFESSED IGNORANCE

Published only a few months after *On the Origin of Species,* Hawthorne's last finished romance, *The Marble Faun; or, The Romance of Monte Beni,* blurs the age-old opposition between humans and animals by introducing a faunlike creature into the setting of then-present-day Rome.[5] The young Donatello, count of Monte Beni, is thought by his friends to bear a striking resemblance to sculptor Praxiteles's marble faun, which depicts a mythical, hybrid being, "neither man nor animal."[6] At first sight, the marble creature seems to resist taxonomic categorization. Yet when its animality is ultimately confirmed by "two definite signs" (the faun's ears, "terminating in little peaks, like those of some species of animals"), paradoxically, it resists being known at all: "The animal nature," we are told, "is a most essential part of the Faun's composition. . . . Praxiteles has subtly diffused throughout his work that *mute mystery* which so hopelessly perplexes us whenever we attempt to *gain an intellectual or sympathetic knowledge* of the lower orders of creation" (9–10; emphasis added). Whereas the marble faun's ears indisputably categorize him as animal (and consign it to unknowability), it is never made explicit whether Donatello himself is or is not a faun. The intrusion of this ambiguous specimen into what is otherwise a realist setting precipitates the epistemological fuzziness that characterizes *The Marble Faun* and registers the romance's resistance to the paradigm of capture that drives the taxonomic impulse. The story ends with the character of the American sculptor Kenyon politely refusing to offer a definitive answer to the question of Donatello's possible animality. When asked if Donatello's ears are as pointy as those of the titular figure, he only smiles inscrutably and says: "I know but may not tell. . . . On that point, at all events, there shall be not one word of explanation" (467).

On that point—that of Donatello's ears—the author himself remained obstinately tight-lipped. When readers wrote to the publisher to express their frustration with the enigmatic treatment of the character of Donatello and other ambiguities left unresolved in *The Marble Faun,* Hawthorne consented to add an explanatory postscript in the new edition of the book. His postscript, however, would only prove more vexing, for, instead of explaining, the author chastises his readers for wanting to know too much. He further disappoints them by referring to "the Author" in the third person, abandoning the omniscient voice he used for most of the romance:

> The idea of the modern Faun loses all the poetry and beauty which the Author fancied in it, and becomes nothing better than a grotesque absurdity, if we bring it into the actual light of day. He had hoped to mystify this anomalous creature between the Real and the Fantastic, in such a manner that the reader's sympathies might be excited to a certain pleasurable degree, *without impelling him to ask how Cuvier would have classified poor Donatello,* or to insist upon being told, in so many words,

> whether he had furry ears or no. As respects all who ask such questions, the book is, to that extent, a failure. (463–64; emphasis added)

How are we to understand this appeal to ignorance? What role does animality play in the epistemic, ethical, and poetic economy of the period, and in the genre of the romance—which at the time of Hawthorne's writing was already passé, out of step with its time? These questions are inextricable from one another: it is not by accident that animality frames debates about knowledge, whether "intellectual or sympathetic," at this particular point in the nineteenth century, and it is not by accident that the question of knowledge and categorization is bound up with questions of fictional genre (genre being itself a taxonomic category).

If we believe Hawthorne's *Notebooks,* the romance was initially conceived as a story of felicitous affinities between wild deities and human beings:

> I looked at the Faun of Praxiteles, and was sensible of a peculiar charm in it; a sylvan beauty and homeliness, friendly and wild at once. The lengthened, but not preposterous ears, and the little tail, which we infer, have an exquisite effect, and make the spectator smile in his very heart. . . . It seems to me that a story, with all sorts of fun and pathos in it, might be contrived on the idea of their species having become intermingled with the human race; a family with the faun blood in them having prolonged itself from the classic era till our own days. *The tail might have disappeared, by dint of constant intermarriages with ordinary mortals; but the pretty hairy ears should occasionally reappear in members of the family*; and the moral instincts and intellectual characteristics of the faun might be most picturesquely brought out, without detriment to the human interest of the story. Fancy this combination in the person of a young lady![7]

Hawthorne did not pursue the idea of a female faun, but he did center his romance around issues of filiation and hybridity.[8] Considering that Hawthorne wrote this romance on the eve of the Civil War, and given the racism that saturated antebellum scientific discourses, this work has often been regarded as a parable on the perils of miscegenation and the corruption of America's racial and cultural integrity.[9] Yet there is little anxiety in the extract above, and, unless one adopts a strictly anthropocentric point of view, *The Marble Faun* is hardly reducible to an apologia for racial purity.[10] In light of the epistemological debates that agitated Europe and the United States at the time, I propose instead to read the romance of the modern faun as an allegory of taxonomic knowledge—as a critical examination of how the newly prominent epistemology of capture altered the view and knowledge of animals. This framing does not dispel so much as displace the specters of racism and xenophobia that permeate the romance, as it shifts racial concerns from classical to modern taxonomy—or, as Benjamin Murphy suggests, from taxonomy to genealogy (to determine Donatello's "faunship," Kenyon explicitly proposes to "investigat[e] the pedigree . . . of his forefathers" [82]).[11]

Taxonomy, in its classical version, inventories knowledge about the natural world; it distributes beings horizontally in a tabulated space, a series of side-by-side boxes, like the drawers of the naturalist's specimen room, into which various critters should neatly fit. Comparative anatomy, in contrast, verticalizes this tabulation by introducing time as a variable; this paves the way for phylogenetic and biopolitical conceptions of race and species, which are now situated along a temporal axis of transformation and evolution (a set of relationships that Darwin would come to figure by the branching and ramifying of an enormous tree). Classical taxonomy assumes an immediate correspondence between knowledge and vision; modern taxonomy also relies on vision, but a vision that has lost the privilege of immediacy: observable details now read as shifting markers indicative of relative stages of development. Not only does comparative anatomy seek to correlate the outside with the inside (as Britt Rusert argues of the changing nature of racial science in the antebellum period), but it also troubles what it means to see something when that something is part of a living being.[12]

It is precisely the visual exposure of Donatello's intimate "parts" that the romance withholds from the reader, inviting her instead to be content with superficial impressions, stubbornly refusing to go "deeper." Seeing superficially is not refusing knowledge but spurning a certain type of knowledge, which the romance equates with the investigations of a "genealogist . . . tracing out link by link, and authenticating [a pedigree] by records and documentary evidences" (180). *The Marble Faun* challenges the taxonomic presumption associated with Cuvier, whose name is a metonym for the rigid worldview that dominated biology and geology in Europe during the first half of the century and, later, the United States under the influence of Louis Agassiz. The pursuit of anatomic knowledge—a particular type of diagnostic and classificatory knowledge—seems irresolvably in tension with the work performed by the romance, as the disclosure of a small anatomical detail that would index Donatello's animality threatens to puncture the edifice of Hawthorne's fable. Figuring an alternative to the systematic tendencies of anatomic classification, *The Marble Faun* provides an exemplary case study for assessing the fate of fiction after Cuvier. The romance suggests that an ineradicable conjectural impulse animates Cuvier's systematics and that "poetic" speculation necessarily supplements taxonomic knowledge.[13] Pointing to this speculative element by no means impedes the "purifying" work that genealogy (in Darwin's sense) has often been enlisted to perform in the modern age. As a matter of fact, uncertainty is the very condition for a biopolitical management of race insofar as biopolitics imagines that the racial other does not threaten it "from elsewhere" but from within—and, as it were, from before.[14] Yet the insistence on the romance's function in this new grand narrative also recognizes an immanent possibility for taxonomic fabulation within this new regime of knowledge, a chance for imagining alternative economies of relation, other forms of kinship.

The Marble Faun was in Hawthorne's time his most popular romance, yet critics have consistently considered it something of a failure. In this they follow Ralph Waldo Emerson, who reportedly called it "a mere mush," and Henry James, for whom the Italian romance is "of slighter value than its [American] companions" because it lacks their completeness and mastery: "The art of narration, in

Transformation [the title of the English edition], seems to me more at fault than in the author's other novels. The story straggles and wanders, is dropped and taken up again, and towards the close lapses into an almost fatal vagueness."[15] For French critic Pierre-Yves Pétillon, *The Marble Faun* is "above all a novel 'out of focus' [*un roman flou*], in the photographic sense of the term."[16] Pétillon is perhaps hinting at the strange fate of the book, which was almost immediately taken up as a guidebook for British and American tourists, and for which the German editor Tauchnitz prepared an interleaved edition in 1860 for readers to insert personal drawings and photographs of the works referenced in the romance. The book's generic undecidability, it seems, prompted a different kind of response and compelled a different kind of attention. Its blurring effect resulted from a careful work on the reliability of the point of view, which Hawthorne deliberately left out of focus, but this makes little difference; the author himself admits that the book can only be, for the realist reader, "a failure" (464).

The treatment of Donatello's character is exemplary of the romance's nebulosity. Henry James comments:

> Every one will remember the figure of the simple, joyous, sensuous young Italian, who is *not so much* a man as a child, and *not so much* a child as a charming, innocent animal, and how he is brought to self-knowledge and to a miserable conscious manhood, by the commission of a crime. Donatello is *rather vague and impalpable*; he says *too little* in the book, shows himself *too little,* and *falls short,* I think, of being a creation.[17]

Riddled with seminegations, James's assessment suggests that Donatello's portrait is vague because the creature is categorically out of place, "as if a painter, in composing a picture, should try to give you an impression of one of his figures by a strain of music."[18] He finds the specimen literally ungraspable and therefore literarily disappointing: "The fault of *Transformation* is that the element of the unreal is pushed too far, and that the book is neither positively of one category nor the other. . . . This is the trouble with Donatello himself."[19] It was not only the readers or the critics that were reluctant to accept Donatello's generic ambiguity. The characters themselves are also fixated upon establishing Donatello's common ancestry to his marble counterpart, interested in classifying him as related to or distinct from the faun, wishing for "a substantial fact" that "may be tested by absolute touch and measurement" to allow them to pin him down (7). To ascertain whether he shares the faun's "pointed and furry ears" ("the sole indications of his wild, forest nature") his friends tauntingly ask him to move aside his brown curls and expose his ears to their scrutiny (10). But Donatello begs his companions not to examine him too closely: "'I entreat you to take the tip of my ears for granted.' . . . 'I shall be like a wolf of the Apennines . . . if you touch my ears ever so softly. None of my race could endure it. It has always been a tender point with my forefathers and me'" (12). The play on the "sensitivity" of his ears (and his sensitivity on the subject of his ears) underscores the book's erotic subtext, played up by its echoes of Titania's spellbound attraction for Bottom's furry ears in *A Midsummer Night's Dream.*[20]

Donatello's protestations, his repeated refusal to submit his body fully to legibility, call to mind what Daphne Brooks calls the "spectacular opacities" staged by black subjects to "confound and disrupt conventional constructions of the racialized and gendered body."[21] The most infamous case of this "'dominative imposition of transparency' systematically willed on to black figures" is that of Sara "Saartjie" Baartman, a Khoikhoi woman exhibited as a curiosity in Europe at the beginning of the nineteenth century because her secondary sex characteristics (her breasts, buttocks, and genitalia, including both external and internal organs) were viewed as abnormally large. After Baartman's death at the age of twenty-six, Cuvier made a plaster cast of her body before dissecting it and extracting her brain and genitalia, which were exhibited in the Museum of Natural History until 1974. The anatomist, who compared Baartman to an orangutan on account of a suspiciously selective set of criteria,[22] was particularly obsessed by her sexual organs, whose perceived hypertrophy inverted the "ideologies of anatomical size that governed investigations of brains and skulls where largeness was equated with superiority and civilizing potential."[23] It is thus telling that the "point" that rouses inquisitiveness and on which Donatello's friends' understanding stumbles is sexually marked. It is just a detail, but details are precisely what demarcate one species from another. Comparative anatomy is, indeed, a matter of detailing (from the French *tailler,* "to cut"), of cutting (from the Latin, *ana-tomia,* "cutting up"), of dissecting, and, according to Michel Foucault, of "dividing [bodies] into distinct portions" in order to disclose "the great resemblances that would otherwise have remained invisible."[24]

It is precisely this anatomizing logic, which dismantles bodies in the name of a hidden, transhistorical, unitary principle—life, heredity, sexual drive—that the romance so dramatically rejects.[25] *The Marble Faun*'s avowed unfinishedness, its blurring of categories both taxonomic and generic, is thus less a symptom of the writer's fatigue than the sign of a poetic and ethical calculation. For Emily Miller Budick, the sort of generic indeterminacy on display in *The Marble Faun* is the trademark characteristic of the American romance, which operates in direct contrast with the realist conventions of the European novel.[26] Hawthorne himself famously makes the distinction between novel and romance in the preface to *The House of the Seven Gables,* claiming for the romance "a certain latitude both as to its fashion and material," whereas the novel "is presumed to aim at a very minute fidelity, not merely to the possible, but to the *probable and ordinary* course of man's existence."[27] Consciously running the risk of "failure," Hawthorne plays the romance's fabulous taxonomy against the taxonomic fabulations of the realist novel.

FICTION IN THE AGE OF CUVIER

Of course, not all fiction is imperiled by the type of knowledge Cuvier personifies. The French naturalist's influence on a novelist like Honoré de Balzac, who claimed to have modeled *The Human Comedy* after his system of comparative anatomy, is well known.[28] "Is not Cuvier the greatest poet of our century?" exclaims the narrator of Balzac's *The Wild Ass's Skin*:

> Certainly, Lord Byron has expressed in words some aspects of our spiritual turmoil; but our immortal natural historian has *reconstructed worlds from bleached bones,* has, like Cadmus, rebuilt cities by means of teeth, peopled anew a thousand forests with all the wonders of zoology thank to a few chips of coal and rediscovered the races of giants in a mammoth's foot. . . . He calls æons back into being without pronouncing the abracadabra of magic; he digs out a fragment of gypsum, describes a footprint in it, and cries out: "Behold!" *And suddenly marble turns into animals* [*les marbres s'animalisent*], dead things live anew and lost worlds are unfolded before us![29]

What Balzac's narrator extols is the synecdochic genius of Cuvier's method, which connects seemingly insignificant details to otherwise lost, invisible wholes. It is easy to understand what resource a realist novelist, who "unfolds the poeticality, the historicity written on the body of ordinary things," could derive from an epistemological model where every trivial thing becomes a "clue" unlocking worlds of knowledge for whoever is capable of reading it.[30]

The polar opposite of Hawthorne's romance, which prioritizes "the possible" over the "the probable," detective fiction is the genre that best employed and dramatized Cuvier's diagnostic genius, making the most of what historian Carlo Ginzburg calls the "evidential paradigm" (whose emergence Ginzburg situates in the second half of the nineteenth century across fields as varied as criminology, psychoanalysis, and art history).[31] In the ambitious genealogy he outlines in his essay, Ginzburg notes that Voltaire's Zadig prefigures the characters of Dupin and Sherlock Holmes when he deduces with uncanny precision the species and shape of some animals by simply looking at their tracks. It comes as little surprise, then, that Cuvier's name crops up at the end of Poe's "The Murders in the Rue Morgue." Detective fiction is the genre that corresponds to a universe ruled by conjecture and probability (it is the ourang-outang's improbable presence, we remember, that subjected him to the detective's capture). Cuvier himself, when he praised the new science of paleontology, compared its deductive powers to those of Voltaire's proto-detective:

> Today, anyone who sees only the print of a cloven hoof might conclude that the animal that had left it behind was a ruminator, and this conclusion is *as certain as any in physics and in ethics.* This footprint alone, then, provides the observer with information about the teeth, the jawbone, the vertebrae, each leg bone, the thighs, shoulders and pelvis of the animal which had just passed: *it is a more certain proof than all Zadig's tracks.*[32]

Given this literary origin, and given the eminently narrative character of the diagnostic paradigm—which Ginzburg associates with the hunter's ability to convert disparate and seemingly insignificant details into a coherent sequence of events—what are we to make of Hawthorne's professed antipathy toward Cuvier?[33] His aversion, I contend, pertains to the metonymic arrogance of the anatomist's epistemological model when it purports to situate "with certainty" a singular entity in relation to a given reality.[34]

Cuvier's unfavorable comparison of Zadig's method with paleontology suggests that the naturalist was not entirely satisfied with the diagnostic paradigm Voltaire narrativizes. His dissatisfaction, we can speculate, stems from the fact that the paradigm is by definition "conjectural" and thereby, to a degree, as Ginzburg concludes, "unscientific," if *scientific* means exact, systematic, and unequivocal.[35] Inherited from immemorial venatic lore and divinatory practices, the diagnostic method is "far removed from higher forms of knowledge which are the privileged property of an elite few"; instead, it is the property "of hunters, of sailors, of women," and it "binds the human animal closely to other animal species."[36] In that regard, it appears incompatible with the totalizing and systematic aspirations of the naturalist's "anatomical" model.[37] What Cuvier praised in the diagnostic method, therefore, is less the method itself (which includes an

PLATE 1. John Syme, *John James Audubon*, 1826. Oil on canvas, 35 ½ × 27 ½ inches. White House Historical Association: 485.

PLATE 2. John James Audubon, *Golden Eagle, Aquila chrysaetos,* 1833. Watercolor, pastel, graphite, and selective glazing, 38 × 25 ½ inches. Collection of the New-York Historical Society. Digital image created by Oppenheimer Editions. United States public domain.

PLATE 3. Jacques-Louis David, *Bonaparte franchissant le Grand-Saint-Bernard,* 1800. Oil on canvas, 101 × 87 inches. Collection of the Musée national des châteaux de Versailles et de Trianon.

PLATE 4. Walton Ford, *Delirium,* 2004. Watercolor, gouache, ink, and pencil on paper, 62 5⁄8 × 43 1⁄8 inches. Courtesy of the artist and Paul Kasmin Gallery.

ineradicable element of chance) than its underlying epistemology, the metonymic structure that correlates the singular with the general. (It is precisely this romantic devotion to wholeness that impressed Emerson so deeply when he first encountered Cuvier's work during his visit at the Jardin des Plantes in 1833.[38]) Comparative anatomy absolutizes the hunter's hunch by presupposing the existence of a single, all-encompassing principle that Cuvier names "life": "the only cause of all compositions—the mother, not only of animals and vegetables, but all bodies which now occupy the surface of the earth."[39] Anatomic details, for him, are significant only insofar as they are subordinated to a more general (and more essential) functionality; specimens count only insofar as they represent their species, genus, order, etc.[40] From his perspective, as I argue in the introduction, animals and humans alike disappear in their manifestation of a life that itself remains invisible. To say it with Foucault: "Animal species differ at their peripheries, and resemble each other at their centres; they are connected by the inaccessible, and separated by the apparent. . . . The more extensive the groups one wishes to find, the deeper must one penetrate into the organism's inner darkness, towards the less and less visible, into that dimension that eludes perception. . . . In short, living species 'escape' from the teeming profusion of individuals and species; they can be classified only because they are alive and on the basis of what they conceal."[41]

What Hawthorne (and Donatello) want to play with as metaphor, Cuvier (and the reader) demand to determine as metonymy. When Hawthorne refrains from disclosing small details of Donatello's anatomy, he rejects the correlationist closure of a system that would situate his character within or without a given category (in this case, the human species). When he declines to turn his character's ears into "two definite signs," he eschews the totalizing semiology wherein signs signify to the extent that they are negatively defined in relation with other signs. This formulation evokes not merely Saussure's differential conception of language "without positive terms" but also Rancière's definition of *literature* as the "modern regime of the art of writing"—which Rancière explicitly links to the work of Cuvier—that breaks with the representational model of the belles lettres toward a scriptural regime where "meaning becomes a 'mute' relation of signs to signs."[42] And indeed, there is something comically anachronistic and antimodern in the romance's stubborn refusal to anatomize Donatello, whose affinities with the faun can only be determined by way of a superficial "likeness" and not a structural homology in the arrangement of the organs. It is tempting thus to read *The Marble Faun* as resisting the imperatives of modern biology in its reluctance to privilege internal organizations over external resemblances. It is as if the romance asks whether we can appreciate Donatello not for what or who he is "deep inside" but for what he appears to be, on the surface—and whether this impression might impart any (unscientific yet valuable) knowledge to the observer. *The Marble Faun*'s anatomical reticence is proper not to fiction in general, as Poe and Balzac show, but specifically to the untimely genre of romance, which Cooper had doomed to extinction (see chapter 2), and which Hawthorne makes the preserve of "anomalous creatures" like Donatello:

> [The Author] reluctantly avails himself of the opportunity afforded by a new edition, to explain such incidents and passages as may have been left too much in the dark. . . . He designed the story and the characters to bear, of course, *a certain relation to human nature and human life,* but still to be so artfully and airily removed from our mundane sphere, that some laws and proprieties of their own should be implicitly and insensibly acknowledged. (463; emphasis added)

For Cuvier, knowledge aims at banishing or vanishing all uncertainty, whereas for Hawthorne, certainty is the point at which romantic fiction vanishes. Before asking what might be the meaning of the romance's reticence toward modern anatomic reason and what alternative form of knowledge it makes possible, let us look briefly at a case that exemplifies how Cuvier handles anomalous creatures, what the naturalist calls "doubtful specimens."

CUVIER'S SIREN, DARWIN'S POINT

In *The Open: Man and Animal,* Giorgio Agamben reminds us that Peter Artedi cataloged sirens alongside seals and sea lions in his 1735 zoological treatise. They were then cautiously added to the second edition of Linnaeus's *Systema Naturae* (1735), in the section entitled "Animalia Paradoxa." In *The Platypus and the Mermaid,* Harriet Ritvo records cases of mermaid spotting in England as late as 1822. Claims to have seen these fabulous human/animal hybrids, however, were being systematically disproven by anatomists.[43] Ritvo, for instance, relates the case of Captain Eades, who brought back a specimen of mermaid (or merman) from his journey to the Fiji islands. Upon inspection, William Clift, the curator of the Hunterian collection at the Royal College of Surgeons, proved that the mermaid was inauthentic, a "fraud, constructed of the cobbled remains of an orangutan, a baboon, and a salmon."[44] After that, sirens found shelter only in volumes of cryptozoology (and in P. T. Barnum's museum of "monsters," whose considerable popularity betrayed a desire for a world not yet entirely known and domesticated).[45]

In an 1807 text entitled "Anatomical Research on Reptiles Still Regarded as Doubtful by Naturalists [*Recherches anatomiques sur les reptiles regardés encore comme douteux par les naturalistes*]," Cuvier examines the case of three aquatic creatures that had until then defied classification. Each of the reptiles possessed both gills and lungs and, because of their large size, it was uncertain whether they were larvae or adult specimens. Up to that moment, the only known amphibian animals had been tadpoles, whose gills shriveled and disappeared as their lungs developed. The first reptile Cuvier studied bore the name of "siren" (*sirène*), presumably named after the mythical creature for its two front legs and a long tail. Sent from the Americas to Linnaeus in 1765, the creature was at first classified as an amphibian. But in 1785, Dr. Camper, a Dutch zoologist and pioneer in the new science of comparative anatomy, dissected a specimen of the siren that was owned by the British Museum of London and discerned no lungs, changing the creature's classification to "fish." In order to settle the dispute between his predecessors, Cuvier ordered that a fresh siren be sent from the New Continent. The autopsy confirmed that the animal possessed both gills and lungs and that its lateral appendages were legs, not fins. After a minutely detailed description of the animal's bone structure, Cuvier concluded that it was an adult specimen. To remove any remaining "doubt," the naturalist created a new order, the Perennibranchiata (a name that indicates that the batrachians' gills, or branchia, are perennial, persisting into adulthood). But this addition did not really add anything; it only filled in the gaps of an infinitely capacious taxonomic system. About Cuvier's method (and its material correlative, the organization of the natural history museum at the Jardin des Plantes), Lee Rust Brown observes that "nothing could be discovered that did not have an open place waiting for it." Any new specimen only confirmed, retroactively, the system's wholeness. "In the largest sense," Brown explains, "specimens did not so much fill these *lacunes* as they disappeared into them. . . . The Muséum could afford to welcome all new facts precisely because it was sure that every new fact would disappear into one *lacune* or another, and bring its encyclopedic representation of the world a step closer to perfection."[46] Thus, the fabulous siren disappeared, leaving the mythic waters of the Strait of Messina to be thrust into the rational universe of modern science.[47]

But if Cuvier contributed to the vanishing of hybrid animals into the mists of cryptozoology, there is nonetheless in his method something that appears monstrous to our post-Darwinian sensibility. Although he spearheaded the development of modern biology, breaking with the neatly tabulated spaces of Classical Age taxonomy to inject "historicity" into what had been a relatively static science, the founder of comparative anatomy unwaveringly believed in the immutability of species.[48] The predetermined character of Cuvier's classificatory system, not to mention its relative arbitrariness and blatant racism, would be questioned some fifty years later by Darwin's work, which revives (without fully endorsing) Buffon's continuist and Lamarck's transformist intuitions. Yet Cuvier's notorious fixism is not antithetical to Darwin's evolutionism, as Foucault shows that the former paved the way for the theory of evolution by positing the existence of an invisible unified plane connecting all living beings despite their surface differences (the "invention of life" discussed in the introduction). What truly sets the two scientists apart, Foucault contends, is less their views on species transformation than the priority Cuvier grants to general categories over empirical individualities:

> Darwin acknowledges that all the taxonomic frames proposed for classifying animals and plants are, to a certain point, abstract categories. For Darwin, then, there is one reality that is the individual and a second reality that defines the "varietivity" [*variativité*] of the individual: its capacity to vary. Everything else (be it species, genus, order) is a kind of construction built from this reality's starting point: the individual. In that sense, we can say that Darwin is absolutely opposed to Cuvier.[49]

Instead of thinking from the species down to the specimen, Darwin identifies numerous borderline cases where it is difficult to distinguish between species and variety; where Cuvier is anxious to incorporate anomalous cases into clearly defined species categories, Darwin highlights their irregularities to challenge the idea of the predetermined and immutable category of "species." In the first edition of *On the Origin of Species* (1859), Darwin elects the platypus and the siren—not Cuvier's North American siren but the *Lepidosiren paradoxa,* a South American lungfish—as his aberrant specimens of choice to explain his theory of evolution by natural selection:[50]

> The affinities of all the beings of the same class have sometimes been represented by a great tree. I believe this simile largely speaks the truth. The green and budding twigs may represent existing species; and those produced during each former year may represent the long succession of extinct species. . . . From the first growth of the tree, many a limb and branch has decayed and dropped off; and these lost branches of various sizes may represent those whole orders, families, and genera which have now no living representatives, and which are known to us only from having been found in a fossil state. As we here and there see a thin straggling branch springing from a fork low down

> in a tree, and which by some chance has been favoured and is still alive on its summit, *so we occasionally see an animal like the Ornithorhynchus or Lepidosiren, which in some small degree connects by its affinities two large branches of life, and which has apparently been saved from fatal competition by having inhabited a protected station.*[51]

Darwin views these aberrant creatures not as "doubtful specimens" awaiting taxonomic determination but as living clues pointing to a dynamic, open system founded on a principle of modification that is inherent to every organism.[52]

A decade later, in *The Descent of Man* (1871), Darwin tackles a subject that he had not dared to address in *On the Origin of Species*: the applicability of his theory of "descent with modification" to humans. It is with regard to the exceptional position of Man that Darwin departs most radically from Cuvier. "The greater number of naturalists who have taken into consideration the whole structure of man," he sneers, "have followed Blumenbach and Cuvier, and have placed man in a separate Order. . . . If man had not been his own classifier, he would never have thought of founding a separate order for his own reception."[53] In the first pages of the work, Darwin remarks that a significant percentage of human ears present a congenital condition: a protuberance at the junction of the upper and middle thirds (see Figures 9a and 9b), commonly known as "Darwin's point" (or "Darwin's tubercle"). This oddity inaugurated the scientist's exploration of atavistic features in humans that evidence common ancestry with other primates. The small auricular mutation was mentioned to the naturalist by Thomas Woolner, a Pre-Raphaelite sculptor whose attention "was first called to the subject whilst at work on his figure of Puck, to which he had given pointed ears" and was "thus led to examine the ears of various monkeys, and subsequently more carefully those of man."[54] It is perhaps not fortuitous that a sculptor who was creating long, pointed ears for a humanlike cryptid was the first to spot "Darwin's point," when most professional anatomists (trained in Cuvier's tradition) dismissed this detail as an irrelevant malformation. There is a long history of the influence of anatomy on Western painting and sculpture, but in this case we witness the reverse influence of an artist on an anatomist.[55] Darwin, who jokingly referred to the excrescence as the "Angulus Woolnerianus," would later consult Woolner to write *The Expression of the Emotions in Man and Animals* (1872), in which he argues that human emotions are not essentially different from instinctual animal behaviors. Although he deplored the artists' tendency to "sacrifice truth for the sake of beauty," he praised sculptors and painters for their unusual powers of observation.[56] About Woolner's discovery, Darwin notes that it is "probable that the points in question are in some cases, both in man and apes, vestiges of a former condition."[57] By highlighting the "co-descendence" of apes and humans, Darwin blurs the sharp species demarcation that Cuvier sought to enforce.[58]

This is where the affinities between *The Descent of Man* and *The Marble Faun* become troubling. It seems as if Hawthorne, attentive to Praxiteles's sculpture, anticipated Darwin's conclusions by more than ten years. The abovementioned passage from the *Notebooks* uncannily describes the recessive character of some phenotypical traits like the pointed ears, which can skip generations and indicate common ancestry between humans and nonhumans: "The tail might have disappeared, by dint of constant intermarriages with ordinary mortals; but the pretty hairy ears should occasionally reappear in members of the family."[59] Just like Darwin makes atavistic signs a function of "sexual selection," Hawthorne imagines the pointy ears as an indication of a past kinship. Instead of dispelling doubtful specimens by boxing them in new taxonomic categories, as Cuvier does with the siren, Hawthorne and Darwin use cryptids as "pointers" that reveal something that Cuvier made thinkable but could not admit, especially when it came to Man: that is, that Nature does not only work in spurts, catastrophically making some species extinct and providentially maintaining others, but that it is moved by a continual, aleatory process of "selection" that binds all living organisms. The pointy ears, for both, indicate that what is could have been otherwise and that Man is neither the beginning nor the end of the story.

If it overturned long-held hierarchies that saw Man as the crowning jewel of the natural world, the Darwinian revolution in no way

A

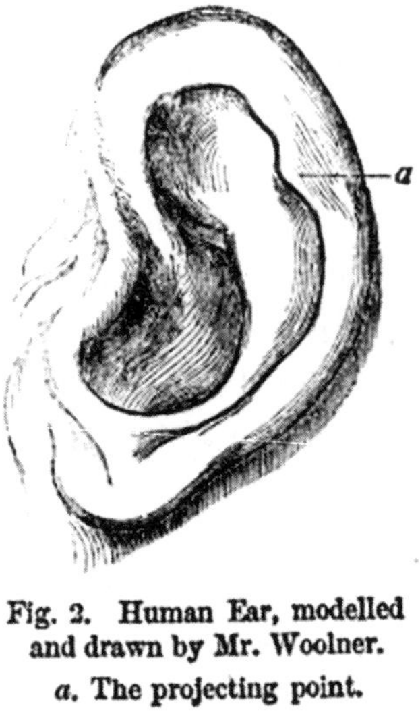

B

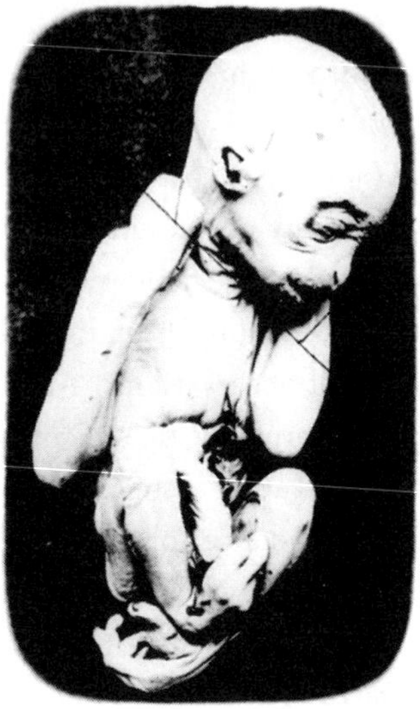

FIGURE 9. *(a)* "Human Ear. Modeled and drawn by Thomas Woolner. *a.* The projecting point." Darwin, *Descent of Man,* 32. *(b)* "Foetus of an Orang. Exact copy of a photograph, showing the form of the ear at this early age." Darwin, *Descent of Man,* 33.

"stopped" the relentless labors of anthropogenesis, that machine for creating Man; instead, as Agamben observes, it prompted the inversion of its mechanism. In the ancient variant, "the non-man is produced by the humanization of an animal: the man-ape, the *enfant sauvage* or *Homo ferus,* but also and above all the slave, the barbarian and the foreigner, as figures of an animal in human form."[60] In modern anthropological thinking, however, the animal threatens Man from the inside. The modern anthropological machine "functions by excluding as not (yet) human an already human being from itself, that is, by animalizing the human, by isolating the nonhuman within the human: *Homo alalus,* or the ape-man."[61] This new machine follows a subtractive process, extirpating the animal from out of the human to reveal Man alone, unmixed with lower species and races.[62] This is why biopolitics is so relevant in the modern age, for biopower is the attempt to isolate and control the animal life that secretly abides in Man.

(Recall that in my discussion of "The Murders in the Rue Morgue," I argued that the criminalization of marginalized humans began to be internalized, with criminality being seen as an instinctive behavior attributable to an animal within, which must be controlled lest it explode in violence.) The rise of evolutionary theories in the nineteenth century marks the moment of shift from the ancient to the modern anthropological machine: the animal, which can no longer be neatly confined in a safe "elsewhere" or in hermetic taxonomic "cases," will have to be excised from within the human. Hence, we can speculate, the insistence with which *The Marble Faun*'s readers wished to lift Donatello's curls to ascertain his animality and perhaps his criminality (Donatello's guilt is said to have "kindled him into a man" [134], suggesting that it is his animal instincts that pushed him to murder Miriam's persecutor).

Symptomatically, Darwin's evolutionary theory was appropriated by Cesare Lombroso only five years after the publication of *The Descent of Man.* Lombroso, who argues in *L'Uomo Delinquente* (*Criminal Man,* 1878) "that most criminal behavior is atavistic, a reversion to evolutionary primitive actions," takes ears as exemplary sites for identifying the criminal body.[63] As Michael Sims writes, Lombroso played "into the fear of our animal nature exemplified throughout mythology, in which one of the bestial attributes of satyrs is their pointed ears."[64] A few years later, Francis Galton, Darwin's cousin and the "father" of eugenics, notoriously used "composite photography" to capture the biometric "ideal-type" of the criminal and devised the method for classifying fingerprints that we still use today.[65] He later "attempted to distinguish racial peculiarities in the fingertips, but without success; he declared, however, that he would pursue the research on Indian tribes in the hope of discovering there 'a more monkey-like pattern.'"[66] Nietzsche warned against reading the title of *The Descent of Man* teleologically, for evolutionism does not stage the emergence of humanity as the ultimate chapter in the history of the world.[67] Yet this teleologization is precisely what occurs in Lombroso's and Galton's racist and classist targeting of the allegedly less evolved (i.e., less human) specimens of humanity. Retrieving the animal in the human is not enough to "jam" the anthropogenic machine, however, because this "ironic apparatus" feeds on the lability of the human/animal partition.[68] Anomalous creatures or aberrant morphologies can always be enlisted as representatives of an immature stage in the "progress" of evolution. (Think, for example, of the enduring myth of the "missing link," which is plentifully deployed in post-Darwinian racist discourses.)[69] Needless to say, this is a gross misreading of Darwin's theory, which rejects the notion that nature gradually moved from defective, rudimentary prototypes toward the more perfect specimens that people the present. Darwin's point, "bearing the stamp of inutility," is not the sign of a residual animality out of which Man (should have) evolved but simply the marker of a common ancestry—not a link in an unbroken chain but a branch of the family tree of life.

What, then, should we make of Darwin's siren, the "living representative" of a quasi-extinct species that "connect[s] to a certain extent orders at present widely separated in the natural scale"?[70] In his pathetic portrait of the siren, "which has apparently been saved from fatal competition by having inhabited a protected station," Darwin registers the animal's anachronistic endurance, its uncanny maintenance in a present that seems no longer its own. A vestige of a bygone era, this "living fossil" belongs at the same time to the past—by genealogic necessity—and to the present—by geological chance. With this survival of the unfit, we are confronted with the heterogeneous temporality of evolution, where the lateral "unity of type" (to which Cuvier gave priority) momentarily defies the vertical, temporal march of natural selection—which was, for Darwin, an even "higher law" than the logic of descent. How can we account for this ephemeral present without turning it into the waiting room of evolution?[71] Can we resist the urge (one that even Darwin felt, betrayed by his elegiac tone) to see the siren's "presence" as meaningful only in relation to the inexorable march of natural selection—in the terms imposed by the temporality of capture, which assumes the animal(ized) as essentially fugitive and passing? This precarious position, as Sylvia Wynter warns, makes individuals eminently susceptible to the racist logic that shadows the biocentric and taxonomic reinvention of Man as species.[72] It is precisely a foray into this strange intercalary time, neither momentary nor geologic, that *The Marble Faun* stages. The book's conceit is the unexpected persistence of an anomalous specimen after its presumed extinction, and the book itself is also calculatedly anachronistic: as a romance, it stages its survival from an older time, marooned in a sea of modern realist novels.

BETWEEN TIMES

From the very first lines of the preface of *The Marble Faun,* Hawthorne speaks as from beyond the grave. Faithful to the "antique fashion of Prefaces," he appeals to the benevolence of a reader, a "congenial friend," who may or may not still be "extant now": "The Gentle Reader, in the case of an individual author, is apt to be extremely short-lived; he seldom outlasts a literary fashion. . . . If I find him at all, it will probably be under some mossy grave-stone, inscribed with a half-obliterated name, which I shall never recognize" (2). Whether it is the author or the reader that is now at rest, *The Marble Faun* comically mourns the improbable (yet not impossible) elective affinity between itself and its readers. Hawthorne, whom Henry James sneered was the "last specimen of the more primitive men of letters," declares his consciousness of having outlived his time as a writer. Hawthorne thus appears as an avatar of the antique faun, wandering in modern life. This prefatory confession should of course be taken with a grain of salt, as should the "thoughtful moral" the author seeks to "evolve"—a rather curious word choice—out of his romance (3). This moral is spelled out in the last chapter by Kenyon, pressed one final time by his friend Hilda to reveal if Donatello was "really a Faun":

> "If you had ever studied the pedigree of the far-descended heir of Monte Beni as I did," answered Kenyon with an irrepressible smile, "you would have retained few doubts on that point. . . . It seems the moral of his story, that human beings of Donatello's character, compounded especially for happiness, have no longer any business on

earth, or elsewhere. Life has grown so sadly serious, that *such men must change their nature, or else perish, like the antediluvian creatures,* that required, as the condition of their existence, a more summer-like atmosphere than ours." (459; emphasis added)

When Hilda refuses to accept her friend's stern lesson, he quickly replies: "'Then, here is another; take your choice!" (460). The second moral, an adaptation of the theory of the felix culpa to Donatello's story, does not appear to be any more satisfactory to Hilda. The romance thus refuses the closure (the boxing in, the determination, the full and definite knowledge) of its morals—which risks, as the author of *The House of the Seven Gables* warned, "impal[ing] the story . . . as with an iron rod,—or rather, as by sticking a pin through a butterfly,—thus at once depriving it of life, and causing it to stiffen in an ungainly and unnatural attitude."[73]

Instead of this pinning down of the story, the reader instead is invited to become momentarily lost (like Kenyon at the end of the romance) in the euphoric openness of a carnival (which uncannily resonates with the messianic banquet Agamben describes at the end of *The Open,* as we will see shortly). Here is Hawthorne's description: "Hereupon, a whole host of absurd figures surrounded [Kenyon], pretending to sympathize in his mishap. Clowns and particoloured harlequins; orang-outangs; bear-headed, bull-headed, and dog-headed individuals" (446). These celebrants are all strange cryptids, hybrid animal/humans (and note that the orang-outang makes an appearance, echoing Poe's murderous animal). Ultimately, Kenyon and Hilda leave an Italy they deem impure (for Hilda, the impurity is religious, but in light of the themes of animality and evolution that subtend the romance, the term seems also to invoke the impurity of humanity, with its admixture of animality). They return "home to America," while Miriam consents to the monstrous community offered by Donatello. But things soon go awry. Everything has an end in *The Marble Faun*: Donatello ends up captive in a jail of the Vatican and Miriam's final appearance shows her to be mute:

> When the kneeling figure beneath the open Eye of the Pantheon arose, she looked towards [Hilda and Kenyon] and extended her hands with a gesture of benediction. Then they knew that it was Miriam. They suffered her to glide out of the portal, however, without a greeting; for those extended hands, even while they blessed, seemed to repel, as if Miriam stood on the other side of a fathomless abyss, and warned them from its verge. (461)

Miriam's intimacy with Donatello has banished her from the community of humans, removed from her the power of speech assumed to distinguish Man from the animal. While *The Marble Faun* opens up the possibility of hybridization, imagining "a being in whom both races meet on friendly ground," it also, crucially, raises the specter of a dystopic dissolution into the unknown. "*To-day* Donatello was the sylvan Faun; *to-day* Miriam was his fit companion, a Nymph of grove or fountain; *to-morrow*—a remorseful man and woman, linked by a marriage bond of crime" (435; emphasis added). Miriam falls silent, contaminated by the "mute mystery" that, for the romance, characterizes the animal in whose name it is impossible to speak, if improperly (10). Does Hawthorne's romance, which reduces Miriam to be spoken of but unspeaking, in the end announce Cuvier's victory? Perhaps. If there is one thing that we are taught by the irony of the postscript to *The Marble Faun,* however, it is that no end is definitive, no case is perfectly closed, and something always returns, "after all." Pondering Miriam and Donatello's miscegenation, their "bond of crime," Kenyon tells Hilda, "'You do not know . . . what a mixture of good there may be in things evil; and how the greatest criminal, if you look at his conduct from his own point of view, or from any side point, may seem not so unquestionably guilty, after all. So with Miriam; so with Donatello." "And, *after all,*" the narrator tells us, "the idea [of the faun] may have been no dream, but rather a poet's reminiscence of a period when man's affinity with Nature was more strict, and his fellowship with every living thing more intimate and dear" (10–11; emphasis added). What remains, after all, then, of the story of Donatello? The romance points toward a posthistorical time that, after *all*, might be a time of reconciliation between humans and animals.

Agamben opens and closes his biopolitical meditation on the "question of the animal," *The Open: Man and Animal,* with the image of a messianic banquet (found in a thirteenth-century Hebrew bible) in which the representatives of a "concluded humanity" are "depicted with animal heads."[74] If these righteous men are indeed those who are "still alive at the moment of the Messiah's coming," as the Rabbinic tradition assumes, what are we to make of their hybridity? Agamben reads it as resulting from the suspension of the "metaphysico-political operation in which something like 'man' can be decided upon and produced" in contradistinction with the animal.[75] He sees in their composite form a counterpoint to the relentless "animalization" of human beings under biopolitics (insofar as animalization here preserves the categories of animal and human). While he deplores this animalization, Agamben sees in the biopolitical moment an unprecedented opportunity to gauge the possibility of a "different economy of relations between animal and human" that could "render inoperative" the "anthropological machine" that tirelessly demarcates between humans and animals.[76] Dominick LaCapra denounces Agamben's cautious optimism as an "empty utopianism of pure, unlimited possibility," in part because animals in *The Open* "are not figured as complex, differentiated living beings but instead function as an abstracted philosophical topos."[77] LaCapra is not wrong to denounce the reduction of the animal to a mere philosopheme—Derrida would say "theorem," something seen but that cannot return the seeing—but his attack misses its mark, for Agamben's avowed ambition is never animals qua animals but the category of "the animal"—the animal as anthropogenic concept, as distinguished from Man. And this concept, pace LaCapra, is not transhistorical, if only because *The Open* posits that it underwent a profound mutation with the advent of biopolitics.

For Agamben, biopolitics can be said to inaugurate the "end of history" insofar as history is conceived as a deeply anthropocentric paradigm. In other words, taking seriously the premise of biopolitics demands that we envision the end of a politics addressing autonomous subjects and the end of a history only made of and by conscious and volitional actors. This envisioned future "other-than-anthropocentric" history is gestured to by LaCapra; at the end of his essay, he calls for "situating the question of the human and the animal in a broader but differentiated ecological perspective or wide-ranging networks of relations." But this gesture (avowedly) constitutes the "limits" of his own essay and methodology.[78] This is not to say that I side with Agamben's esoteric "solution" to the problems posed by the supposedly "idling" anthropological machine of biopolitical modernity. I share LaCapra's skepticism toward *The Open*'s "all-or-nothing paradoxicalism" and his irritation with Agamben's condescending tendency to delegitimize any reformist politics as inauthentic or misguided because it does not have the pretention to overturn the structure of biopolitics, which while only recently articulated is arguably as old as Western politics itself.[79] But I take issue with LaCapra's assertion that Agamben summons Benjamin at the end of his book "as a deus ex machina or distancing lever with respect to Heidegger."[80] To be sure, Agamben follows rather unquestioningly Heidegger's definition of the animal as "poor in world"; his reading of the work of biosemiotician Jakob von Uexküll on the tick suggests that Agamben embraces Heidegger's dubious ethological claim that the animal is entirely absorbed, benumbed, or "captivated" by its environment and therefore deprived of access to the world "as such" (contrary to Man). Nevertheless, when Agamben invokes Benjamin, it is as a messianic figure glimpsing redemption not through history—which is what LaCapra would want Agamben to propose, although Agamben makes clear that Man's "becoming historical" is already an effect of the "anthropological machine"—but *in* history.[81]

To say the least, Agamben's interpretation of Benjamin's "saved night" is cryptic, but it does not gesture toward a nontime of festive reconciliation between humans and animals. Such an eschatological conception would run counter to his reflections on "the practical and political mystery of separation" between Man and animal.[82] Instead, Agamben proposes to rethink the concept of history and its possible suspension through the image of Benjamin's "dialectics at a standstill." Rereading Foucault's famous prophecy at the end of *The Order of Things,* Agamben sees the disappearance of Man not as a geological accident but as a political event, a hybridization to come that would represent not "a new declension of the man-animal relation so much as a figure of the 'great ignorance.'"[83] This ignorance, which signals the suspension of the tireless partitioning of the anthropological machine, forms a "zone of nonknowledge—or better, of aknowledge," a zone "beyond both knowing and not knowing"[84]—a refusal that recalls Kenyon's Cheshire cat smile in *The Marble Faun*'s final words: "I know, but may not tell. On that point, at all events, there shall be not one word of explanation" (467).

"I know, but may not tell." There is knowledge here, but it is beside the point. By concluding on an utterance that retracts itself, an unapologetic performance of reserve, *The Marble Faun*'s profession of ignorance does not ultimately promote a naïve or reactionary antiscientific attitude but an alternative economy of meaning and attention. Of course, Kenyon's words are spoken from a position of privilege: not all are allowed his reserve when silence can be used against you—as we saw with Poe, lack of recognizable speech can be a (negative) sign of culpability. Reserve can always be converted into muteness (as with Miriam) and thereby find itself absorbed or resorbed in an overarching semiotic system—a clue to be deciphered or a symptom to be decoded (tellingly, ears in *The Marble Faun* are primarily things to be seen, symptoms, or clues rather than mediums of hearing, indices of the faun's aural powers). Only once anomalous animals are muted (dissected, pinned by an iron rod like a moral in a story or a butterfly on a board) do they become legible to "Cuvier's hermeneut of osseous textuality"; only once they are petrified or fossilized—in other words, once they are conceived as "inanimate signs of what is not"—are they susceptible of "disclosing the secret of life."[85] Cuvier turns marble into animals, as Balzac raves, but his animals all belong in an irrevocably bygone epoch.[86] It is quite different with Hawthorne, whose fiction seeks to animate a past that is never fully extinct. Not only do atavistic features threaten to resurface at any moment in *The Marble Faun,* but the romance literally turns marble into an "animate sign." Hawthorne had initially envisaged titling his romance *Marble and Life,* and one of the themes of the book is the false sense of timelessness and purity conveyed by the immaculate sculptures strewn all over the Eternal City. Hawthorne shows that marble, too, is susceptible to time: he bemoans the Italian weather for its "fossilizing" quality that leaves not only art but entire cities "without enough of life and juiciness . . . to be any longer susceptible of decay" while repeatedly insisting on the slow but inevitable corruptibility of marble, a material that in the very first paragraph of the romance appears "yellow with time" (5). Marble, in its customary association with pristine whiteness and white superiority in antebellum culture, is from the outset subjected to the force of decay that is life. Textually importing the Faun of Praxiteles to the cloudier climes of New England, the author vivifies old European marble into a living allegory of the new yet already outdated American art of the romance, which "like ivy, lichen and wall-flowers, need[s] Ruin to make [it] grow" (3).

The precarious temporality of the romance is perhaps best exemplified by Kenyon's reconstruction of a statue of Venus from what strikes him at first glance to be a "shapeless fragment of stone." Not unlike in Poe's "The Murders in the Rue Morgue," where Dupin shows us that the astronomical Venus appears to whoever views her "in a side-long way," the Goddess of Beauty emerges in *The Marble Faun* when the sun falls "slantwise" on the statue's fragments, which Kenyon reassembles in characteristic Cuvierian fashion.[87] Finally, for a moment, the statue appears complete, but it inhabits a wavering between present and past, knowability and illegibility: "The beautiful Idea at once asserted its immortality, and converted that heap of forlorn fragments into a whole, as perfect to the mind, if not to the eye, as when the new marble gleamed with snowy lustre. . . . Kenyon . . . almost deemed himself rewarded with a living smile" (329). It seems that Kenyon has brought to life in the present the long-dead model for the statue, made her visible through the lifeless marble itself (echoing Donatello's possible position as the living model for Praxiteles's marble faun). But soon enough "the divine statue seemed to fall asunder again, and become only a heap of worthless fragments" (329)—to retreat back into the impenetrable past from which Kenyon had sought to redeem and preserve. For Hawthorne, then, as Baudelaire theorized around the same time in "The Painter of Modern Life," the Ideal is only a moment of the artistic experience. Contingency is an essential part of art just as transience is the rhythm of life, a transience that can be neither entirely domesticated under the linearity of secular progress (Darwin) nor monumentalized by the timelessness of the Ideal (Cuvier). Indeed, it finds itself constantly threatened by both. Hawthorne's elusive faun, grasped on the brink of either metamorphosis or extinction, is the fragile incarnation of this interstitiality. Dupin finds his cryptic creatures approachable, indeed knowable, only negatively, as the mirror image of human rationality; Hawthorne glimpses the possibility, however faint and ephemeral, however inconceivable and unspeakable within the epistemological frame erected by Cuvier, of a knowledge that extends beyond—or rather between—the taxonomic confines of species determination. This interval, which is not timeless, makes possible Hawthorne's fabulous taxonomy. It opens a space for his romance on the figure of Man, for the dream of Man's transformation into something different altogether, and for an ethics of relating differently to what can only be partially seen and known.

Playing Cuvier's orderly fossils against Étienne Geoffroy Saint-Hilaire's aberrant specimens, Deleuze and Guattari affirm that "Cuvier reacts in terms of discontinuous photographs, and casts of fossils."[88] The unity of life postulated by comparative anatomy remains abstract and hidden in Cuvier, a transcendent principle, a "sovereign vanishing point." Thus conceived, life clearly appears in its historicity and technicity, as conditioned by the rendering still—both mute and immobile—of discretized elements of life, which are turned into mere points, seen as devoid of intensity or motivation. Is it possible to develop a positive image of this untimely animality that appears lost in and for modern life?

— 5 —

THE STOCK IMAGE

(MUYBRIDGE)

> The grand discovery of an eye which would catch and a plate which would register the most evanescent of movements has enabled us to discover what was concealed before, and if we fail to avail ourselves of the teachings of this superhuman professor, it will be a confession of willful perversity and an avowal of stupid, mulish ignorance.
> —*California Spirit of the Times*, article about Muybridge's zoopraxiscope (1880)

In July 2017, the scientific journal *Nature* reported that a team of Harvard scientists had, in an unprecedented feat, encoded a movie in living organic cells.[1] What the scientists encoded was not just any moving picture but British photographer Eadweard Muybridge's iconic 1878 sequential image of the galloping mare Annie G. (Figure 10). The experiment sought to demonstrate that the state-of-the-art gene editing technology could "capture and stably store practical amounts of real data within the genomes of populations of living cells."[2] While DNA had already been successfully used to store information, it had never been used to record a sequence of images that could, as the *New York Times* reported, "be retrieved at will and multiplied indefinitely as the host divides and grows."[3] Among the multiple potential applications of the engineered bacteria (such as using them as miniature spies wandering through living bodies to collect information that is otherwise inaccessible), media coverage emphasized the genome's storage capacities, salivating at the economic prospects opened by the breakthrough in a moment when "data storage is a growing problem": "Not only are significant amounts [of data] being generated, but the technology used to store it keeps becoming obsolete, like floppy disks. DNA is never going out of fashion."[4]

Treating the living as stock—as matter to be reproduced for use or profit—has a long, highly gendered and racialized history. What appears to be new here is the use of live matter as an archiving technology and, more specifically, as a technology for storing time. Stock is traditionally thought in spatial terms as a reservoir or warehouse for merchandise, but here the living cell—itself continually subject to change—is where cinematic time unfolds; it is, so to speak, a time for time. The scientists' nod to Muybridge is doubtless meant to mark the significance of an experiment perhaps no less groundbreaking than their own: the invention of cinema. And the two experiments mirror each other, for while the "father of the moving picture" encoded animal motion on film, trying to record and reproduce the "original movements of life," the Harvard scientists instead encoded a film on living cells—using the living itself to host lifelike representation.[5] More subtly, the nod sheds light on the kinship that binds genetic editing procedures and cinematic montage, a kinship that is discernible in the method shared by these techniques, of disassembling something, removing parts of it, and reassembling it in a new configuration.[6] This return to the primal scene of Muybridge's early stop-motion experiments indicates an unsuspected continuity between the apprehension of living bodies through apparatuses of capture (particularly the moving image) and the modern notion that living organisms themselves function as, and perhaps even are, technologies of capture.[7]

Mary Ann Doane has demonstrated how profoundly the advent of cinema altered our conception of time, contributing to its conversion from a lived, subjective experience into an externalized, atomized, and uniformly consistent unit of measurement conducive to the emergence

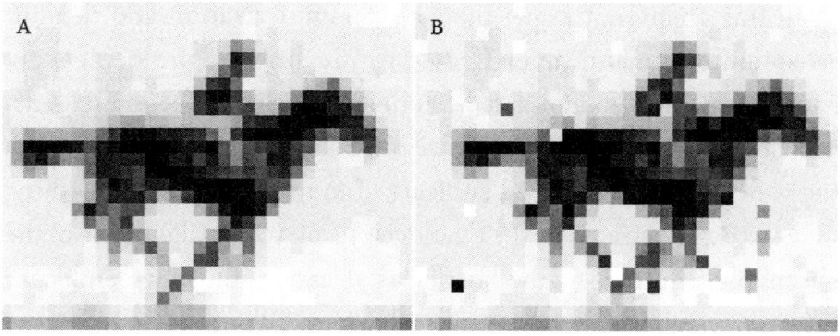

FIGURE 10. *(a)* An image from the film encoded in bacterial DNA. *(b)* The same image retrieved from another cell. Courtesy of Seth Shipman.

of industrial capitalism, while paradoxically valorizing contingency, ephemerality, and spontaneity.[8] Doane argues that the conceptions of time as both measurable and contingent may appear contradictory, but they are not incompatible; in fact, their interdependence is what defines modern temporality—what she calls "cinematic time." I take the groundbreaking feat of the Harvard geneticists as an invitation to consider whether cinematic grammar—which is not reducible to the mechanical scansion we traditionally associate with capitalist production—might also accommodate the trace of an embodied and subjective duration (although one that is by no means irreconcilable with capitalist reproduction). The critical literature on Muybridge overwhelmingly reads his stop-action experiments as dismantling continuous motion into discrete gestures that are vulnerable to analysis and adjustable to the cadences imposed by assembly lines. This visual (an)atomizing is undeniable, and its consequences are very real, but I detect in Muybridge's early chronophotography (a technique by which movement is decomposed into a series of snapshots) the expression of something like "horsetime," which has little to do with the horsepower fetishized by industrial capitalism.[9] The horses in Muybridge's 1870s photographs were taking their own pictures (each photo was taken when the horse passed over a trip wire that triggered a camera) in what may have been the first "selfies," even as the apparatuses that captured the horses and mechanically reproduced their images contributed to stripping them of any traditional notion of selfhood or singularity.

In this chapter, I argue that the defamiliarization and denaturalization of life and time effected by Muybridge's protocinematic experiments can be mobilized to ethological and biosemiotic ends. Muybridge's work compels a radical rethinking of subjectivity, for both the viewing and the viewed subjects of moving images—something that was demonstrated by the ethologist Jakob von Uexküll's use of the chronophotographic method in the last decade of the nineteenth century. Chronophotography was central to Uexküll's efforts to represent what the milieus (*Umwelten*) of various organisms might look like from the organisms' own point of view—in the words of Uexküll himself, to penetrate "worlds [that] are not only unknown [but] also invisible."[10] The term *Umwelt* "has proved notoriously recalcitrant to translation," semiotician Thomas Sebeok notes, and *milieu* might not be the most accurate term (Sebeok proposes "subjective universe," "phenomenal world," and "self-world").[11] I choose to translate *Umwelt* as *milieu,* however, to mark a connection between Uexküll and Foucault by way of Canguilhem.[12]

Canguilhem traces the genealogy of this indispensable "category of contemporary thought" from the present day back to Newtonian mechanics, with a stop on the way at Lamarckian biology and another, more surprisingly, at Balzac, who gives the milieu its *lettres de noblesse* in his *Comédie humaine.* It is easy to reduce the milieu to a mechanistic system of external influences on living organisms, a conception evocative of Descartes's infamous "animal machine" thesis. The definition of the milieu is what is at stake, Canguilhem remarks, in the famous polemic that tore Darwinians and Lamarckians apart in the second half of the nineteenth century. Canguilhem sums up the theses of the two camps as follows: on the one hand, for Lamarckism, the effort comes from the living being and works against a milieu that appears indifferent to its existence; for Darwinism, on the other hand, the initiative originates (though not always and not uniformly) in the milieu itself.[13] It is into this debate that Uexküll intervenes to argue that a living being does not merely survive in or adapt to a given milieu but actively configures its milieu.

> A living being is not a machine, which responds to excitations with movements, it is a machinist, who responds to signals with operations. . . . Out of the abundance of the physical milieu, which produces a theoretically unlimited number of excitations, the animal retains only some signals (*Merkmale*). Its life rhythm orders the time of this *Umwelt,* just as it orders space. . . . Lamarck used to say that time and favorable circumstances constitute the living bit by bit. Von Uexküll turns the relation around and says: time and favorable circumstances are relative to certain living beings.[14]

Not only does Uexküll reverse Lamarck's proposition, but he contests the cold teleology of Darwin's "natural selection" by advancing the idea of something like a "natural election," the notion that every living being actively participates in the composition of its milieu. By considering animals, not just humans, to experience the world from their own subjective capacities and interests, Uexküll's ethological work expands on Immanuel Kant's transcendental epistemology.[15] More deeply, his work can be said to operate a Kantian revolution in that it awakens the human observer not just to what they cannot perceive but to the constitutional limit of what is humanly perceptible—to what Walter Benjamin calls the "optical unconscious," or the registration of "images which escape natural optics altogether."[16] Beyond an analytical method for glimpsing into the worlds of animals, the cinematic technique offered Uexküll the foundational intuition that what we see is contingent on the finitude of our sensorial faculties—an intuition that was spurred by the capture of a motion too rapid to be registered by the human eye. Meaningfully, one of the first cinematic insights into our "optical unconscious" was that of a galloping horse.[17]

"THE POSSIBILITY OF A HORSE"

The man who named himself Eadweard Muybridge[18] began working on animal locomotion at the urging of railroad mogul and one-time governor of California Leland Stanford, who asked for the photographer's assistance in settling a debate: whether horses lift all four hooves off the ground at any one time when running. So goes the legend, at least. In fact, Stanford, who owned one of the largest "stock farms" in the country, had commissioned Muybridge's work for the purpose of breeding racehorses. Stanford's interest in heredity and genetics was not limited to horses, as attests his choice of eugenicist David Starr Jordan as the founding president of Stanford University, but the horse was the ideal subject for the magnate's bioengineering experiments.[19] As territorial expansion was drawing to a close, the horse, which was materially and symbolically inseparable from the conquest of the West, became a new frontier to conquer: it could be made better, faster, more efficient, if its inscrutable workings could be unraveled. "When I began breeding horses," Stanford boasted, "I commenced studying the anatomy of the horse, until at the end I could take the steed apart and put it together with the accuracy that distinguishes a skilled watchmaker."[20] Despite this mechanistic analogy, which puts his technique on a par with divine creation, Stanford avowed a deep fascination for the "great mystery" of life: "the old writers on animal mechanics . . . would test vital force by the laws governing the motion of the pendulum or those of gravity," reads the introduction to *The Horse in Motion* (the product of Stanford's collaboration with Muybridge), but they ignore "a power that must enter into all our estimates of vital force, and that is the *will.*"[21] For the rich industrialist, mechanistic and vitalist views were surprisingly not incompatible but rather complementary.

Sometime in the spring of 1872, Muybridge successfully photographed Occident, one of Stanford's fastest racehorses, at full speed. To say that Muybridge thought highly of his own accomplishment is an understatement: he prided himself to have solved a mystery as old as art itself, at least as old as Paleolithic cave paintings.

> In the spring of the year 1872, . . . there was revived in the city of San Francisco a controversy in regard to animal locomotion, which we may infer, on the authority of Plato, was warmly argued by the ancient Egyptians, and which probably had its origin in the studio of the primitive artist when he submitted to a group of critical friends his first etching

> of a mammoth crushing through the forest. . . . In this modern instance, the principal subject of dispute was the possibility of a horse . . . having all four of his feet, at any portion of his stride, simultaneously free from contact with the ground. . . . Having constructed some special exposing apparatus . . . the author commenced his investigation on the race track at Sacramento, California, in May 1872, where he in a few days made several negatives of a celebrated horse named Occident, while trotting laterally, in front of his camera. . . . The photographs resulting from this experiment . . . exhibited the horse with all four of his feet clearly lifted, at the same time, above the ground.[22]

Muybridge had successfully designed the first contraption capable of recording a movement too rapid for the naked eye. A few years later, he conducted his chronophotographic studies more systematically, laying the groundwork for what we now know as motion pictures. He began this work under the patronage of Stanford, who, inspired by the contemporary French physiologist Étienne-Jules Marey's treatise on animal locomotion, *La machine animale,* encouraged Muybridge to use a zoetrope (a device consisting of a slotted disk spun in front of a mirror, giving the impression that a discontinuous sequence of images is one single moving image) to faithfully reproduce the appearance of animal motion.[23] In order to create the characteristic serial images of racing horses that we associate with his name, Muybridge and his collaborators devised a complex apparatus in which a battery of cameras was triggered by a horse running on a track latticed with trip wires (Figure 11). Muybridge would modify his system when he began conducting his research on animal locomotion at the University of Pennsylvania in 1884. Instead of cameras activated by the horse's passage over a series of trip wires, Muybridge used three batteries of twelve cameras equipped with a motor clock. Not only did the electrical motor help prevent accidents (avoiding registering "abnormal" behavior), it also went off at pretimed moments rather than when the horse crossed the wire.[24] In lieu of equidistant snapshots, there were equal intervals between each exposure. This standardization marks a transition from "horse time" to "human time," or rather "machine time": the animal was henceforth expected to move at a given pace, where before its gait had been the source determining the length of the intervals.[25]

There were only a few years between Muybridge's invention of an apparatus to capture velocities indiscernible to the human eye and his imposition of a predetermined, uniform temporal pattern, an interim during which Muybridge's animal models had not yet been fully subordinated to the mechanized order of modern temporality. It is in this interim that I find a space for thinking about what cinematic technique can contribute to biosemiotics and ethology. For Étienne-Jules Marey, Muybridge was but an "ingenious experimenter" who "did not succeed at taking his instantaneous photographs at equal intervals of time." In other words, Muybridge "decomposed motion into space" instead of time. Marey saw this as evidence of Muybridge's lack of scientific rigor:[26] by segmenting space instead of time, Muybridge made it impossible to determine with exactitude how much time elapsed between two frames and how the photographed subject "moved from one position to the next."[27] In his criticism of the trip wire system, tellingly, Marey almost seems to blame the horses as much as Muybridge for their lack of temporal constancy and precision.[28] His judgment, however, assumes an "objective" notion of time as an indifferent, empty, infinitely divisible milieu—as a homogenous principle of commensurability between heterogenous embodied experiences.

Marey was himself a chronophotographer working to record the movement of animals on the other side of the Atlantic. Unlike Muybridge, who linearly juxtaposed separate stills to imply temporal progression, however, Marey's images typically superimposed several phases of movement on one photographic plate, collapsing several spatial positions into a single temporal frame. His attempt to record movement without fragmenting it into discrete images stems from a desire to "represent *all* time" without loss, as Doane argues. Marey's blurry photos have a rather dreamlike, fantastic quality, yet as Jonathan Crary keenly observes, Muybridge's "first images from Palo Alto in 1878 . . . are finally more disturbing than anything" done by Marey. Crary writes:

FIGURE 11. Eadweard Muybridge, *General View of the Experimental Track, Plate F for Attitudes of Animals in Motion,* 1881. Toned cyanotype on print-out paper. Iris & B. Gerald Cantor Center for the Visual Arts at Stanford University; Stanford Family Collections.

> [Marey's work] was based on a reciprocal operation of decomposition and reunification: his analysis of movement, within the frame of a single visual field, preserved a vector of spatial and temporal coherence, giving to movement a new form of legibility and rationality, even if through unprecedented representational practices. Muybridge conducts a more intransigent and blunt dismantling of the apparent continuities of movement and of time. . . . No relations of causal necessity link the positions or sections that are presented in sequence, only an imprecise and disjunct sense of before and after. Hence those who criticize Muybridge as being less "advanced" than Marey because he did not introduce the variable of time into his work are thinking in terms of an impoverished model of time.[29]

The same chrono-anarchic element that expands our conceptions of time, however, also has the power to destabilize our sense of reality. When Muybridge's serial photographs fragment subjectively experienced units of time, or moments (from *movere,* "to move"), into abstract points of time, or instants (from *in-stare,* "to stand")—when they convert movement into a series of stills, space into fractions of time—they introduce the unsettling notion that reality itself can be divided, disassembled, then rearranged at will.

Muybridge, in other words, invented a way of dissecting the real that made it uniquely vulnerable to capitalist exploitation insofar as capitalism, in the words of Karl Marx, supposes the "eradication of space by time."[30] Construed as distance and deferral, as a cause of "friction" hampering the circulation of goods and people, space is reframed under capital as a function of time. Paradigmatic of this "eradication of space" in the U.S. context is the completion of the Transcontinental Railroad in 1869, an event celebrated with great fanfare by Leland Stanford, who planted the "Last Spike" that hitched together the tracks of the Central Pacific and Union Pacific and connected the eastern and western coasts. Discounting the hazardous conditions under which thousands of men—mostly veterans and immigrants—had built the railway, the *San Francisco Bulletin* touted the accomplishment as "a triumph bloodless, deathless, but no less glorious to the Nation and the State: a victory over space, the elements."[31] This new "epoch of annihilated space," as Hawthorne calls it, often figured as a cataclysm in the literature of the middle of the century (though for some, like Frederick Douglass, it also heralds the promise of a borderless, less inegalitarian world).[32] For Henry Adams, the simultaneous irruption of the steamboat, the train, and the telegraph heralded the end of the world: a "new world was ready for use, and only fragments of the old met his eyes."[33] The fate of the horse, subject of Muybridge's first studies, perfectly epitomizes this transformation. While it "had been for thousands of years the primary mode of vehicular movement in human societies," the horse became "symbolically dismantled into quantified and lifeless units of time"—so too were culture, labor, human experience, even time itself, newly subsumed by a standardized economy, running on mechanical time.[34]

Underlining the convergence of Stanford's epistemic investment in animal locomotion with his financial investment in locomotives, John Ott argues that the "Muybridge photos encouraged viewers to imagine the horse, and by extension, all of nature, as merely another kind of machine. Fixed within a cold, monotonous grid of six, twelve, or twenty-four, the serial print demanded that viewers reconceptualise a sweaty, snorting, quivering mass of horseflesh as a dynamo performing an endless repetitive sequence of actions."[35] Ott articulates the now-dominant view that Muybridge served, perhaps unwittingly, a socioeconomic regime that privileged the mechanized "industrial gaze" over natural optics. He rightly underlines that the skepticism with which Muybridge's images were met at the end of the nineteenth century was less a reactionary attachment to retinal vision or a shortsighted hostility toward "progress" (which for Stanford was synonymous with industrialization) than a discerning opposition to the "new corporate industrial order buttressed by scientific authority, managerial supervision, and complex, capital-intense technologies."[36] Characterizing the violence of industrial capitalism in terms of the mechanization of animal life, however, risks presenting animals (and nature more broadly) as pretechnological entities newly vulnerable to the operations of industrial capital. In fact, animals—and horses in particular—had long been a technologically produced laboring machine; as Michael Lawrence notes, the "many centuries of developing . . . various kinds of horses for the purpose of working" that preceded the Industrial Revolution means that "the technological methods utilized to produce these particular images were thus in important respects continuous with the means deployed to produce the subjects of the images."[37]

If he warns against the temptation to regard Muybridge's stop-motion studies as a radical rupture in the technological subjugation of animal life,[38] Lawrence ultimately shares Ott's perception that Muybridge is irredeemably aligned with "a capitalist regime of image production organized around alienation and misrecognition."[39] He wishes to counteract the technocapitalist amnesia that frames the animal as immaterial and insignificant by focusing on an experimental cinematic archive that disrupts the "Muybridgean approach to animal being" and restores the horse's material and historical "thereness," producing it again as a "meaningful being"—a subject in its own right.

To that end, he endows the animal with a form of "livingness" irreducible to the lifelikeness cherished by capitalist film culture, assuming (somewhat dogmatically) that "the animal will *always* refer to the 'outside [of] the film itself.'"[40] Yet the "thereness" of filmed animals does not index their externality to film so much as their entanglement with the apparatus of capture.[41] That is, instead of supposing that the animal constitutes the "other" of technocapitalist reproduction, what might we gain by considering animals as cinematic subjects? Instead of holding singularity and autonomy as a priori conditions of subjectivity, might we not envision subjectivity as an effect of reproducibility? Let us put this in Benjamin's terms: instead of privileging the notions of naturality and unicity that pertain to the auratic and the irreproducible, can we discern in technological reproducibility a conception of animal life that does not automatically feed into the biocapitalist agenda described by Ott, Lawrence, and Shukin?[42] Is there not an alternative legacy to Muybridge's experiments?[43]

In the breakdown of what had before Muybridge seemed to be the natural syntax of motion, I see an opportunity to decouple chronophotography from the representational grammar of biocapitalism. Muybridge's photographic experiments do not merely atomize animal motion but model a computational logic—one that Philip E. Agre calls "capture." In "Surveillance and Capture," Agre explains that the well-known model of "surveillance" employs visual metaphors, following Foucault's work on panopticism. In contrast, "capture" employs linguistic metaphors and is modeled after information technologies, "taking as its prototype the deliberate reorganization of industrial work activities to allow computers to track them in real time."[44] Capture, Agre explains, devises a grammar of representation that converts hitherto unformalized actions into a series of "parsable" gestures (here we glimpse Foucault's "anatomopolitics of the body"). These gestures constitute "minimal replicable units"—what artificial intelligence calls "primitives"—that can then be arranged in a variety of ways, like words in a sentence. But capture's standardizing work, Agre insists, is not a simple mechanical process. Capture does not simply gather data about people, objects, or places, for what it gathers has no reality prior to the act of capture. The data acquires its ontological dignity *as data* (as given) as a result of a "kind of representational crusade," which is itself "part of a much larger material process through which these new social ontologies, in a certain specific sense, *become real.*"[45] Capture therefore denotes a realist relation between sign and referent insofar as it assumes a "real" out there that can be faithfully expressed by signs, but Agre shows this realism to be the product of a performative operation. Capture is "attended by a kind of mythology according to which the newly constructed grammar of action has been not 'invented' but 'discovered.'"[46] This realist orientation underpins much visual representation (e.g., photography's conventional pretensions to objectivity and realism), but Muybridge's work breaks down these assumptions about the relationship of sign to referent. By disjointing time from motion, Muybridge's proto-animations expose the uncanny temporality of the becoming-real of animal movement. They show that the "real" is not a data so much as a capta, not a given but a taken—or perhaps a given that is haunted by a disavowed, unaccountable form of *giving.*[47] Seeing the biocapitalist grammar of capture as the outcome (rather than the condition) of a representational crusade that is ongoing and can be challenged, we obtain a different picture of the horses caught in the net of Muybridge's apparatuses of capture.

MUYBRIDGE'S GRIDS

In a manner reminiscent of Chomel's *tonnelle* (Figure 8), Muybridge's apparatus turns space (the space of the track on which the horses run) into a gigantic trap, an attempt to capture the horses' motion through time that is visually condensed in the trip wire lines across the track. The motif of the trap is continued in the striated backdrops against which the silhouette of Occident materializes (Figure 12). (The parallel lines in the background, which resemble nothing more than prison bars, and later the photographs taken from three different angles, seem to announce the technology of the mug shot developed by criminologist Alphonse Bertillon a few years later.)

The trapping motif intensifies as Muybridge's technique evolves; when Muybridge starts working at the University of Pennsylvania,

FIGURE 12. Eadweard Muybridge, "Instantaneous Photographs of Sallie Gardner," from *The Horse in Motion*, 1878.

the parallel lines give way to a checkered grid made up of silk threads divided in five-centimeter squares. It is not incidental, Marta Braun observes, that Muybridge first deployed this grid in capturing the image of the "mulatto pugilist" Ben Bailey. Unlike Audubon's grid, Muybridge's were not primarily intended "to ensure the accuracy of the proportions in [his] picture"; the grid in *Animal Locomotion* was an anthropometric instrument "borrowed from one devised by English ethnologist J. H. Lamprey . . . to assist in comparative morphological measurement in his photographs of Malay natives."[48] A tool of scientific racism in the lineage of physiognomy and phrenology, the grid was meant to assist in the production of categories. Here, it helped to produce the category of whiteness, as it worked to distinguish visually between various racial "types" and valorize white male bodies as the norm;[49] in other cases, it served to distinguish between "normal" and "pathological" bodies and behaviors, as in Muybridge's photographs of subjects with disabilities;[50] and in the hands of criminologists, it would be used to profile "the criminal."[51] Breaking down everyday actions into measurable discrete gestures, the grid also contributed to forging what Paul Lawrie calls a "laboring race" by subjecting the human body—particularly the male nonwhite body—to increased scrutiny in the name of efficiency, hygiene, and progress.[52] Subjected to the depersonalizing effect of the metrological grid, Muybridge's images of Bailey remind us how post-Reconstruction African Americans came to be routinely criminalized and pathologized, "positioned as captive to their bodies" and characterized as "a depraved race destined for extinction."[53] This uneven targeting of certain populations was enabled by a technology that presumed, paradoxically, the fundamental commensurability of bodies marked by different races, genders, classes—and, of course, species, as suggested by the title Muybridge chose for the twenty thousand images composing his "Electro-Photographic Investigation of Consecutive Phases of Animal Movements."

Through the lattice of Muybridge's anthropometric grid, we can thus glimpse how chronophotography colluded with the heightened supervision and administration to which human and nonhuman bodies were being subjected at the end of the century. The gridification at the level of the body intensifies a larger cultural logic that extends from grids that mapped dead and disappearing animals onto representations (as in Audubon's painting techniques), to speculative techniques for the occupation of uncharted territories (as in Cooper's *The Prairie*), to the gridded layout of city streets (as in Poe's "The Man of the Crowd"). Before working at the University of Pennsylvania, Muybridge was mostly known for his photographs of North and South American landscapes. Though he was primarily interested in these landscapes' picturesque dimension, his work had occasionally been commissioned by the U.S. government; he accompanied General Halleck to the recently purchased territory of Alaska in 1868 and mentions interrupting his work as a surveyor to work on Stanford's Palo Alto Stock Farm in 1872. By fully devoting himself to motion studies at the end of the 1870s, notes Rebecca Solnit, "Muybridge had given up place without motion for motion without place, and mountain ranges had been replaced by a gridded white wall."[54] The grid, Solnit observes, "was everywhere in nineteenth-century America":

> Thomas Jefferson's great land survey of 1785 had imposed an imaginary grid spreading west from the Appalachians. . . . The grid had been the mental and governmental logic that allowed Americans to proceed into the terra incognita of the West. . . . The grid meant rationality in its regularity and democracy in its equal apportionment of space. It was also a resonant emblem of science in the nineteenth century, of a science that like settlement was trying to manage the wild abundance of the natural world.[55]

The grid was everywhere, but while it had remained inconspicuous in the structuring of Audubon's paintings and the settling of the United States, it had now come to the surface. I see the materialization of the grid in Muybridge's work above all as a testament to its influence on scientific representation.[56] After seeing Muybridge's instantaneous photographs in the French scientific journal *La Nature,* Marey—the same Marey whose book had inspired Stanford, the same Marey who would later declare Muybridge's images unscientific—asked Muybridge to help him find a way to record the flight of birds. Reporting that he was "filled with admiration for Mr. Muybridge's instantaneous photographs," Marey explained that he was "dreaming of a kind of *photographic gun,* to seize the bird in a pose, or even better, in a series of poses marking the successive movement of its wings," a gun that he would invent in 1882.[57] The results of Marey's invention are mesmerizing images showing multiple exposures of birds on a single negative, like a Vitruvian animal (Figure 13).

In Audubon's elaborate compositions, the "truth" of the species is conveyed by the representation of one archetypal specimen; in the work of Muybridge and Marey, it is shown by a serialized set of pictures of one or several "average" specimens. Audubon's paintings highly dramatize his animal encounters, demonstrating "his preference for the uncommon or unique event over the repeatable"; the chronophotographers seek to register what hides in plain sight, the everydayness of "normal" animal locomotion.[58] Audubon's animals are "drawn from nature," flushed out of hiding and brought into visibility by the hunter-naturalist's artistic talents; in contrast, Muybridge

FIGURE 13. Étienne-Jules Marey, transverse flight of a tethered pelican, c. 1882.

and Marey's (already captured) animals, deemed "unseeable" by the naked human eye, defy visibility on a different level altogether.[59] For Audubon, invisibility is a faculty that animals display in a variety of forms and manners (mimicry, camouflage, ruse); for Muybridge and Marey, it is a property of animality itself. This was true for both, but whereas Muybridge seemed content with the images generated by his apparatuses, Marey despaired over chronophotography's "need for a hiatus between exposures," which explains why his photographs were consistently blurry (Figure 14a).[60] To represent animals for Marey no longer means to show what they "look like" but to produce a visual analog of the secret processes that animate them.[61]

The author of *La machine animale* is usually classified—and classifies himself—as a mechanist thinker, but Marey's relentless tracking of an ever-active and all-explaining "force," betrayed by the desire to invent a mode of representation faithful to the assumed continuity of physiological time, confers a vitalist dimension to his work.[62] Jonathan Burt is right to note that both Marey's photographic gun and Muybridge's trip wire system derived from hunting techniques, but their objective—the capture of live motion—is antipodal to that of the hunt.[63] What chronophotography retains from the hunt is a stilling effect that, however minimal, Marey found intolerable. The apparatuses that Marey devised to capture animals' movements required that animal bodies quite literally disappear from representation, for the scientist "suppressed in black" portions of his (human and nonhuman) models to adapt them to the demands of the camera: "stripes were used: the horse, bird or human subject was coated from head to foot in black except for a few thin streaks of shiny metal, or little dots of white paper stuck to appropriate areas."[64] The models thus found themselves geometrized and desubstantialized so that they could be made intelligible—so that their capturability could be optimized. In Marey's "partial photographs," the grid migrates from the background onto the models themselves (Figures 15a and 15b).

Around the same time, American painter and photographer Thomas Eakins used a gridded horse—a living butcher's chart—as the model for one of his paintings (Figure 16). (Famously, as his first assignment in painting classes, Eakins required students to visit a local slaughterhouse to dissect horses.) Before working with Muybridge at Penn, Eakins had written to the photographer to express his interest in his images, though he complained that the distance between the horse and the gridded wall made it difficult to establish the size of the model.[65] Eakins's collaboration with Muybridge confirms Marey's prediction that the stop-motion method would revolutionize artistic representation, as does Muybridge's influence on realist artists like Jean-Louis-Ernest Meissonier and Frederic Remington. But Muybridge's images did more than provide "photographic evidence" to correct erroneous ideas about the gait of horses; they radically altered the coordinates of the visible, an alteration that is most perceptible in the significant role they played in redefining the mission and nature of art at the turn of the century.[66] The new epistemology encapsulated in Muybridge's and Marey's photographs had a direct impact on some of the most influential artists of the twentieth century, from Degas and Duchamp to Francis Bacon, Sol LeWitt, and more recently experimental filmmakers Hollis Frampton and Marion Faller (who parodied Muybridge's work in *Sixteen Studies from Vegetable Locomotion,* in which they dropped a watermelon over a gridded plate).

Indirectly, we can see Muybridge's grids—both the backdrops against which his subjects were photographed and the gridded

A

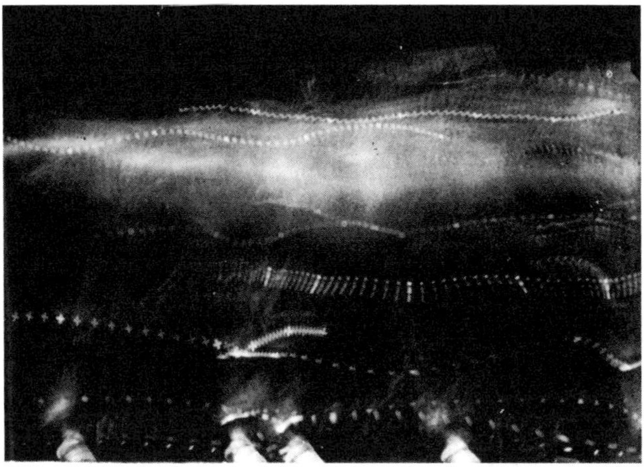

B

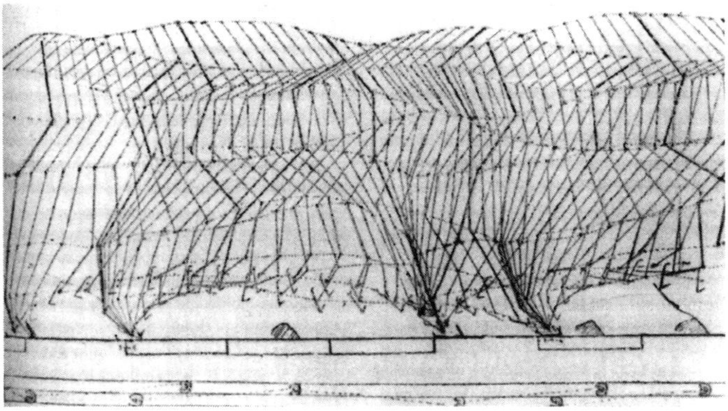

C

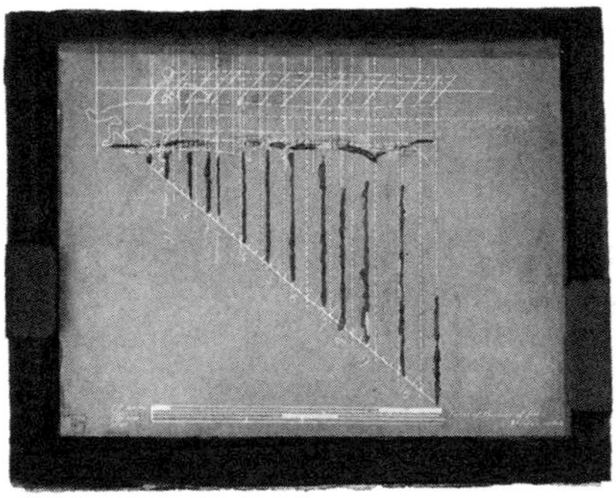

FIGURE 14. *(a)* Étienne-Jules Marey, geometric chronophotograph of horse with stripes, c. 1886; *(b)* Étienne-Jules Marey, diagram of the right leg of horse walking; *(c)* Thomas Eakins and Ellen Wetherald Ahrens, analysis of horses in motion (after Muybridge), 1884.

A

FIGURE 15. *(a)* Étienne-Jules Marey, model in "homme squelette" suit; *(b)* Étienne-Jules Marey, "Geometric chronophotography," from *Movement* (1886).

B

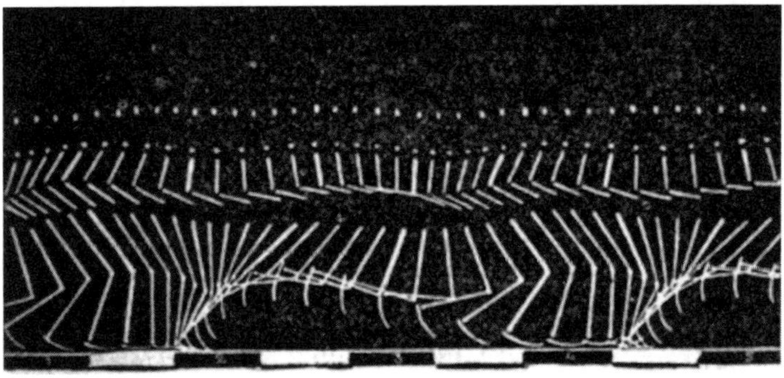

composition of the pictures in *Animal Locomotion*—as inaugurating what Rosalind Krauss identifies as the modernist passion for grids. The form of the grid emblematizes modernity, Krauss explains, because, by "abrogating the claims of natural objects to have an order particular to themselves," it rejects art's naturalist or mimetic pretensions.[67] While the grid is ubiquitous in twentieth-century art, Krauss sees it "nowhere in the art of the last one [the nineteenth]," and fifteenth- and sixteenth-century studies of perspectives formalized by Alberti are in no way the precursors of artists like Mondrian, Malevich, or LeWitt.[68] Krauss contends that the Albertian perspective is premised on a mimetic continuity between the material world and its

FIGURE 16. Thomas Eakins, *Horse (Chalk Grid Drawn on Body)*, c. 1895. Platinum print on cream wove paper.

figuration. This is the source of its value for a science premised on representation. In contrast, the modernist grid supposes an irreducible disjointedness between the artwork and the world, relinquishing any pretension to re-present the real. Recognizing Muybridge's influence on the artists she mentions invites us to revise Krauss's chronology and brings into relief the epistemological purchase of the modern grid. Contra Krauss's autotelic interpretation, the modern grid does not discover a radical discontinuity between reality and representation so much as it inverts the primacy of one over the other. Through the grid, representation no longer comes after the real it seeks to reproduce; it is reproducibility that defines what counts (albeit retroactively) as original. It is reproducibility, metaleptically, that engenders the aura of the original. This reversal has a bearing on the image of animals composed by modern representational grammars, which produce

A

B

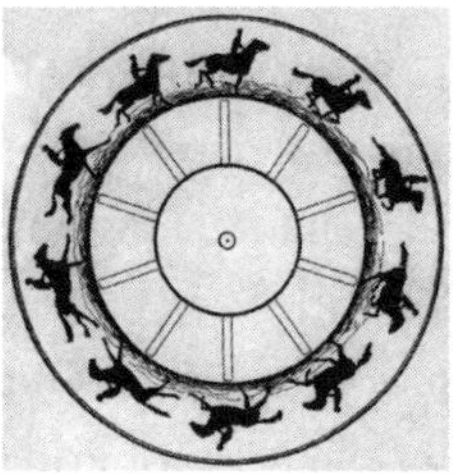

D

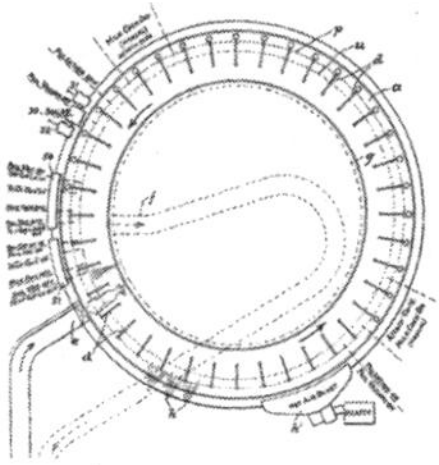

C

E

FIGURE 17. *(a)* Eadweard Muybridge, Plate 673 from *Animal Locomotion,* 1887 ("Sow; walking"); *(b)* pig gestation crates in a concentrated animal feeding operation; *(c)* zoetrope, made with photographs by Eadweard Muybridge; *(d)* patent detail for "Cow Milking Apparatus" (industrial rotolactor), patented by C. H. Hapgood in 1930; *(e)* film still from *New Jersey. "The Rotolactor" — hygiene's latest — automatically washing and milking 50 cows at one time in 12 ½ minutes — inaugurated by Mr. Thomas Edison.*

nostalgia for something construed as essentially fugitive and vulnerable and, in a sense, already lost.

How can we account for the fact that the animal figures so prominently as this obstinately elusive yet highly exploitable "real" glimpsed by the modern eye of Muybridge's camera? Perhaps it is, as Lippit suggests, that Muybridge was "racing against the imminent disappearance of animals from the new urban environment."[69] Yet the animals in his catalog were hardly the most marginalized (to use Berger's terminology), nor were they the most immediately threatened by extinction—indeed, the first volumes of *Animal Locomotion* feature pigeons, cats, and dogs alongside human beings performing mundane activities such as walking, jumping, or pouring water.[70] Animals—including humans perceived as animals—were not merely exemplary case studies for the development of motion pictures; instead, they actively "participated" (albeit not always voluntarily) in shaping modern technologies of capture. But first, they had to be reconceptualized from the perspective of their reproducibility (Figures 17a–e).

THE ANIMAL IN THE AGE OF ITS TECHNOLOGICAL REPRODUCIBILITY

In the age of mass slaughter and manmade extinction, some animals can barely reproduce fast enough to survive, while others have been made eminently reproducible. This reproducibility was effected both materially, with the advancement of industrialized breeding and factory farming, and symbolically, in the deluge of images precipitated by the advent of photographic and cinematic reproduction. Much has been written about the coeval development of cinematography and the relentless exploitation of animal life. Derek Bousé, for instance, has shown that the killing or harming of charismatic animals for aesthetic and dramatic purposes was integral to the development of cinema. Meant to serve as a "guarantor of authenticity,"[71] the "practice of setting up an actual killing for the cameras" began as early as 1884, "when Muybridge arranged at the Philadelphia zoo for a tiger to be set loose on an old buffalo who may even have been tethered," and Thomas Edison produced in 1903 a short film called *Electrocuting an Elephant,* which depicted just that: the sensational sacrifice of a rebellious female Asian elephant, Topsy.[72]

Beyond their mistreatment as "disposable subjects" of cinema, animals have bequeathed an operative mode (animation) and a medium (gelatin) to cinema. Lippit observes that during the second half of the nineteenth century, as animals rapidly vanished from the industrialized West, they were at the same time clandestinely reintroduced by modern technological apparatuses, appearing not only as images on our screens but also through the very notion of animation. Building on (and against) Lippit's claim, Shukin lays bare the profound interimplications of the "consumption of animal disassembly as affective spectacle," which normalized "tours of the vertical abattoir, the material rendering of animal gelatin for film stock," and "the mimicry of seamless animal motion integral to cinema's and automobiles' symbolic economies."[73] This collusion between the mass slaughter of animals for human consumption and the advent of the moving image (and automobility), she argues, was prefigured and made possible by the Chicago slaughterhouses' *dis*assembly lines (the inspiration for Henry Ford's moving assembly lines) as a primal cinematic scene. Yet the modern tangle of animal mass production with technological reproducibility also demands that we examine how the emergence of this new technological economy altered not only the representation of nature and its figures but the very nature of representation. Recalling that Benjamin extends the significance of his insights on the fate of art in the age of technological reproducibility "far beyond the realm of art," I briefly return to his essay to examine what became of "the animal" when animals came to be subjected on an unprecedented scale to carnal and figural processes of reproduction.

Capital, and biocapital a fortiori, are predicated on the conflation of production and reproduction (a conflation exemplified by the current ecological crisis, caused in large part by the exploitation of nonrenewable resources as if they were renewable).[74] Capitalism is thus assisted and subtended by cultural forms that simultaneously encourage and normalize a certain type of reproduction. But Benjamin's essay goes further. It posits that while culture ought not be reduced to propaganda in the service of capitalist (re)production, it must be understood as being profoundly shaped by reproduction, for it has assimilated reproduction in and as its very procedures. Shukin makes a similar claim when she advocates in favor of a "biopolitical critique" that debunks the common assumption that the semiotic and the somatic should be treated independently from one another. Biopower's penetration of all aspects of life, she contends, "never operates solely through the power to reproduce life literally, via the biological capital of the specimen or species, nor does it operate solely through the power to reproduce it figuratively via the symbolic capital of the animal sign, but instead operates through the power to hegemonize both the meaning and matter of life."[75] Here she invokes the double logic of "rendering," which "signifies both the mimetic act of making a copy . . . and the industrial boiling down and recycling of animal remains," to denounce the modern "complicity of representational and material economies in the reproduction of (animal) capital."[76] While Shukin emphasizes that rendering is made possible by Western culture's abiding investment in the "fetishistic currency of animal life"—a life invoked and put to work precisely as that which eludes capital's inherent constraints, magically "working" without laboring, undying therefore infinitely killable, etc.—my analysis focuses on the technological disposition of modern culture to merge representation and reproduction.[77]

Here I follow Lippit, whose analysis is grounded in a notion of reproduction that refers "not to the duplication of something that already exists . . . but rather to the introduction of . . . something other through a technology of representation."[78] For him, the paradigmatic technology of representation-as-reproduction is cinema, which finds in animal reproducibility a prototype of sorts:

> The function of unheimlich reproduction, the vicissitudes of affect, the dynamics of animation and projection, the semiotics of magnetism, and the fundamental properties of memory can be seen as the basis of cinema, but also of the animal. Cinema is like an animal; the *likeness* a form of encryption. From animal to animation, figure to

> force, poor ontology to pure energy, cinema may be the technological metaphor that configures mimetically, magnetically, the other world of the animal.[79]

The implications of Lippit's thesis, I believe, have not yet fully been reckoned with, and Lippit himself might not stress enough that cinematic technologies do not just mimetically borrow from animals certain characteristics (reproduction, animation, magnetism) but actively contribute to inventing the modern concept of "the animal" (as undying, as pure energy, as ontologically poor). I would not go so far as to lament with Shukin that Lippit "ends up buying the idea of the undead animal," thereby unwittingly conspiring with biocapitalist forces that profit from idealizing the animal as a pure, preideological intensity.[80] However, I recognize that casting the animal as the mute trope of modernity—as signifying in spite of itself—might foreclose the potential opened by cinema for conjuring the "other world of the animal," for perceiving and conceiving animals as subjects (unless at stake is a mute subjectivity and not a mere subjection to muteness).

The fetishized concept of animal life to which Shukin refers is less condition than effect, less the provision than the legacy of mass reproduction. By forcing her reader to confront the fact that "capital has become animal," Shukin suggests that mimesis has been entirely coopted by and subsumed under the figural economy of capitalist biopower and thus cannot be a viable method of either eluding or resisting the all-pervasive market logics. Shukin asserts that all thinkers who do not see mimesis as entirely absorbed into capitalism—Benjamin foremost among them—are guilty of an idealist, primitivist form of escapism that is complicit with said market logics.[81] But when Shukin plays tautology (capital has become animal) against Lippit's simile (cinema is like an animal), she perfectly aligns mimesis with reproduction and reduces any form of alterity to fetishism. Is she not, then, "buying" (to reflect her own criticism of Lippit) the idea that the animal is pure reproducibility? The circuitous logic she (rightly) identifies as integral to capital's workings makes it seem as if there was nothing outside of capitalism, as Tobias Menely observes.[82] Moreover, by equating capital with animal, she implicitly endorses the view that reproducibility constitutes the essence of animality, whereas I would suggest that the reproducibility of the animal should be seen as itself an event in the history of animals, one that constitutes as epochal a shift in the animal condition as any genetic or migrational mutation. Yet here I do not wish to emphasize what stubbornly exceeds biocapitalist reproducibility (for Menely, it is the "animal claim," the addressive capacity by which nonhuman animals have historically been accounted for by various political communities). Rather, following Benjamin's brand of immanent critique, I suggest that bioreproduction contains its own antithesis. It is a question of looking not *elsewhere* but *otherwise*—of looking at it "slantwise," as Hawthorne suggests, at the question of reproducibility.

Benjamin's insights on the work of art in the age of its technological reproducibility prefigure the modern conditions of (re)production of animal bodies, which are well disposed to "neutralize a number of traditional concepts" often manipulated in the interests of biocapitalism. Benjamin's essay, we recall, hinges on two fundamental insights: First, that technologies of reproduction substitute "a mass existence for a unique existence," undermining the concepts of unicity and authenticity that are traditionally associated with the original work of art; the artwork's aura—its "here and now," what it is said to retain from its unique physical origin—dwindles in proportion to its replicability. Second, he asserts that the unprecedented inflation in quantity afforded by modern conditions of production triggers a qualitative mutation in the works themselves, whose value and function become determined by their degree of reproducibility. One may sum up Benjamin's contention by paraphrasing Hegel's famous adage: with the advent of technologies of reproduction, what is reproducible is real, and the real is reproducible.[83]

I offer two insights, parallel to Benjamin's, about the lot of animals in the age of their technological reproducibility. First, because to be mass-produced in factory farms animals must be dis-located from their natural habitats, and because industrial slaughter is incompatible with ritualized killing, the animal can be said to have lost its aura, which, for Benjamin, is an intrinsic attribute of "natural objects." In fact, destroying the aura of the object is a necessary step toward its commodification, as the auratic is by definition that which resists standardization and appropriation.[84] This explains why conservation efforts to preserve endangered species sometimes seek to restore the aura of animals "naturally" bad at reproduction: giving proper names to endangered lions and rhinoceroses, underlining the rarity and thus value of endlings (the last known exemplars of a species), etc. Second, with the advent of factory farming, industrialized countries do not "produce" the animals they traditionally consumed; instead, they consume the animals that they can most efficiently and cheaply reproduce. Animals are viewed less as individual specimens than as profitable and manipulable breeds; similarly, from a conservation perspective, animals are primarily regarded through the lens of their impending extinction, perceived as either viable or endangered. Both perspectives view animals statistically, in aggregate, at the level of population or breed—from the vantage of their reproducibility.

This schematic recapitulation is consonant with Foucault's theory that populations and species, not individuals, constitute the new "subjects" of biopolitical governance.[85] Animals fully enter the calculus of biopower once reproducibility has become the principle by which the reality of animal life is apprehended. But at the moment when animals appear to be catastrophically vulnerable to biocapitalist exploitation, a new image of the animal emerges. Cary Wolfe has shown that biopolitics offers a valuable "frame" for posing anew the "question of the animal." In *Before the Law,* he deconstructs the relentless "enframing" operations performed by apparatuses of biopower that work to position what is enframed as mere stock or "standing-reserve," exposing an untold number of animals to a "noncriminal putting to death" insofar as they appear endlessly reproducible. Wolfe, however, also underlines the "fundamental ambivalence" of Foucauldian biopolitics, which points to a fracturing in the categories of animal and species as no longer constitutive (yet still operative) in a biopolitical frame. Biopolitics, he shows, has historically been beneficial to some animals, "not in spite of the fact that they are 'animals' but *because* they are 'animals'" (pets and endangered species being a case in point).[86] The entrance of life into the domain of politics, in other words, has allowed the management, regulation, control, exploitation, overproduction, and extermination of the living at an unprecedented scale, but it has also afforded different ways of caring for and relating with the living.

I share Wolfe's theoretical premise, but I shift the emphasis away from the ontological and legal economies of "enframing" to the epistemological and representational technology of what I have called "capture." Addressing the epistemic and aesthetic dimension of capture does not mean disregarding its material conditions and effects. On the contrary, it means examining how new technologies like photography and cinema have altered our conceptions of animals and, at the same time, how animals have materially and figurally informed these technologies to compose the representational grammar of biopolitical modernity. Along with the sea change undergone by representational practices and protocols in the middle of the nineteenth century, a fragile but revolutionary potential arises—an opportunity to gain a new awareness of how the living is enmeshed with technologies of reproduction. I now return to Eadweard Muybridge to argue that the advent of technological reproducibility does not simply mark a transition in the way we perceive and conceive animals. Instead, animality becomes the site of a profound metamorphosis in the nature of knowledge and representation; the technological reproducibility of animals occasions a radical rearticulation of the age-old opposition between *physis* and *technè.* The issue at hand is thus not to bring animals back "in focus" but to understand what new animal figures emerge under capture, what becomes newly visible, and how this crisis in representation might indeed "change everything" about the question of the animal.

COUNTERPOINT: EXPRESSIONIST CREATURES

One can hardly emphasize enough the seismic transformation occasioned by Muybridge's time-motion studies on the way we see—and, in particular, on the way we see animals.[87] Animal photography until then had been an art of the still life, and the few nonhuman animals visible in Muybridge's early pictures were taxidermied animals or the skeletal remains of bison destined to serve as fertilizer.[88] Although the amount of time required to fix the photographic image through daguerreotypes was rapidly getting shorter and shorter—from thirty minutes at the inception of photography in 1839 to thirty seconds in 1841—the interval was still too long for the capture of animals in motion.[89] It is little surprise, therefore, that the very first moving image with a "real subject" that Muybridge produced with his zoopraxiscope staged not a living horse but a horse skeleton imported from New York in 1881 (Figure 18). The irony was double: what was presumably the first animation ever made with unretouched photographs was both artificially composed and a paradoxical fabrication of lifelikeness that relied on its subject's death. (Remarkably, Marey called the black and white garments with which he captured human motion his "homme squelette"—"skeleton man"—suits [Figure 15].) This was not live action but a danse macabre. Kittler reminds us that the very first illustration of a print shop figured a "dance of death," and here, the first animation produces a galloping skeleton, which we can read as the allegory of the entropy on which the medium itself is often thought to be predicated.[90] To produce the likeness of life, animation paradoxically seemed to require that the living be stilled.[91]

Yet cinematic lifelikeness need not be construed as inimical to life. We can also see it as revealing an alternative image of the living predicated on discontinuity and reproducibility. Capture does not consist in arbitrarily reanimating visual fragments that are themselves nonsignificant, like letters in the alphabet ("lifeless units of time and movement," in Crary's words);[92] rather, it supposes an attunement to a residual motivation in the gesture that is extracted from an apparently continuous motion. In modernity, writes Agamben, "every image is animated by an antinomic polarity: on the one hand, images are the reification and obliteration of a gesture (it is the *imago* as death mask or as symbol); on the other hand, they preserve the *dynamis* intact (as in Muybridge's snapshots or any sports photograph)."[93] The emphasis has often been placed on the reifying moment, and the dynamis has been reduced to a fetishized energy in the service of reification. But

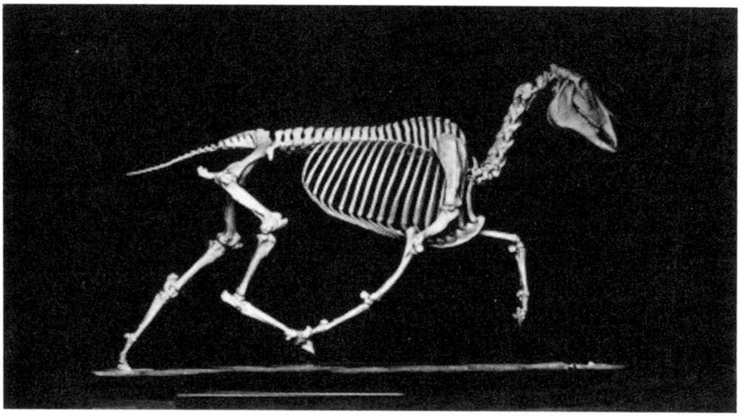

FIGURE 18. Eadweard Muybridge, "Some Phases in the Gallop of a Horse," 1881.

what is gained in Muybridge's sequential images is the sense that every still is the fragment of a gesture that in turn expresses the technohistorical milieu in which it took place: "The gesture is the exhibition of a mediality," Agamben writes: "it is the process of making a means visible as such." This is the only way that "the obscure Kantian expression 'purposiveness without purpose' acquires a concrete meaning."[94] We can reframe Agamben's intuition in terms of what Benjamin calls the "optical unconscious," which designates the "salutary estrangement between man and his surroundings [*Umwelt*]" effected by cinema.[95] By its capacity to immerse us in another *Umwelt*, cinema makes us aware of our environment *as environment*, not as the world "as such." Reflexively, the subject at the center of this environment is invited to embrace its own mediality. Subjectivity here does not index the immutable essence of a living being but reveals its inextricable enclosure in a singular *Umwelt.* Thus, the subject is refashioned as interface, as medium—as itself an elective technology of capture, cutting up or editing the world according to various interests and sensorial aptitudes.

Among the various techniques that orchestrate the new representational regime of capture, Benjamin cites the close-up, slow-motion footage, and bird's-eye-view perspectives as expanding the realm of the humanly visible and the editing process as artificially recomposing an impression of naturalness. In the hypermediated age of technological reproducibility, perception becomes second nature—a synthetic product. The hallucinatory dimension with which the world becomes imbued, in Benjamin's account, has often been read as modern man's fall into technology and loss of nature all over again. This reading is not solely a function of the ever-increasing interpenetration of reality and technology in the latter half of the century but more deeply of the recognition of the technological nature of reality—the recognition that reality is not passively awaiting to be uncovered but is, in effect, constituted by the observer (who, as Crary shows, is construed as a "technique").[96] Muybridge's stop-motion studies played a key role in prompting this recognition. With "his modular segmentation of images," Crary explains, Muybridge "breaks down the possibility of a 'truthful' syntax, and his aggregate presentations set up an atomized field that an observer cannot seamlessly rebind" but that can be artificially bound through the process of editing.[97]

These individual images, "although ostensibly part of a linear sequence and syntax," acquire with Muybridge "a newly autonomous, floating identity" prone to render them complicit with forces of capitalist deterritorializing. Yet for Benjamin, it is precisely this deterritorializing force that holds a revolutionary promise by offering us a means to situate ourselves, if no longer within nature, at least in what he calls our environment, or milieu. "Film can be characterized not only in terms of man's presentation of himself to the camera," Benjamin observes, "but also in terms of his representation of his environment [*Umwelt*] by means of this apparatus."[98] It is this ability to contextualize the self that, for Benjamin, produces the revolutionary potential of film:

> On the one hand, film furthers insight into the necessities governing our lives by its use of close-ups, by its accentuation of hidden details in familiar objects, and by its exploration of commonplace milieu through the ingenious guidance of the camera; on the other hand, it manages to assure us of a vast and unsuspected field of action [*Spielraum,* literally "room for play"]. Our bars and city streets, our offices and furnished rooms, our railroad stations and our factories seemed to close relentlessly around us. Then came film and exploded this

> prison-world with the dynamite of the split second, so that now we can set off calmly on journeys among its far-flung debris. . . . *Clearly, it is another nature which speaks to the camera as compared to the eye.* "Other" above all in the sense that a space informed by human consciousness gives way to a space informed by the unconscious.[99]

The camera does not denature reality so much as it defines "another nature," inviting us to glimpse beyond our conscious human world. It is little surprise then that Uexküll, with whose work Benjamin was familiar, found in photography, and chronophotography in particular, a powerful method for studying and conceptualizing human and animal *Umwelten.* Uexküll uses what he calls "the grid method" to produce approximations of how various animals experience space according to their singular perceptive capabilities (showing how different the same room will look from the point of view of a human, a fly, and a mollusk). His experiments assume the commensurability of different visual perceptions, but not of the subjective experience of the perceiving subjects. If the "world as seen through a fly's eye must seem significantly coarsened as compared to its being seen through a human eye," it does not entail that humans see better, only differently. Such a perspective allows one to understand how, for instance, "the threads of a spider's web are completely lost to sight" for a fly.[100]

Chronophotography also offers Uexküll a way to approach how different animals experience time. Though he learned chronophotography from Marey, whose Paris laboratory he visited in 1899, Uexküll's conception of animals was antipodal to that of the French physiologist. As Inga Pollmann explains, "Marey's chronophotography was based upon a Helmholtzian notion of the body as energetic machine." In contrast, Uexküll used chronophotography to analyze the movements of animals, not simply "with respect to their function and efficiency," but in order to explore the animals' "ability to organize and reorganize [their attitudes] depending upon the circumstances in which [they find themselves]."[101] Put differently: Marey posits time as the shared, objective milieu of all living beings, whereas Uexküll refutes the idea of a homogenous concept of time, instead imagining a manifold of subjective temporalities specific to each organism.[102] To illustrate this claim, Pollmann takes the example of a snail (*Helix pomatia*) for whom Uexküll devises an apparatus to determine what he calls the "snail's moment" (Figure 19). Here I quote Uexküll at length:

> A snail is placed on a rubber ball which, because it is floating on water, can slide freely past beneath the snail. The snail's shell is held in place with a clamp. The snail is thereby free to crawl and also to stay in the same place. If one places a stick at the foot of the snail, it will crawl upon it. But if one strikes the snail from one to three times a second with it, the snail will turn away. However, if the blows are repeated four or more times a second, the snail begins to crawl onto the stick. In the snail's environment, a stick that moves back and forth four or more times a second must be at rest. We can conclude from this that the perception time of the snail takes place at a speed between three and four moments a second.[103]

Uexküll compares the snail's haptic perception and the human's optical perception of their respective environments by using a cinematographic analogy: there is a threshold of perceptibility below which the snail does not feel the stick's quivering, he finds, just as there is a threshold of visibility below which a human eye does not register the flickering of images.[104] Of course, the experiment is imperfect, and Uexküll himself is well aware that he can only speculate what the *Umwelt* of another species (or, indeed, of another individual specimen, animal or human) looks and feels like. As Pollmann suggests, what chronophotography affords Uexküll is neither the objective image traditionally associated with photography nor the subjective experience of nonhuman living subjects but a view that is "other or alien."[105] When Uexküll invites his reader to peer at universes that are both "unknown" and "invisible," he does not promise to make the invisible visible, nor does he promise to bring into view what was heretofore unseen. He aims instead to disclose these invisible worlds *as invisible*, without piercing their mystery. Uexküll founds his ethology on the intuition that one can recompose an image of that other that the animal is, however

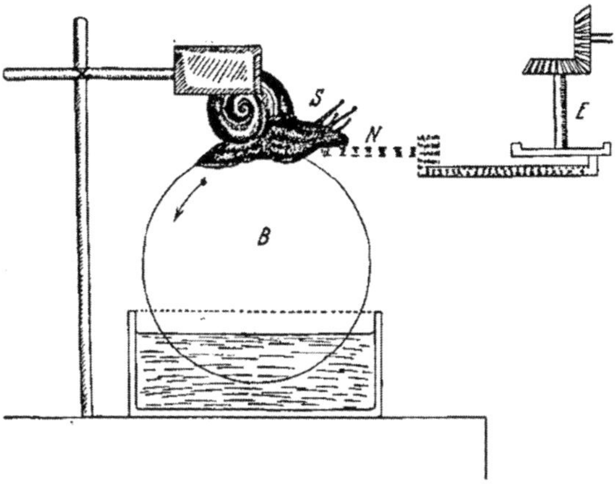

FIGURE 19. Jakob von Uexküll, "The snail's moment," in *A Foray into the Worlds of Animals and Humans*, 1934. B = ball, E = eccentric, N = stick, S = snail.

alien it may be, by observing how it interacts with, and composes, its milieu. In this intuition lies the ethical impetus of Uexküll's ethology, in the Spinozan sense of ethics.[106] Muybridge's trip wires and grids should be seen not as a Cartesian trap rationalizing and mechanizing animal gestures but rather as a spiderweb, recalling Nietzsche's intuition that "in the last resort, we achieve nothing more by cognition than the spider achieves by weaving its web, hunting and sucking the blood of its prey."[107] Or in Uexküll's words: "Every subject spins out, like the spider's threads, its relations to certain qualities of things and weaves them into a solid web, which carries its existence."[108]

Uexküll uses the image of the spider to figure what type of "relation" a given animal entertains with its *Umwelt* and with other animals. Since the spider weaves a web "before it has ever met a physical fly," it cannot be said to hunt a particular fly, nor even that it builds its web in order to catch flies; its web, rather, "represents the *primal image* [*Urbild*] of the fly, which is physically not at all present."[109] The web fits the fly like a tailored suit, Uexküll continues: the spider is fly-like insofar as "it has taken up certain motifs/motives of the fly melody in its bodily composition."[110] Deleuze and Guattari elaborate: "The spider's web contains 'a very subtle portrait of the fly,' which serves as its counterpoint. . . .

This is not a teleological conception but a melodic one in which we no longer know what is art and what nature ('natural technique'). There is counterpoint whenever a melody arises as a 'motif' within another melody, as in the marriage of bumblebee and snapdragon."[111] This oft-cited image of the "marriage of bumblebee and snapdragon" can easily be misread as an idealization of "Nature" construed as flawlessly harmonious but ultimately meaningless. Envisioned in "perfect communion" with its environment, the animal appears locked in an unmotivated chain of causality. But what Uexküll describes is precisely not a causal relation: "The web—but never the fly—can be called the goal of forming the web," he insists. "But the fly does indeed serve as the counterpoint, as the motive for the formation of the web."[112]

In his courses at the Collège de France on *Nature*, Merleau-Ponty invokes Uexküll to counter the causalist and correlationist views promoted by behaviorism with a conditional and chiasmatic perspective:

> The organism is not defined by its punctual existence; what exists beyond is a theme, a style, all these expressions seeking to express not a participation in a transcendental existence, but in a structure of the whole. The body belongs to a dynamic of behavior. Behavior is sunk into corporeity. The organism does not exist as the thing endowed with absolute properties, as fragments of a Cartesian space.[113]

For Merleau-Ponty as for Uexküll, animal behavior cannot be reduced to a series of mechanical reactions to stimuli; the animal is a semiotic subject decrypting what constitutes its lifeworld, its body a site of sensorial impressions and expressions. Marey's avowed dream, we remember, was to reduce the living animal to its functional mechanisms, to break down the continuous motion of the living into a series of discretized points. "For Marey," Doane observes, "the mathematical representability of motion/time was dependent upon the concept of the point."[114] But in its isolation, the point betrays its epistemological promise because it loses sight of the movement it seeks to make intelligible. Doane plays Marey's point (the symbol of perfect rationalization) against Peirce's point (the mark of contingency, the promise of a real that escapes all predeterminations) only to show their complementarity. The point, she concludes, emblematizes modernity's passion for the fugitive and its inexorable desire to control it.

When confronted with a taxonomic form of knowledge that accounts for living beings in terms of correlated points, Hawthorne, as we saw in chapter 4, prefers not to disclose what he knows, intimating his reader instead to imagine a different mode of relating to the animal. Uexküll takes stock of the lesson of taxonomy—that organs can be isolated from living organisms and turned into insignificant points—but challenges the idea that any point is thinkable absent its counterpoints, which compose the *Umwelt* of a given animal. This is the complementary lesson of ethology, which understands living beings on the basis of purposefulness (a purposefulness without purpose) and not of functionality or causality. Ethology asks what a particular animal "takes" in its world and what it remains unaffected by: "Every point has its counterpoints: the plant and the rain, the spider and the fly," writes Deleuze.[115] "So an animal, a thing, is never separable from its relations with the world. The interior is only a selected exterior, and the exterior, a projected interior." Although the combination of "carriers of significance" is immanently orchestrated on an infinite symphonic plane of composition, Uexküll's view is resolutely not deterministic, leaving room for unforeseen assemblages and becomings. The animal is never "free" insofar as it is bound to a certain *Umwelt*—figured at times as a "soap bubble" or a "bodily house"—but neither is it ever fixed insofar as it has the power to improvise and express itself. The word *animal* here has little to do with the "'real' animal," which for Deleuze and Guattari "is trapped in its molar form and subjectivity."[116] Hyphenated to a dynamic process of becoming, *animal* signals the possibility, not of an abstract notion of "freedom," but of a contingent and conditional power to "escape" (think of Kafka's ape in "A Report to an Academy," evolving out of necessity by imitating his human captors, preferring to "freedom" the pragmatic possibility of a "way out").[117]

Like the spider's web and its trace of the fly, like the whale secretly shaping *Moby-Dick,* Muybridge's experiments contrapuntally draw the portrait of the horse—a portrait of a specific human-machine-horse configuration, a snapshot of a certain historical assemblage. Muybridge's first apparatus of capture was Uexküllian avant la lettre insofar as it did not stop, decompose, and spatialize animal motion according to a predetermined temporal pattern. In these early experiments, Muybridge's horses were not (yet) indifferent objects; they were active participants, for the pictures were indexed on their "own times." Indeed, it is chronophotography's indexical potential (Peirce's point) that Muybridge's trip wire system reveals, to the extent that the index, in the words of Doane, "seems to acknowledge the invasion of semiotic systems by the real."[118] Thinking in terms of indexicality allows us to consider Muybridge's animal subjects as leaving on the film expressive traces of their passage. The manner in which these traces disappear for our senses does not just show us that we do not "really" see animals; what they reveal is their entanglement with our own (technologically inflected) *Umwelt*. We do not see the fly—just the web. But in the web, we can glimpse a "subtle portrait of the fly." Not seeing becomes a specific mode of engagement with our own environment. The ethics of this engagement demands not just that we recognize our own hand in the process of capture (especially because, as we saw with Audubon, capture is premised on the elision of the human hand) but also that we acknowledge that the "hand" animals have in the nature of their representation is fundamentally historical and subject to change.

Horses have always taken their own picture—they have always existed in a way that informed the procedures of their representation—but the trip wire used to be a shrine, a ritual sacrifice, a hunt. The relations humans have with different species imbue the technics of a given cultural era. Cinema, as the paradigmatic aesthetic technology of reproduction, is itself an index of the modern epoch, a period when the West's relation to the living came to be conceived predominantly in terms of reproducibility. Reproducibility does not erase material or historical consciousness, nor does it freeze the animal in some kind of timeless formalin or embalming fluid; it is the principle that underlies the animal condition in the age of its capture.

CONCLUSION

LIFE IN CAPTURE

> I held it so tight that I lost it
> Said the Child of the Butterfly
> Of Many a vaster Capture
> That is the Elegy—
> —Emily Dickinson, "I Held It So Tight That I Lost It"

In the early 1800s, the passenger pigeon made up almost half of the entire bird population in North America. But by the 1900s, only a handful of specimens remained, all in captivity, all kept alive by breeders, scientists, and zookeepers.[1] In less than a century, the passenger pigeon went from being an indomitable force of nature to a symbol of nature's imperilment by the irrepressible onrush of modernity. The story of the passenger pigeon traces in miniature the transition from hunt to capture theorized in this book. In what follows, I use the extinction of the passenger pigeon as a lens both for apprehending the dire consequences of the rise of capture and for glimpsing the ethical imperative that emerges out of this devastation.

Audubon's 1813 entry on the passenger pigeon famously describes interminable flocks darkening the sky for days at a time. Noting settlers' mass hunting of the birds, the naturalist reassures his reader that it poses no risk of extinction.[2] Just a decade later, however, Cooper devotes an entire chapter of *The Pioneers* to the settlers' ruthless "carnage" of a pigeon roost to warn against the transformation of the hunt (as that which targets one object at a time) into something else altogether: an increasingly one-sided, automatic, and indiscriminate slaughter characterized by shooting blindly, killing en masse, and using nets and other unsportsmanlike stratagems. At the end of the chapter, Judge Temple expresses remorse when he belatedly grants his victims the power to return his gaze: "I see nothing but eyes, in every direction, as the innocent sufferers turn their heads in terror. Full one-half of those that have fallen are yet alive; and I think it is time to end the sport, if sport it be."[3]

As the passenger pigeon became inextricable from its tragic fate under capture, a new condition of the animal emerged that cast it as essentially elusive. The precipitous decline of the species would usher in a new era of game management and biodiversity conservation laws. The pigeon's incapacity to reproduce by "natural" means prompted a mutation in the biopolitics of conservation—what Irus Braverman calls a shift "from 'letting be' to 'making be.'"[4] But assisted reproduction had no effect on the gregarious animal, which needed large flocks to have viable reproduction rates. Unable to stem the passenger pigeon's disappearance, conservationist efforts typically framed its demise as a late awakening to the reality of anthropogenic extinction, which could no longer be ignored.[5]

By 1910, only one specimen remained. Martha, the last of the passenger pigeons, named for Martha Washington (the nation's original First Lady), outlived the rest of her species by four years.[6] During these solitary years, Martha was not just the last representative of her species; she *was* her species, a metonym of herself, the tragic culmination of the move from animals to "the animal." On September 1, 1914, Martha's lifeless body was found lying at the bottom of her cage at the Cincinnati Zoo. For the first time in history, the extinction of a species could be dated with certainty. Upon Martha's death, her carcass (now safely stored in a drawer at the National Museum of Natural History) was shipped to the Smithsonian in Washington, D.C., where it was photographed, dissected, and taxidermied for display. Of the last photograph taken of Martha while alive (Figure 20), Robert Wilson Shufeldt, the renowned anatomist who autopsied the bird (and incidentally, Audubon's great-son-in-law), wrote: "It is quite unnecessary to comment on the value of this picture or its uniqueness, as it represents one of those things that can never be repeated."[7]

The value of the photograph, as Shufeldt makes clear, lies not in its aesthetic qualities but in the nonreproducibility of its referent. Martha became a celebrity in the last years of her life and a national icon in death. Today, a color hologram of her taxidermied body rotates in a 360-degree animation on the Smithsonian's website: a flightless pigeon in perpetual motion—a spectral manifestation of the bird caged by the movement of the thaumatrope.

For all the Cincinnati Zoo's efforts to find Martha a mate, she produced no offspring; although she was infertile, she remained seen through the prism of reproducibility, owing her fame to her inability to perpetuate her species. She had become what Darwin calls a "living fossil." The practices that encase Martha's memory for us today—zoo and natural history museum promotional discourses, photography, taxidermy—seek both to stave off and to compensate for nature's loss. "To make an exact image," writes Donna Haraway of taxidermy, "is to insure against disappearance, to cannibalize life until it is safely and permanently a specular image, a ghost."[8] Ghostly creatures like Martha—those "living dead" animals that would not live without conservationist efforts[9]—are the hypervisible counterparts to the billions of "zombie" animals bred to be killed every year behind the closed doors of factory farms.[10] This dimension of capture appears to trap the animal in a melancholy narrative that, like the child in Emily Dickinson's poem, compulsively conjugates preservation with loss: "I held it so tight that I lost it / Said the Child of the Butterfly / Of Many a Vaster Capture / that is the Elegy."[11]

But capture does not have to be elegiac. As capture defines a new epoch in the history of animality, it also provides the basis for an ethics of life in capture. In the last chapter of this book, I locate the kernel of this ethics in a strand of twentieth-century ethology invested in a relationship to animals that is not based on shared

FIGURE 20. "The Passenger Pigeon in Life." Martha in 1912, in Cincinnati Zoo. Photograph by Enno Meyer. From R. W. Shufeldt, "Published Figures and Plates of the Extinct Passenger Pigeon," *Scientific Monthly* 12, no. 5, May 1921.

experience or proximity but predicated on the recognition of an unbridgeable distance between living beings. This approach was most famously theorized in the work of Jakob von Uexküll, a foundational figure for twentieth-century biopolitical thought, who argues that every living subject is enclosed in a milieu fully meaningful only to it—what he calls the *Umwelt.* Such a view implies a radical change of perspective from the anthropocentric epistemological fervor that fueled the rise of capture in the nineteenth century: a way of looking at animals not as objects to be seen but instead as subjects that see:

> We must therefore imagine all the animals that animate Nature around us . . . as having a soap bubble around them, closed on all sides, which closes off their visual space and in which everything visible for the subject is also enclosed. . . . Only when we can vividly imagine this fact will we recognize in our own world the bubble that encloses each and every one of us on all sides.[12]

Uexküll's call for a different economy of attention models an epistemology and ethics of cohabitation, a way of inhabiting absolutely enclosed yet irreducibly entangled worlds. This form of attention means being attuned to the semiotic and operative capacities of various living subjects and to the manner in which they experience and configure their milieus, only to discover that what we take to be the world is but a worldview conditioned by the horizons of our own singular perceptual faculties.

What is adumbrated in the structure of capture is a new conception of the disappearing animal. But against capture's mandate to preserve, secure, and manage animals through mechanisms of enclosure, we find in Uexküll's ethology a different ethics of relation to this elusive animal: neither at hand nor at large, beyond both restitution and loss. Advocating for an ethics of capture does not mean valorizing the conditions from which capture emerged, which are profoundly entrenched in white settler colonial and biocapitalist histories of exploitation and extermination. Nor does it mean sanctuarizing distance, as with the "setting aside" of nature promoted in most early twentieth-century conservation rhetoric or the dispassionate detachment championed by scientific objectivity. What it does mean is the acknowledgment of distance as the ground for a new ethics of care and knowledge, as the condition for regarding other animals as well as ourselves.

ACKNOWLEDGMENTS

This book began as a dissertation written in the Department of Comparative Literature at Brown University. It took shape during years spent as an assistant professor of comparative literature at Cornell University and came to completion during my time as an assistant professor of comparative literature and English at the University of Michigan. I gratefully acknowledge the institutional networks that sustained and enlivened this work and the many individuals who helped make it possible.

I thank my colleagues in the departments of comparative literature and English language and literature at Michigan for ensuring I had the resources I needed to complete the book under the best possible conditions. I am grateful for the vibrant intellectual communities I find in both departments. I have benefited greatly from the support of my department chairs and associate chairs: Yopie Prins, Silke Weineck, David Porter, Lucy Hartley, and Gaurav Desai. I am extremely fortunate to have the mentorship of Marjorie Levinson, Peggy McCracken, and Scotti Parrish, who have engaged, read, and supported me with great care and intellect. A warm thank you to the administrative staff, and particularly to Amy Argersinger, Julie Claus Burnett, Katie Colman, Judy Gray, Jane Johnson, and Joe Johnson for their consummate professionalism and infinite patience.

I am deeply grateful for the support I received while a junior faculty member at Cornell University from 2013 to 2015. Many thanks to Andrea Bachner, Anindita Banerjee, Cathy Caruth, Cynthia Chase, Jonathan Culler, Brett de Bary, Laurent Dubreuil, Paul Fleming, Tom McEnaney, Tracy McNulty, Natalie Melas, Jonathan Monroe, Karen Pinkus, Nancy Pollak, and Naoki Sakai for their warmth and generosity. A special thanks to Timothy Murray for welcoming me to the Society for the Humanities' seminar table when I first arrived in Ithaca.

As a graduate student at Brown University, and only a recent transplant from the French system, I was especially fortunate to learn from and enjoy the support of many professors: Réda Bensmaïa, Anthony Bogues, Kenneth Haynes, Kevin McLaughlin, Karen Newman, Marc Redfield, Gerhard Richter, and Zachary Sng. I cannot thank Barbara Herrnstein Smith enough for her unparalleled critical rigor. Her contagious enthusiasm for Nietzsche and Foucault, brilliant asides, and sense of humor will continue to influence my scholarship for years to come. My time at Brown would have been less happy if not for the wonderful Charles Auger and Carol Wilson-Allen and for the companionship of my graduate cohort in comparative literature, in particular Silvia Cernea Clark and Natalie Adler. The early stage of my research was supported by a fellowship at the Pembroke Center for Teaching and Research on Women at Brown University, for which I thank Suzanne Stewart-Steinberg. I also thank those professors at Brown who were especially supportive during my time as a Fulbright Scholar in 2007–2008, which first gave real legs to my desire to pursue a career in the United States: Susan Bernstein, William Keach, Kevin McLaughlin, Deak Nabers, and Len Tennenhouse.

This book benefited immensely from the provocative insights of Dana Luciano and Cary Wolfe, whose scholarship has long shaped my thinking. I am humbled by the rigor and generosity with which they engaged my work. Scotti Parrish and Peggy McCracken's trenchant comments and thoughtful criticisms invaluably sharpened my thinking.

For reading drafts of chapters at various stages of completion, I am grateful to Irina Aristarkhova, Lauren Benjamin, Michael Boyden, Walter Cohen, Duygu Ergun, Laura Finch, Lucy Hartley, Kenneth Haynes,

Danny Herwitz, Justin Joque, Yael Kenan, Silvia Lindtner, Tomoko Masuzawa, Joshua Miller, Benjamin Murphy, Benjamin Paloff, Yopie Prins, Mauro Resmini, Anton Shammas, Xiaobing Tang, Stéphane Vanderhaeghe, and Daniel Vandersommers. For crucial displays of support and encouragement at key turns, I thank Monique Allewaert, Nancy Armstrong, Branka Arsić, Jane Bradley Winston, Timothy Campbell, Rey Chow, Lee Edelman, Kim Evans, Anne-Lise François, Lynne Huffer, Gregg Lambert, Joe Litvak, Don Pease, Lloyd Pratt, Nasrin Qader, Matthew Solomon, Len Tennenhouse, and Michelle Ty.

I have had the privilege of presenting and workshopping material from this book at talks and conferences at the Institute for the Humanities and the Central Concepts in Contemporary Theory Working Group at the University of Michigan; the A19 (19th Century Americanists) Group at the Université Paris Diderot; the Department of French and Italian at Northwestern University; the Department of English at the Université Paris 8; the Department of Comparative Literature and the Expanded Communities and Posthumanity Symposium at Cornell University; the Department of English at Lille III; the Pembroke Center for Teaching and Research on Women at Brown University; the Center for 21st Century Studies at University of Wisconsin–Milwaukee; the American Comparative Literature Association; the Society for Novel Studies conference; the American Society for Environmental History; the Society for Literature, Science, and the Arts; the Society of Early Americanists; the Association Française d'Etudes Américaines; and Interdisciplinary Nineteenth-Century Studies.

This book was revised and revised and revised in the company of several exceedingly supportive writing groups. At Cornell, I want to thank the members of the animal studies group: Elisha Cohn, Peter Gilgen, Tyran Grillo, and Sam Zacher. I also thank members of the working group on *Besetzung*: Bruno Bosteels, Paul Fleming, Amanda Jo Goldstein, Nathan Taylor, and Johannes Wankhammer. At Michigan, I thank the members of the LFF writing group for suffering many versions of my Introduction and for allowing me to take advantage of their individual and collective genius: Hadji Bakara, Ingrid Diran, Sarah Ensor, Anna Watkins Fisher, and Molly Lynch. For the final push, I had the good favor of benefiting from the intellectual community of the Institute for the Humanities' Summer Faculty Fellowship program. For their helpful feedback and good cheer, I thank Peggy McCracken, Philip Christman, Henry Cowles, Enrique García Santo-Tomás, Annette Joseph-Gabriel, Shelley Manis, Christine Modey, and David Morse.

I have been fortunate to collaborate with many exceptional thinkers and friends over the past few years. These collaborations have roused my thinking and buoyed my spirit. Special thanks to Naminata Diabate for speculating with me about biopolitical futures; to Amanda Jo Goldstein for mulling over our uncommon natures; to Tobias Menely for moving the conversation from finitude to surplus; to Seb Franklin for the exhausting but exciting workshop on capitalist capture at King's College London; and to Ingrid Diran for countless sessions spent decalcifying our fossil imaginaries. Ingrid deserves special mention here as she has read every chapter more times than anyone ever should, each time making them incomparably better and smarter. I remain forever indebted to Thangam Ravindranathan for her idiosyncratic brilliance and for the many insights gained in long conversations with her about the ever-elusive animal.

I am grateful to treasured friends, new and old, for so many good times: Amanda Alexander, Diana Allan, Merike Andre-Barrett, Farid Aouiachia, Grégoire Archière, Amanda Armstrong, Gavin Arnall, Michael Ashkin, Marion Bacrot, Lynn Badia, Hadji Bakara, Tim Bewes, Ariane Blayac, Bénédicte Boisseron, Anna Bonnell Freidin, Leslie Brack, Curtis Brown, Vincent Bruyère, Vivian Choi, Pierre Corbeil, Henry Cowles, Clare Croft, Manan Desai, Retika Desai, Xavier D'Halluin, Ingrid Diran, Sarah Ensor, Kim Evans, Raphaëlle Frija, Amanda Jo Goldstein, Patty Keller, Vanasay Khamphommala, Aliyah Khan, Athena Kirk, Bertrand Lécuyer, Blandine Lécuyer, Rafaële Lécuyer, Joseph Lee, Annie Lewandowski, Silvia Lindtner, Alex Livingston, Molly Lynch, Viviana Maggioni, Ted Martin, François Massonnat, Annie McClanahan, Sara McClelland, Tom McEnaney, Andrew Moisey, Roger Moseley, Jonathan Mullins, Sarah Murray, Emily Nacol, Ben Parris, Ben Piekut, Verity Platt, Thangam Ravindranathan, Mauro Resmini,

Charlotte Rosier, Ana Sabau, Romain Savreux, Nandi Theunissen, Kris Trujillo, Flora Valadié, Audrey Vermersch, Agnès Volle, Brian Weeks, Gillian White, and Jan de Wilde.

I thank my cherished French teachers, mentors, and interlocutors, who instilled, encouraged, and share my interest in the way philosophical and literary discourses traverse and redefine one another during my time as a student for the agrégation at Ulm, as a graduate student at Université Lille 3, and as an instructor at Université Paris 8: Yves Abrioux, Noëlle Batt, Thomas Constantinesco, Agnès Derail-Imbert, Mathieu Duplay, Pierre-Louis Patoine, Ronan Ludot-Vlasak, Cécile Roudeau, Anne Ullmo, and Stéphane Vanderhaeghe.

I gratefully acknowledge the pathbreaking work of my friends and colleagues in animality studies, who have affected my thinking in ways they may or may not know: Sarah Bezan, Colleen Boggs, Irus Braverman, Matthew Calarco, Istvan Csicsery-Ronay, Ted Geier, Akira Lippit, Susan McHugh, Tobias Menely, Alain Romestaing, Nigel Rothfels, Marta Segarra, Daniel Vandersommers, and Kari Weil. Deep thanks are due to Deb Zureik, who took the time to give me a private tour of the Cincinnati Zoo and gave me access to the zoo's archives on Martha.

While a faculty member at the University of Michigan, I have had the honor of getting to teach, but mostly to learn, at Macomb Correctional Facility. A special thank you to my friends who are or have been incarcerated there: Chris, Cowboy, David, Donald, Jay, Jemal, Julio, Justin, Mario, Oscar, Q, Randy, Steve, Tyrone, and in particular Bantu—teacher and philosopher extraordinaire. I am everyday inspired by the transformative work you're doing inside. My gratitude also to the outside members of the Theory Group for their incredible work on restorative justice: Amanda Alexander, Imani Byrd, Paul Draus, Molly Manley, Heather Mooney, Jeff Morenoff, Becca Pickus, Gerard Robertson, and Ruby Tapia.

The book is much better for the thoughtful and perceptive feedback I received from the two anonymous readers of the manuscript. At the University of Minnesota Press, I have been fortunate to work with Doug Armato, who expertly shepherded this book through the review process. I am grateful to Gabriel Levin, Zenyse Miller, Rachel Moeller,

Mike Stoffel, and Anne Wrenn for guiding me through the final steps of completion. Many thanks to Ziggy Snow for his attentive copyediting and to Sandra Friesen for her gorgeous cover design. I also acknowledge the helpful vote of support that Cary Wolfe and Cesare Casarino offered me along the way.

The book became immeasurably more cogent under the keen editorial eyes of Kim Greenwell and Heath Sledge. Thanks also to Elizabeth McNeill for her superb research assistance.

Deep thanks are due to my families on both sides of the Atlantic for their continuous support and encouragement. Thank you to my parents, Christian and Catherine, my siblings Florence and Étienne (and their families), and my in-laws, Gwen and Evans.

I am grateful for the welcomed distractions of my favorite writing companions—Henry, Birdie, and Mabel—whose *Umwelten* make mine incomparably richer.

Finally, I thank my first, last, and best reader, Anna. Thank you for making this book, and everything in my life, better and more exciting. Your encouragement and countless brilliant insights have inspired me and this project in ways words could never begin to capture.

NOTES

INTRODUCTION

1. Specification forming part of Letters Patent No. 286,447, dated October 9, 1883.
2. Advertisement for Kilburn Gun Camera. Reproduced from Scovill product catalog, appended to J. T. Taylor, *Photographic Amateur.*
3. Susan Sontag famously characterizes photography as a form of "sublimated hunt," writing that guns "metamorphosed into cameras" when nature "ceased to be what it always had been—what people needed protection from. Now nature—tamed, endangered, mortal—needs to be protected from people. When we are afraid, we shoot. But when we are nostalgic, we take pictures" (*On Photography,* 64, 15). One can glimpse the debt photography owes to firearms in the predatory attitude the camera actuates and the appropriative relation it entertains with its objects. On the predacious dimension of photographic gestures, see Arnheim, *New Essays on the Psychology of Art*; and Flusser, *Towards a Philosophy of Photography.* On the camera as an instrument of colonization, see Bryden, *Gun and Camera in Southern Africa*; MacKenzie, *Empire of Nature*; Dunaway, "Hunting with the Camera"; and Ryan, *Picturing Empire.* On the terminology and technology shared between guns and cameras, see Kittler, *Gramophone, Film, Typewriter.* On camera hunting

more specifically, see Haraway, *Primate Visions,* 42–46; and Brower, *Developing Animals,* 25–82.

4. Kilburn's invention had several precursors in Europe. Around 1860, two British inventors filed patents for contraptions that modeled a camera after a gun—the "pistolgraph" and the "photorevolver"—and by 1878, French physiologist Étienne-Jules Marey had begun devising a "photographic gun" capable of recording the flight of birds.
5. To "photograph a bird in flight is not just to hunt for the bird," notes Jason Puskar, "but to hunt for the elusive motion of the bird, that part of the animal that remains invisible to the naked eye even when the bird is fully in view. . . . To shape a camera like a gun is thus not just to fantasize about masculine power, but to acknowledge the fleeting and evasive nature of action" ("Pistolgraphs," 523).
6. The mantra of objectivity, for Allan Megill, is "untouched by human hands" (*Rethinking Objectivity,* 10). The tenets of capture are largely compatible with sciences invested in what Lorraine Daston and Peter Galison call "mechanical objectivity"—i.e., sciences suspicious of subjective observations and grounded in mechanized modes of representation (Daston and Galison, *Objectivity*).
7. As Donna Haraway observes of the motivation to exchange guns for cameras, "Once domination is complete, conservation is urgent" ("Teddy Bear Patriarchy," 28).
8. Foucault, *History of Sexuality,* 138. Crucially for us, biopower names a form of power that enlists truth, rather than force, to justify itself. As arbitrary forms of sovereign power give way to enlightened discourses and practices of knowledge, the workings of power appear naturalized, and its violence is less visible.
9. Scholars have begun to refine or challenge Foucault's Eurocentric account of the emergence of life as an epistemic reality and an analytic of power by confronting his theories to alternative knowledges produced in the colonies. Susan Scott Parrish, for instance, shows that Foucault's account of the modernization of natural history depended on, but also was contested by, the empirical expertise of Euro-American, indigenous, and Afro-American specimen collectors (*American Curiosity,* 9). Monique Allewaert and Christopher Iannini contest Foucault's chronology in *The Order of Things*. Allewaert, for instance, identifies

an ontology of life—the attribute not of biological organisms but of matter itself—in the tropics. By spotting a "vitalist materialism" in naturalists like Bartram and Humboldt, she complicates Foucault's assumption that the eighteenth century was obsessed with grids and fixed taxonomies (*Ariel's Ecology,* 52). Iannini, as for him, shows that the "emblematic" description of nature—a technique that Foucault associates with the episteme of the Renaissance—perdured "well into the eighteenth century" and "especially in the colonial Americas" (*Fatal Revolutions,* 26). My book looks at a later period, the transition to the "modern" episteme, when there were stronger pressures to harmonize and globalize scientific practices: this for me takes the form of the hegemony of Cuvierian epistemology, which did not impose itself synchronously or homogeneously on both sides of the Atlantic but whose influence nonetheless strongly affected the nineteenth-century U.S. scientific and cultural imaginary (as I argue in chapter 4). On biopolitical practices specific to the nineteenth-century U.S. context, see Luciano, *Arranging Grief* (on the literary deployment of sentiment as a regulatory technology); and Schuller, *Biopolitics of Feeling* (on the influence of oft-overlooked scientific traditions like Lamarck's theory of plasticity).

10. Tocqueville, *Democracy in America,* 663. The specificity of American despotism, for Tocqueville, lies in its apparent peacefulness, which is achieved by covering "the surface of society with a network of small, complicated, minute, and uniform rules" (663).

11. Elias Canetti helpfully distinguishes between the two types of power represented by hunters and herdsmen: "Over all the animals that man keeps captive hangs his death sentence. It is, it is true, *suspended,* and often for a long time, but it is never remitted. . . . The span of life he allows them is as set as his own. . . . As herdsman, he has more power than any hunter. His animals are all in one place and do not flee from him. The duration of their lives is in his hands. He does not have to kill them when and where he finds them. The *force* of the hunter has become the *power* of the herdsman" (*Crowds and Power,* 199).

12. Foucault, *Security, Territory, Population,* 473.

13. The term *realist* often implies a sense that the real is passive and stable, waiting to be uncovered, experienced, or mimetically re-presented. For

me, it names the attempt to understand how things manifest or produce themselves to an observer/reader and how they can be reproduced without betraying their constructedness. Realism, in other words, tends to collapse representation and reproduction.

14. For a detailed analysis of the grid as a hegemonic economic, political, and epistemological form in nineteenth-century U.S. culture, see chapters 2 and 5. On the rectangular survey as an instrument of modern colonial governmentality and speculation, see Siegert, *Cultural Techniques,* 111. On the land grid pattern and the industrialization of farming practices in the United States, see Cronon, *Nature's Metropolis,* 101–2. Cronon shows how standardization made animals "governed as much by the nature of capital as by the nature that gave them life" (259).
15. Today the culmination of the logic of capture is everywhere apparent. Whether physically subjected to extreme conditions of confinement under agrocapitalism or closely monitored for preservation purposes in refuges and parks, animals can no longer be thought to belong to some wild or exotic elsewhere. A staggering number of animals are relegated to spaces of enclosure: confined animal feeding operations (CAFOs), hatcheries and battery farms, pounds and kennels, zoos and aquaria, research labs, breeding facilities, canned-game ranches and hunting reserves. Florence Burgat argues that our epoch "has paradoxically become one when animals look back at us from the shadow of the places where we hold them captive. Indeed, 'detention' . . . affects an unheard-of number of animals cloistered and confined to various ends; it has been systematized to the point of becoming the norm for the life of billions of mammals and birds" (Burgat, *Une autre existence,* 23, my translation). On agrocapitalism and animal confinement, see C. Taylor, "Foucault and Critical Animal Studies"; Holloway and Morris, "Exploring Biopower in the Regulation of Farm Animal Bodies"; Twine, *Animals as Biotechnology*; Novek, "Pigs and People"; and Thierman, "Apparatuses of Animality." On the (bio)politics of wildlife preservation, see Braverman, *Wild Life*; and Purdy, *After Nature*.
16. On hunting in the American cultural landscape, see Frost, *Heroes and Hunters of the West*; and Herman, *Hunting and the American Imagination.*

On the erection of the hunter as a national hero, see Slotkin, *Regeneration through Violence,* 313–68.

17. D. Lawrence, *Studies in Classic American Literature,* 133.
18. The matter is further complicated by the facts that the novel was first published as *The Whale* in England (Melville changed his title for the American market) and that "Moby Dick" is conventionally hyphenated in the title but not in the body of the book.
19. Melville, *Moby-Dick,* 223.
20. Whether exclusive or inclusive, the copula "or" that yokes "Moby-Dick" to "The Whale" indexes either a mere tautology (that Moby Dick is but another name for the whale) or an irreducible inadequacy (that the proper name fails to capture the general reality it is after). The title stumbles on this innocuous-seeming "or," this grammatical hinge that binds the singular animal to the name of its species.
21. Matt Cartmill explains: "Hunting is an end in itself for the hunter, and he wants the beasts he kills to be endlessly replaced so that his sportive battle with the wilderness can go indefinitely. . . . Throughout European history, hunters have tended to see themselves as enemies of the individual animals but friends of the animal kinds" (*View to a Death in the Morning,* 31). The dual allegiance of the hunter accounts for the topos of hunting narratives, predominant in American literature, where the hunter identifies with his animal victim and undergoes a kind of "becoming-animal."
22. In the chapter entitled "The Affidavit," Melville's narrator explains that some sperm whales have been so ferocious that they have gained "ocean-wide renown." Not only does "each of those famous whales enjoy great individual celebrity . . . , not only was he famous in life and now is immortal in forecastle stories after death, but he was admitted into all the rights, privileges, and distinctions of a name" (*Moby-Dick,* 223). With a proper name, what the animal paradoxically acquires—more accurately, what it is granted—is immortality as an effect of its mortality (an end of one's own).
23. Melville, 82.
24. Whereas Ishmael acknowledges the consequences of overhunting on the continent, he curiously shrugs off this possibility for the whale

(Melville, 501–2). As if to reassure itself, the chapter marshals statistical data and mythical references to deflect the fatalist predictions of "some philosophers of the forecastle" about the diminishing number of sperm whales. Near the chapter's end, Ishmael pronounces the whale inextinguishable: "We account the whale immortal in his species, however perishable in his individuality" (503–4). The hunt can safely go on, its sustainability secured by this way of "accounting" the animal. Melville, observes Colin Dayan, "understood how the very forms of speech and heights of artifice went hand in hand with a history of extermination," a history "always masked by the veneer of enlightenment" (*With Dogs at the Edge of Life*, xiii).

25. Melville's appropriation of the agricultural term *harvest* in relation to the whaling industry bespeaks the nascent industrialization of fishing and the euphemization of animal killing discussed by Noëlie Vialles in *Animal to Edible*. On the anonymization of flesh, the elaborate making "inoffensive" of the rendering industry, and the withdrawal of slaughterhouses from urban environments in Europe and North America, see Shukin, *Animal Capital*, 49–86. Shukin recovers the forgotten history of Henry Ford's assembly lines, which were inspired by Ford's visit to Chicago's stockyards, to show that the assembly line, "so often taken as paradigmatic of capitalist modernity," was "mimetically premised on the ulterior logistics of animal disassembly" (87). This forgetting is not fortuitous, she claims, but it signals the degree to which animal killing and rendering have been made transparent in our culture. On *Moby-Dick* and the emergence of an "extinction-producing economy," see Barnard, "Cod and the Whale," 853. On the disavowed "reliance on animal death" that powered the bourgeois "culture of sentiment" in antebellum America, and on the orientalist bias that subtends this disavowal, see Schuller, "Specious Bedfellows," 18.

26. At first glance, his quest seems antithetical to the enterprise of Peleg and Bildad: fixated on the unique, nonsubstitutable, auratic animal, Ahab seems to stand for the precapitalist logic that refuses to "engage in exchange." But as Cesare Casarino shows, Ahab's monomania "only pave[s] the way for a higher level of subsumption" (*Modernity at Sea*,

86). Ishmael himself suggests in passing that Ahab's obsession with "the ultimate capture of Moby Dick" might easily extend to "all sperm whales." In the chapter soberly titled "The Chart," the reader witnesses Ahab scrupulously trace the ocean-lines (or "veins") formed "with undeviating exactitude" by the leviathans in hopes of finding the solitary creature that obsesses him (Melville, *Moby-Dick,* 216). Ultimately, the whale escapes these Euclidian formalizations, but as it disappears it leaves behind it a mess of lines, charts, and data that profoundly alter the maritime landscape. Melville mentions oceanographer Lieutenant Maury, who compiled statistics from a great number of logbooks in order to "divid[e] the ocean into districts of five degrees of latitude by five degrees of longitude" (216). Maury was not just mapping the probable presence of whales, he was using whale hunting to chart the world, and the grid he imposed onto the globe was responding not only to economic imperatives but also to the whales' biological needs (feeding grounds, mating habits, etc.).

27. Philip Armstrong argues that the nineteenth-century whaleman is an exemplary transitional figure in that he "was both a romantic adventurer into wild space and a prototype of the industrial laborer, farmer, and meat processor. . . . No wonder that *Moby-Dick,* like its sources, oscillates so vigorously between apparently opposed attitudes to the whale: wonder and contempt, mundane nonchalance and transcendent awe, humanized fellow feeling and the calculus of market value and profit" ("'Leviathan Is a Skein of Networks,'" 1040).

28. A testament to the rise of gun culture after the Civil War, the entanglement of photography and hunting emblematized by Kilburn's gun camera also exposes a new obsession with technologies capable of engaging with a "nature" newly perceived as endangered. While species extinction was still a much-debated scientific hypothesis in the 1800s, by century's end it had become an empirically observable phenomenon that led the self-proclaimed "wilderness hunter" Theodore Roosevelt to implement unprecedented protectionist measures. On the prominent role hunters played in conservation, see Cioc, *Game of Conservation*; Ritvo, "Destroyers and Preservers"; Reiger, *American Sportsmen and the Origins of Conservation*; and Warren, *Hunter's Game.*

29. On the resignification of hunting from a "barbarian" activity (as Jeffersonian agrarianism had framed it) to a performative practice foundational to America's frontier identity, see Jones, *Epiphany in the Wilderness.* Of course, hunting had been performative before westward expansion, carrying out important symbolic functions in early settler and indigenous hunting cultures, and hunting played a crucial role in the material economy and politics of a nineteenth-century United States reshaped by westward expansion. But attending to the hunt as performance allows us to heed what Jones calls the evolving "afterlife of the hunt"—i.e., the historically determined cultural artifacts and mythoi that hunting practices have engendered and that contribute to the "invention of tradition" (18). The resignification Jones focuses on comes into relief when "natural resources of the West began to run out": "Witnessing the decline of game stocks, a diverse range of constituencies—from sportsmen-preservationists to camera-hunters and American Indians—proselytized on the imperilment of hunter's paradise and its necessary salvation" (21).
30. From his 1830s expeditions, George Catlin reports that one could see "several thousands [of buffalos] in a mass, eddying and wheeling about under a cloud of dust" (quoted in Cronon, *Nature's Metropolis,* 215), and John James Audubon famously observes in his *Ornithological Biography* that the "air was literally filled with Pigeons; the light of noon-day was obscured as by an eclipse" (321). Over the course of the nineteenth century, the number of bison in the United States plummeted from thirty million to a dramatic twenty-three, and the passenger pigeon went extinct at the beginning of the twentieth century. I return to the extinction of the passenger pigeon in the conclusion.
31. Discourses on extinction emerged in Europe at the turn of the nineteenth century in the wake of epic enterprises of comparative anatomy and classification, themselves reliant on the importation of foreign species facilitated by the extraction of resources in the colonies and the intensification of the transatlantic trade. A distinctive epistemic frame, first formalized by French naturalist Georges Cuvier in 1800 in his "Mémoire sur les espèces d'éléphans vivantes et fossiles" and later confirmed by Charles Lyell in his 1830 *Principles of Geology,* was needed

to explain why fossils had no living counterparts, to render *visible* the absence of some animals—although the reality the term *animals* covers here must already have changed, since extinction demands that animals be viewed primarily as species (i.e., from the vantage of reproducibility and viability). As for mass slaughter, many critics have shown that its possibility rests on an invisibilization of animals through the development of an elaborate semiotics of denial and the structure of what Carol J. Adams calls the "absent referent" (*Sexual Politics of Meat,* 19–44). More deeply, mass slaughter is premised on mass reproduction, which deindividualizes animal beings to present them as stock (see chapter 5). Once cataloged into recognizable species, animals could be saved en masse (as with conservation efforts aiming to avoid species extinction) or produced (and killed) ad infinitum. In both cases, what is at stake is a profound mutation in the conception-perception of animals—a mutation subtended by a transformation in their material and figural apprehension.

32. I borrow the phrase "mute mystery" from Hawthorne's *The Marble Faun* (9). I elaborate Hawthorne's views on animality in chapter 4.
33. The "rule of capture" is a common-law rule that stipulates that the first person to capture "fugitive" natural resources becomes their legal owner. In the 1889 case *Westmoreland and Cambria Natural Gas Co. v. De Witt*, the Supreme Court of Pennsylvania stipulated that "water and oil, and still more strongly gas, may be classed by themselves, if the analogy be not too fanciful, as minerals *ferae naturae* [because] in common with animals . . . they have the *power and the tendency to escape without the volition of the owner*" (quoted in Daintith, *Finders Keepers?,* 22; emphasis added). Tellingly, after 1892, records show no mention of the capture of wild animals in litigations between neighbors. Animals disappeared from legal arbitrations, subsisting merely, in their fugitivity, as fanciful analogies. Though not uniquely an American phenomenon, the rule of capture "assumed particular importance in the United States," according to legal scholar Terence Daintith, "where the process of westward expansion constantly opened up new resources that might be available for appropriation by the prompt and energetic" (4). Melville saw it well when he writes in *Moby-Dick*: "What was America in 1492 but

a Loose-Fish, in which Columbus struck the Spanish standard by way of waifing it for his royal master and mistress?" (435).

34. As I discuss in chapter 2, "primitivizing" the hunt served two purposes: it presented indigenous populations as unable to graduate to civilized modernity and it made nature and Native cultures available for colonial appropriation. On the fetishistic attachment of white settlers to Aboriginal cultures, see Wakeham, *Taxidermic Signs.*
35. Roderick Nash observes that in 1888, "with a view to implementing his ideas, Roosevelt organized the Boon and Crockett Club. Its stated purpose was the encouragement of big-game hunting, but the character of the hunter was the real object of concern. . . . Of course, Americans had always shot game, but this group of wealthy hunters coupled their sport with unprecedented primitivistic philosophy" (*Wilderness and the American Mind,* 152). Presented as a prophylactic against the degeneracy of the white race, hunting, "once a utilitarian activity, had been given a new rationale" (153). Donna Haraway shows how the ideologies attached to hunting continued to fuel the national imaginary in the first half of the twentieth century while appearing superfluous to the material economy of the country: this apparent superfluity or primitivity is symptomatic of a historical alteration in the approach of nature and its animal(ized) representatives ("Teddy Bear Patriarchy").
36. Industrial capitalism, for instance, promotes a conception of animals as endlessly reproducible rather than individual, continually available yet never fully present—it "is biopolitically invested," Nicole Shukin explains, "in *producing* animal life as a spectral body" (*Animal Capital,* 38).
37. "To live, for each animal, means to cross the visible by hiding in it . . . even before the hunt learned the infinitely varied modes and the speeds of this dissimulation, it seems that the veracity of the animal world had to establish itself, for itself, on this elusive backdrop of flights and refuges: territories, which can be defined as surfaces . . . where each animal exposes itself, can at the same time be considered as networks of hideaways" (Bailly, *Le visible est le caché,* 14–16, my translation).
38. This dual impossibility of hiding and appearing is consistent with Anna Lowenhaupt Tsing's contention that the systematic destruction of

refugia—those hideaways or "places of refuge" necessary for the regeneration of biological diversity—marks the transition point between the Holocene and the Anthropocene (quoted in Haraway, *Staying with the Trouble,* 100).

39. Berger's 1977 essay "Why Look at Animals?" (*About Looking,* 3–28) has been widely influential in the recent field of animal studies. It is the point of departure for Akira Mizuta Lippit's *Electric Animal* (2000) and Steve Baker's *The Postmodern Animal* (2000), both groundbreaking studies in this field. Jonathan Burt's *Animals in Film* (2002), by contrast, positions itself against Berger, whom Burt accuses of fetishizing the (lost) possibility of an unmediated relation between humans and animals.
40. Berger, *About Looking,* 21.
41. Berger, 28. Many have criticized Berger's thesis for its perceived utopianism, dismissing it as naively lamenting the loss of an authentic or "unmediated" relation between humans and animals. What Berger diagnoses is not the loss of a "direct relation to animals" (Brower, *Developing Animals,* xv)—for him, there always was "an abyss of noncomprehension" between humans and animals (Berger, *About Looking,* 5)—but the invention of the animal as lost. Nostalgia is not the symptom of a historical "fall" out of nature but the mood by which animals are apprehended in modernity. It does not simply prevent us from seeing what is really happening to animals; it trains us to see animals as disappearing. I do not dispute that some aspects of Berger's analysis are debatable. What he writes about pets, for instance, ignores the interactive and improvisational character of pet-owner relations. In fact, it seems that Western cultures might never have been more attuned to multispecies intra- and interactions, as Haraway's 2008 book *When Species Meet* suggests. But if Haraway multiplies sites of cross-species encounters to counter the fantasized notion of "great divide" between nature and culture, hers are not traditional encounters insofar as "the partners do not precede the meeting": they find themselves "entangled," always-already interdependent (*When Species Meet,* 4).
42. For a comprehensive overview of the shift from the "passion for collecting" (1500s–1700s) to the "need to control" (1800s) and the "yearning for nature" (1900s) see Baratay and Hardouin-Fugier, *Zoos.*

On the scientific mission of zoos, their conversion from "paradise to ark," and the practice of human zoos, see Rothfels, *Savages and Beasts,* 19–20, 175, 81–142. On human zoos, see Blanchard et al., *Human Zoos.*

43. For Berger, the public zoo epitomizes the modern (non)relationship between humans and animals. "In principle, each cage is a frame round the animal inside it. Visitors visit the zoo to look at animals. . . . Yet in the zoo the view is always wrong. Like an image out of focus" (*About Looking,* 23). "The disappearance of animals takes several forms," film scholar Anat Pick elaborates, "some of them paradoxically those of enhanced visibility." According to Pick, it is thus the "disappearance of animals from daily life that renders them utterly visible—that re-presents them—as objects of mastery and knowledge," and this "has only intensified under the conditions of endangerment" (*Creaturely Poetics,* 103–4).
44. Berger, *About Looking,* 26.
45. Lippit, *Electric Animal,* 1. In my discussion of animals' disappearance, I follow Lippit's reframing of disappearance not as a singular moment but as an enduring condition of the animal in modernity. Lippit's work has sometimes been read as oblivious to, even complicit with, the relentless exploitation of animals, the orchestration of their sustained and sustainable disappearance on an industrial scale for capitalist profit. Continually disappearing yet infinitely reproducible, "undying" animals are at once ostensibly unkillable (they are not fully alive) and endlessly exploitable (they never go away). Yet Lippit shows better than most that what we call "animal" underwent a profound transformation in the modern period: "the nature of the animal," he observes, "has shifted in the modern era from a metaphysic to a phantasm; from a body to an image; from a living voice to a technical echo" (21). My analysis departs from Lippit's in two important ways. First, I address the animal question from a biopolitical vantage to engage with issues of power embedded in practices of knowledge, whereas the ethical and political stakes of Lippit's work remain for the most part implicit. Second, by focusing on the nineteenth-century United States, I underline how the consolidation of colonial and capitalist logics subtended the making of a new animal condition.

46. Benjamin, "Work of Art in the Age of Its Technological Reproducibility," 253.
47. The agonistic dramaturgy of the hunt is fundamentally iterative and interminable, hence for Walter Benjamin the hunter is the prototype of the flaneur, who does not know in advance what he is looking for (*Arcades Project,* 801–2).
48. Chow, *Entanglements,* 4.
49. The formula is Tom Gunning's ("Play between Still and Moving Images," 33).
50. Jonathan Crary argues that the thaumatrope, which called attention to "the hallucinatory and fabricated nature of the image and the absolute rupture between perception and its object," exemplifies the radical dismantling of classical vision in the first half of the nineteenth century (*Techniques of the Observer,* 106). This shift transformed the viewer from a passive (but sovereign) receiver into an active (but manipulable) producer of visual information.
51. I treat the thaumatrope as an idealized prototype of capture, but it is important to recognize that the toy, akin to a game of fort-da, was far from working ideally: when the thaumatrope slows down, the bird is released and the cage emptied. Its mechanism required constant repetition, which betrays the idealist dimension of capture as a biopolitics of vision. To acknowledge this is to allow for divergent, skeptical, and resistant forms of viewing.
52. Chow, *Entanglements,* 46.
53. Chow borrows the term *entanglement* from quantum physics to describe these encounters that are not defined by proximity, affinity, or equivalence. In entanglement, particles are mysteriously connected "due to simultaneous reactions they produce." She also cites Uexküllian biosemiotics, in which "the behavior of animals and organisms . . . coevolve by mysterious patterns of symmetry, down to the precise details of their bodily formations" (*Entanglements,* 2). I turn to Uexküll's work in chapter 5, but I want to flag here that the conception of the animal as captive of its milieu, which finds its most potent expression in Uexküll's concept of *Umwelt* (the bounded lifeworld of animal subjects), was definitional for twentieth- and twenty-first-century biological thought

(deep ecology, ethology, biosemiotics) and philosophies of life. On the influence of Uexküll on Heidegger, Merleau-Ponty, and Deleuze, see Buchanan, *Onto-Ethologies.*

54. *Oxford English Dictionary Online,* s.v. "capture (*v.*)," accessed April 26, 2020, https://quod.lib.umich.edu/cgi/o/oed/oed-idx?type=entry&byte=50445499.
55. Both Daguerre and Edison turn to the language of captivity to describe the essential features of the daguerreotype and the phonograph, respectively (on the daguerreotype, see Chevalier, *Guide du photographe*, 19; on the phonograph, see Edison, "Phonograph and Its Future," 530). For a brilliant analysis of the politics of Edison's "fugitive sound" in the context of African slavery and the emergence of copyright laws in the United States, see Best, *Fugitive's Properties,* 29–100.
56. Berger, *About Looking,* 23.
57. Foucault, *Order of Things,* 176.
58. Foucault presents the transition from natural history to biology as a move away from the classical belief that seeing is knowing. The classical age is the age of "representation," Foucault argues, and natural history is "nothing more than the nomination of the visible" (*Order of Things,* 144); modern biology challenges this faith in representation by privileging the unseeable. Tellingly, Sari Altschuler opens her history of the rise of U.S. modern medicine, which privileged physiology over anatomy, with the example of physician and novelist Robert Montgomery Bird, who complained in an 1841 address to medical students that doctors had as yet "no window of Momus to give us vistas of living pathology" (*Medical Imagination,* 1).
59. Foucault, 301.
60. Foucault, 303.
61. Derrida discusses this curious "nonpower at the heart of power" in relation to Jeremy Bentham's revolutionary reframing of the animal question in *Introduction to the Principles of Morals and Legislation* (311n1). When Bentham—a thinker of signal importance for Foucault—famously asks "Can they suffer?" instead of "Can they reason?," Derrida comments, he invites us to view animals from what we "undeniably" have in common with them (on Derrida's surprising recourse

to the rhetoric of undeniability, see Menely, *Animal Claim*, 169–73). Derrida ruminates on the aporia that makes animal suffering simultaneously accounted as undeniable and yet routinely discounted in practice. Such anomaly is possible, he suggests, when one relegates suffering to sheer impotence and "disavows" the singular "power" troubled by nonpower at the heart of the animal's "passion" (*Animal That Therefore I Am*, 28). Nicole Shukin accuses Derrida of disempowering animals, of spectralizing animality, and thus of occluding the historical and material ways in which "capitalism is biopolitically invested in producing animal life as a spectral body" (*Animal Capital*, 38). She rightly insists that we need to investigate further the material and technological conditions for the proliferation of spectral animals, but I see in the elusiveness that Derrida associates with the animal a potential for "resistance," in the Foucauldian sense. The positivity of Foucault's description ("The animal . . . discovers fantastic new powers") conjures up biopolitics' introduction of new modes of subjectivation, not just subjugation, albeit the "biopolitical subject" has little to do with the liberal subject (construed as autonomous, rational, and willful). Cary Wolfe points out that biopolitics acts on bodies that are "not always already abjected" but "enfolded via biopower in struggle and resistance" (*Before the Law*, 32). This book accounts for this "resistance" by delineating an "ethics of capture" attentive to forms of expressions that are made intelligible by capture, arguing that animal subjects express themselves both against and through the very apparatuses that capture them.

62. Foucault, "Cuvier's Situation in the History of Biology," 229.
63. Among the most prominent contributors to the recent "animal turn" in biopolitics, Cary Wolfe's *Before the Law* and Nicole Shukin's *Animal Capital* show the extent to which animals are integral to biopolitical rationality and how biopolitics as an analytic of power can shed new light on the "question of the animal." See also Boggs, *Animalia Americana*; Braverman, *Wild Life*; Broglio, *Beasts of Burden*; Calarco, *Zoographies*; Chen, *Animacies*; McCracken, *In the Skin of a Beast*; Seshadri, *HumAnimal*; Shukin, "Security Bonds"; Stanescu, "Beyond Biopolitics"; and Twine, *Animals as Biotechnology.* My book addresses a different critical archive than most of these books: instead of focusing exclusively

on *History of Sexuality* and the seminars at the Collège de France, my Foucault of reference is the author of *The Order of Things,* who is more directly concerned with the role animality played in the emergence of the discourse of species and the human sciences.

64. Framing, for Wolfe, "decides what we recognize and what we don't, what counts and what doesn't; and it also determines the consequences of falling out of the frame (in the case at hand, outside the frame as 'animal,' as 'zoe,' as 'bare life')" (*Before the Law,* 29–30). Wolfe distinguishes between two frames. The first is the Heideggerian *Gestell,* which threatens to dispose (of) what is enframed as "standing-reserve" (*Bestand*). The frame out of which animals routinely fall is a different one: it is the frame of the law, which sanctions the exploitation and "noncriminal putting to death" of the animal(ized). Playing these two frames against one another, Wolfe opens a third way between dominant biopolitical traditions that "miss" the animal in two different ways. On the one hand, Wolfe blames thinkers like Arendt, Agamben, and Žižek for their dogmatic indifference to nonhuman life, which is always-already framed as zoe, as nonpolitical; on the other hand, he criticizes the utopian in-difference (the lack of differentiation) of someone like Esposito, whom he sees falling for what Derrida denounces as "biological continuism" (56–59).
65. C. Wolfe, 47.
66. The term *capture* has received a fair amount of attention in recent biopolitical discourses since Agamben's dizzyingly capacious definition of *dispositifs* as "anything that has in some way the capacity to capture, orient, determine, intercept, model, control, or secure the gestures, behaviors, opinions, or discourses of living beings" (*"What Is an Apparatus?,"* 14). Though Agamben initially claims that apparatuses operate on "living beings," the "subjects" caught in these apparatuses are unmistakably human (Fabbri, "From Inoperativeness to Action," 96). Rather than lament Agamben's "Heideggerian anthropocentrism," Lorenzo Fabbri proposes instead that we expand his biopolitical investigation to institutions that govern the living in general and animals in particular: "One could combine the archeology of prisons, schools, hospitals, mental asylums, and factories with that of battery farming,

kennel clubs, slaughterhouses, and training schools. . . . In this way, it would be more evident that the captivity of animal lives is deeply intertwined with that of human living beings" (97). Agamben does not simply miss an opportunity to account for animal lives, however. By deploring the modern "animalization" of the human, he surreptitiously condemns animals to a default condition of "captivation" (by which humans, he claims, are unprecedentedly threatened under biopolitical governmentality) instead of historicizing how animals came to be conceived as "essentially captivated" by their environment.

67. By focusing on representation, I heed Susan McHugh's invitation in *Animal Stories* to examine the technopolitical functions performed by specific visual and literary forms (the novel, for McHugh, allows for perspectival experimentations beyond the confines of human subjectivity as it is classically conceived).

68. Animals had to be captured for the animal to emerge just as madmen had to be confined for reason to claim madness as its hidden raison d'être. Jeffrey Nealon traces the "first birth of biopower" to the incorporation of animality as the secret essence of humanity, which no longer defines itself against the presumed alterity of animals. This discursive domestication might be just another instance of the "great confinement" Foucault describes in *History of Madness.* In fact, Nealon compares the shifts charted by *The Order of Things* and *History of Madness* to suggest that the advent of Man—the moment "when philosophy becomes anthropology"—coincides with the moment "when the animal became incorporated into reason" (*Plant Theory,* 9).

69. The deceptive neutrality and apparent timelessness of the "catch-all concept" of the animal—which Derrida has taught us to distrust as a formidable discursive mechanism that enframes "*all the living things* that man does not recognize as his fellows" within "the strict enclosure of this definite article . . . as in a virgin forest, a zoo, a hunting or fishing ground, a paddock or an abattoir" (*Animal That Therefore I Am,* 34)—simultaneously marks and masks the undeniable transformation undergone by animal existence over the last two centuries. In *Une autre existence,* French philosopher Florence Burgat enlists phenomenology to argue that "animals behave in a manner that exceeds

the conceptuality in which we have placed them" (25). Her wager echoes Derrida's conviction, reflecting on his own cat, that the animal stubbornly "refuses to be conceptualized" (*Animal That Therefore I Am,* 9). Burgat and Derrida expose Western philosophy's tacit complicity with what both describe as an ageless war against animals. Ironically enough, philosophy has traditionally sought to distinguish humans from other animals precisely by disputing animals' conceptual competencies. Heidegger, for instance, insists that only humans are capable of a true "grasping" for "the hand holds the essence of man"; animals, by contrast, might have "prehensile organs" but no hand proper. As if contaminated by its supposed inability to capture/conceptualize (*concept* and *capture* both derive from *capere*), the Heideggerian animal finds itself captivated, prisoner of itself. Heidegger's well-known thesis concerning the animal's "poverty-in-world" derives from this essential *Benommenheit,* this "captivation," this capture with no captor that entirely determines the animal's experience of a world to which access is forever barred. Because the animal's behavior is governed through and through by the involuntary activation of sensorial disinhibitors, Heidegger asserts that captivation "is the essence of animality" (*Fundamental Concepts of Metaphysics,* 248).

70. Similar claims have recently been made by scholars working at the intersection of animal studies and biopolitics. Colleen Boggs suggests that the foundation of liberal subjectivity rests on the mutual supposition of the categories of "the human" and "the animal" (*Animalia Americana,* 21–24). Zakiyyah Iman Jackson argues that "anxieties about conquest, slavery, and colonial expansionism provided the historical context for both the emergence of a developmental model of 'universal humanity' and a newly consolidated generic 'animal' that would be defined in nonhuman and racial terms" ("Beyond the Limit," iv).

71. By using the term *animality,* I heed Michael Lundblad's call to examine "how constructions of the animal have shifted historically in relation to the human" ("From Animal to Animality Studies," 498). Animality for me is not a transhistorical category, however, but rather a kindred concept to the "sexuality" and "criminality" that Foucault strategically divorces from the ostensible naturalness of "sex" and "crime."

72. Foucault, *Order of Things,* 139.

73. The advent of life marks a shift not just in the organization of knowledge but also in the focus of epistemic practices. Previously, plants had been the privileged objects of natural history, since the principle of their beings was fully on display, readily available for the scientist's classificatory gaze; when the tabulated (spatial) organization of nature gives way to the comparative (temporal) ordering of beings, animals become the paradigmatic objects of study. "If living beings are a classification," Foucault explains, "the plant is best able to express its limpid essence; but if they are a manifestation of life, the animal is better equipped to make its enigma perceptible" (*Order of Things,* 302). The classical model is predicated on representability. Plants can be seen, thus they can be known; in the modern age, representation is subordinated to a subterraneous force or will that defies the laws of visibility. "In relation to life, beings are no more than transitory figures, and the being that they maintain, during the brief period of their existence, is no more than their presumption, their will to survive. And so, for knowledge, the being of things is an illusion, a veil that must be torn aside in order to reveal the mute and invisible violence that is devouring them in the darkness" (303).

74. The "annihilation of certain species is indeed in process," Derrida observes, "but it is occurring through the organization and exploitation of an artificial, infernal, virtually interminable survival, in conditions that previous generations would have judged monstrous, outside of every presumed norm of a life proper to animals that are thus exterminated by means of their continued existence or even their overpopulation. As if . . . instead of throwing a people into ovens and gas chambers (let's say Nazi) doctors and geneticists had decided to organize the overproduction and overgeneration of Jews, gypsies, and homosexuals by means of artificial insemination, so that, being continually more numerous and better fed, they could be destined in always increasing numbers for the same hell" (*Animal That Therefore I Am,* 26). What Western culture ultimately values, this seeming contradiction suggests, is not animal lives but life insofar as it perpetuates the species. Could we justify mass slaughter if the pool of livestock was not, in principle, endlessly

reproducible—if it was knowingly driving a species to extinction? The paradox echoes the idea that under biopolitics it becomes possible "at once . . . to protect life and authorize a holocaust" (attributed to Foucault, quoted in Agamben, *Homo Sacer,* 3).

75. It is not by accident that Foucault deciphers the figure of Man from the lithic contours of fossils, nor that capitalism is powered by fossil energies and invested in machines strategically destined to obsolescence from the outset. The recent surge of critical interest in the Anthropocene—the "age of Man," alternatively dubbed capitalocene and plantationocene to underline its historical conditions of emergence—spells the recognition of the transience of the human as species, which itself hinges on the recognition of Man's animality. On the historical complicities between capitalist extraction and fossil hunting, see Rieppel, *Assembling the Dinosaur.*
76. Foucault, *Order of Things,* 376.
77. Gilles Deleuze remarks that the "discovery" of Man's animality is a strange event, however, since it is what allows Man to apprehend himself "as an object of new positive sciences" yet as essentially subjected to the obscure and unknowable forces of labor, life, sexuality, and language (*Desert Islands,* 91).
78. The "human being," Foucault writes, "arises in a space hollowed out by living beings, objects of exchange, and words, when, abandoning representation, which had been their natural site hitherto, they withdraw into the depths of things and roll up upon themselves in accordance with the laws of life, production, and language. In the middle of them all, compressed within the circle they form, man is designated—more, required—by them, since it is he who speaks, since he is seen to reside among the animals (and in a position that is not merely privileged, but a source of order for the totality they form: even though he is not conceived as the end-product of evolution, he is recognized to be one extremity of a long series)" (*Order of Things,* 341).
79. Hence race, gender, and species become historicizable as technologies determining "caesuras within the biological continuum addressed by biopower" that make "killing acceptable" (Foucault, *Society Must Be Defended,* 256). Importantly, by "killing" Foucault means not "simply

murder as such, but also every form of indirect murder: the fact of exposing someone to death, increasing the risk of death for some people, or, quite simply, political death, expulsion, rejection, and so on." Broadly defined as a partitioning instrument meant to legitimize killing, racism can be understood as a model for other "natural" categories of difference such as gender and species. On this, see Twine, *Animals as Biotechnology,* 85–86; and Shukin, *Animal Capital,* 10–11.

80. Wynter, "Unsettling the Coloniality of Being/Power/Truth/Freedom," 264.

81. "Because Foucault's account of racial discourse is so endemically detached from the patterned shifts in world-wide imperial labor regimes of which those discourses were a part, we are diverted from the gritty historical specificities of what racial discourse did both to confirm the efficacy of slavery and to capture new populations in the transition to wage-labor." And because *The History of Sexuality* focuses on the context of the European bourgeoisie, Ann Laura Stoler lucidly notes, Foucault makes race a "theme through which sexuality is discussed," whereas bodies in the colonies are "constituted as racially and relationally coded from the outset" (*Race and the Education of Desire,* 91, 53). On Wynter's revision of Foucault through the "idea of race," see da Silva, "Before *Man.*"

82. Alexander Weheliye's *Habeas Viscus,* for instance, denounces the occlusion of racialization and slavery by white European theorists of biopolitics, Foucault and Agamben in particular. Weheliye foregrounds the philosophies of Wynter and Hortense Spillers to show how racialized subjects, though violently denied the legal or biological recognition as "full humans," were not purely abjected as "bare life." They were able to leverage their oppressed position, Weheliye argues, to invent alternatives to liberal bourgeois culture and politics—what Wynter calls different "genres of being hybridly human" (Wynter, "Ceremony Found," 214).

83. Shukin, *Animal Capital,* 119.

84. For sustained engagements with manhunting and biometric tracking as technologies of surveillance and discipline, see Chamayou, *Manhunts*; Browne, *Dark Matters*; and Boisseron, *Afro-Dog.* On the agricultural

origin of the "partus" ruling of 1662, which stipulated that "all children borne in this country shall be held bond or free only according to the condition of the mother," see Morgan, *Partus sequitur ventrem,* 158–59. On race as a "natural" technology in the U.S. context, see Chun, "Race and/as Technology."

85. Boisseron powerfully argues that treating as merely "analogous" the subjugation of black subjects under slavery and the mass exploitation of animals threatens to reinscribe, rather than expose or contest, racist or speciesist logics. She warns against "analogy's inherent vice," which "lies in its propensity to give the upper hand to one entity over the other," and offers instead to "determine how the history of the animal and the black in the black Atlantic is *connected,* rather than simply comparable" (*Afro-Dog,* xiii, xx).

86. Apess, "Son of the Forest," 55, 61. Apess quotes from "Traits of Indian Character," which Irving published anonymously in *Analectic Magazine* while the United States was at war with the Creek Indians (1813–1814). At the end of the war, Andrew Jackson forced the Creeks to surrender more than twenty-one million acres of land.

87. Jacobs, *Incidents of the Life of a Slave Girl,* 795. The autobiographies of Linda Brent/Harriet Jacobs, Frederick Douglass, and Solomon Northup offer the most incisive analyses of the treatment of enslaved individuals as livestock. However illuminating, the correspondence has obvious limits and must be established with care. Douglass, for instance, describes how his master's horses and dogs were treated better and more highly valued than his "human cattle" (*Autobiographies,* 509).

88. On the importance of not conflating the modes of subjugation endured, and the forms of resistance invented, by indigenous and black subjects, see Rifkin, *Fictions of Land and Flesh.* On the gendered dimension of racist animalization, see Z. I. Jackson, "Beyond the Limit."

89. Z. I. Jackson, "Beyond the Limit," iv. The animalization of blackness, Jackson argues, is the repressed condition of the normative conception of "the human" we have inherited from European Enlightenment epistemologies. "Binaristic frameworks such as 'humanization versus dehumanization' and 'human versus animal,'" however, "are inadequate to understand a biopolitical regime that develops technologies of

'humanization' in order to refigure blackness as 'human animality' and extends human recognition in an effort to deem blackness as the animal within the human" (vi).

90. Z. I. Jackson, 1. Building on Wynter's and Hartman's analyses, Jackson demonstrates that "*humanization* and *animalization* are mutually constitutive projects of antiblack violence, working in conjunction rather than in opposition, as is often presumed. (Neo)liberal humanism attempts to humanize black people by turning 'the slave' into the proletariat, but the gendered forms of labor made available to the former slave are deemed 'animal'" (78).
91. Coulthard, *Red Skin, White Masks,* 3.
92. Vizenor, *Fugitive Poses,* and *Manifest Manners*; and Byrd, *Transit of Empire.*
93. Hartman, *Scenes of Subjection*; Best, *Fugitive's Properties*; and Rusert, *Fugitive Science.*
94. Rusert, *Fugitive Science.*
95. In a conference titled "The Mesh of Power," Foucault frames the shift from sovereign violence to biopower as a shift from hunt to capture. He proposes to study power in its positivity, from the vantage of its "technologies," instead of looking at the way power represents itself through laws and decrees. To illustrate his point, Foucault explains the transition between monarchy and capitalist democracy as follows: "The system of power that the monarchy had succeeded in organizing from the end of the Middle Ages presented two major inconveniences for the development of capitalism. First, political power, as it was exercised within the social body, was a very discontinuous power. The mesh of the net was too large, and an almost infinite number of things, elements, conducts, and processes escaped the control of power. . . . Consequently, economic processes . . . required the establishment of a continuous, minute power, in a certain atomizing fashion." The second inconvenience is that this type of power was overly costly because it consisted primarily in "the right and force to collect something": "Power was then essentially tax collector and predator [*percepteur et prédateur*]. In this way, it always performed an economic subtraction, and, by consequence, far from favoring and stimulating economic

flow, monarchical power was perpetually its obstacle and its restraint." What modern power invents, Foucault continues, is a system combining an "anatomopolitics" that renders individual bodies docile and labor-friendly with a "biopolitics" that fosters populations at the biological level.

1. STILL LIFES

1. Foucault, *Order of Things,* 301, 289.
2. Nash, *Wilderness and the American Mind,* 1, 96, 97.
3. The article "Chasse" in d'Alembert and Diderot's *Encyclopédie,* for instance, defines *hunting* as "all the sorts of wars that we wage against animals." J. M. Coetzee's 2003 novel *Elizabeth Costello* exploits this analogy. "We had a war once against the animals, which we called hunting, though in fact war and hunting are the same thing (Aristotle saw it clearly)," the title character explains. "That war went on for millions of years. We won it definitively only a few hundred years ago, when we invented guns. It is only since victory became absolute that we have been able to afford to cultivate compassion" (*Elizabeth Costello,* 104). The idea of war implies a relative degree of symmetry between humans and animals and supposes a shared political ground. Yet as Costello proposes, humans and animals ceased to cohabit under the particular conditions that made Man's victory "absolute" (although some animals seem unaware that the war is over; rats, we are told, have not surrendered).
4. This elision is an abiding tradition in American science that can be traced back to the colonial period. On the reliance of the female, nonelite, and nonwhite hunters, collectors, and other "fossilists" in colonial America, see Parrish, *American Curiosity,* 215–306; and Kolbert, *Sixth Extinction,* 39. On the reliance of European naturalists on specimens imported from the colonies, and from the Americas in particular, see Greene, *American Science in the Age of Jefferson.*
5. Even apologists of the young nation like Jefferson thought that it was not the role of the government to support scientific endeavors. In the first half of the nineteenth century, most naturalists were working alone and funded their own practice. Eminent natural history institutions

like the Academy of Natural Sciences of Philadelphia and the New York Lyceum of Natural History were established in the 1810s, and scientific societies did not proliferate until the 1830s. See Bates, *Scientific Societies in the United States*; and Blum, *Picturing Nature.*

6. New, *Line's Eye,* 80.
7. Patterson, *Missouri River Journals of John James Audubon,* 217. "Audubon's own syntax emphasizes the proximity of gun and art," Patterson notes, quoting Audubon: "'I took a Walk with my Gun this afternoon to see the Passage of Millions of Golden Plovers'" (217).
8. Rhodes, *John James Audubon,* 74–75.
9. By modern standards, notes Andrew J. Lewis, "many naturalists of the early republic were scarcely scientists at all [insofar as they] disdained systematic thinking and theory" (*Democracy of Facts,* 12). Ann Shelby Blum finds the epitome of the early nineteenth-century American naturalist in Alexander Wilson, author of the nine-volume study *American Ornithology* (1808–1814), who praised "outdoor practice as opposed to 'speculations of mere closet theory'" (*Picturing Nature,* 30). On Audubon's inferiority complex toward European naturalists, see Patterson, *John James Audubon's Journal of 1826,* xxvii.
10. Daniel Patterson shows how Audubon's late-nineteenth-century and early-twentieth-century biographers, increasingly concerned by the declining wildlife, bowdlerized his writings to minimize the painter's killing sprees and sometimes gratuitous cruelty. They follow Maria Audubon, who forged entries of her grandfather's journals, to present him as an early conservationist (Patterson, "Audubon's Ethic in the Biographies," in *Missouri River Journals of John James Audubon*).
11. Thoreau, *Walden,* 491. Thoreau inscribes his changing relation to untamed animals in a larger context where he sees New England boys gradually "outgrowing" their juvenile (but healthy) drive to hunt. Caustically, Thoreau attributes this maturing, "not to an increased humanity, but to an increased scarcity of game," making humanity an unintended aftereffect of overhunting. On the "sublimation" of this hunting drive—what Thoreau calls the "animal in us"—into forms of self-perfectionism and an "epic of the captive, in which the adventuring impulse turns inward," see Slotkin, *Regeneration through Violence,* 530–38.

12. "It is a surprising and memorable, as well as valuable experience, to be lost in the woods any time," writes Thoreau. "Not till we are lost . . . not till we have lost the world, do we begin to find ourselves" (*Walden,* 459).
13. This was a consecrated formula used by naturalists to signal that their illustrations derived from firsthand observation. "The word 'draw' in 'drawn from nature,'" writes Christoph Irmscher, "the seal of quality that Audubon put on all the watercolors from which Rober Havell in London produced his plates, is not just accidentally ambiguous: to draw means 'to sketch,' of course, but it can also, in the sense of 'drawn from' or 'withdraw,' signify the act of removing something from its original, in this case natural, context. Art is what nature is not—or rather, is no longer" (*Poetics of Natural History,* 206–7).
14. Audubon, *Ornithological Biography,* part 1, vii.
15. Audubon, "My Style of Drawing Birds," in *Writings and Drawings,* 760.
16. Audubon, letter to the territorial governor of Arkansas, James Miller, 1820, quoted in Patterson, *Missouri River Journals of John James Audubon,* 50.
17. Audubon preferred the golden eagle as the U.S. national symbol, for he shared Benjamin Franklin's misgivings about selecting the bald eagle, or "white-headed eagle," as the "Emblem of my Country": for him, the bird's "ferocious, overbearing, and tyrannical temper," his tendency to steal "the hard-earned fruits of [other birds'] labour," and his feeding off carrion (and human children) made it unfit to model the "peaceful freedom" and the industry Audubon held dear (Audubon, *Writings and Drawings,* 238–47).
18. Audubon, 356. Audubon biographer Hezekiah Butterworth was well aware of the nationalist symbolics attached to the bird. In his 1901 biography, titled *In the Days of Audubon: A Tale of the "Protector of Birds,"* Butterworth substitutes the golden eagle for a "caracara eagle, the Brazilian bird," and the scene of its capture takes place in Florida instead of Boston (quoted in Patterson, *Missouri River Journals of John James Audubon,* 214).
19. Stebbins, "Audubon's Drawings of American Birds," 20.
20. Rhodes, *John James Audubon,* 376.
21. Rhodes, 376.

22. Audubon, *Writings and Drawings,* 765.
23. In this, the painting anticipates Emanuel Leutze's *Westward the Course of Empire Takes Its Way* (1862) and John Gast's *American Progress* (1872), in which a series of archetypal American figures are facing the wild, promising territories of the West. During the American Civil War, Leutze was commissioned by Congress to paint in the Capitol his mural celebrating Manifest Destiny. Gast's painting celebrates the progress of civilization over "savagery," epitomized by Native Americans fleeing westward, and an untamed nature, represented by a herd of bison being hunted.
24. Some critics have read the ubiquitous interspecies violence depicted in *The Birds of America* as a prefiguration of Darwin's theory of natural selection through competition. Seeing that Audubon includes himself in the picture as the archpredator, the hunter's hunter, we see how his pictorial rhetoric might sanction a social or colonial order perceived as immanent, endless, and justified by the laws of nature.
25. Audubon, "Method of Drawing Birds," in *Writings and Drawings,* 754.
26. Roberts, *Transporting Visions,* 184n49. The painter's desire for a lossless translation denotes his deep-seated aversion to abstraction—an aversion that Roberts interprets in light of his financial troubles following the Panic of 1819—and underlines the unbroken continuity Audubon sought to establish between his images and the material world, which was being newly read as evanescent and subject to transformation.
27. Audubon's insistence on drawing specimens at the 1:1 scale was, for Roberts, an act of resistance against the "rampant spatial abstractions of the culture of speculation that had first fueled, and then destroyed, his career as a merchant" (Roberts, 6). The panic, Roberts explains, was not just financial but also "reflected anxieties about geography, circulation, scale, and representation" (110). Audubon worried about the possibility to misrepresent his bird species just as he feared the markets' volatility. Thus, Roberts interprets his commitment to indexicality and the cumbersome materiality of the four volumes of *The Birds of America* as prophylactic defenses against the capitalist and colonialist logics of abstraction and scalability.
28. Roberts, 110. For Audubon, killing the birds is not antithetical to their pictorial preservation. In fact, their death is a sign of the picture's

success: "There is a sense in Audubon's work that representation wholly eclipses the referent, destroying it in the process," Roberts argues. "The life of the bird seems to shift from one body to another; the image is not an immaterial copy that goes out into the world, but the original referent itself" (110).

29. Arsić, *Bird Relics,* 408.
30. Audubon, *Writings and Drawings,* 355.
31. Audubon, 354–55. Blum notes Audubon's tendency to enlarge the heads and eyes of his birds to make them more appealing (*Picturing Nature,* 32). If neoteny and cuteness are biological assets, as Stephen Jay Gould argues in "A Biological Homage to Mickey Mouse," the cute is also that which is defenseless, that which I know I could kill. On this, see Ngai, "Cuteness of the Avant-Garde," 823.
32. On the human–animal rivalries presented in Audubon's paintings, see Blum, *Picturing Nature,* 106; and Irmscher, *Poetics of Natural History,* 229.
33. Audubon, *Writings and Drawings,* 354–55.
34. Audubon, Ornithological Biography, part 1, vii.
35. Derrida, "Eating Well," 112.
36. Derrida, Animal That Therefore I Am, 135. Although Derrida presents himself as a hunter in this text, he rejects the exculpatory license granted by the sovereign "right to kill," which has always been the heteropatriarchal preserve of Man. Instead, he animalizes himself, claiming to "track, to sniff, to trail, and to follow some of the reasons they [humans] adduce for the so confident usage they make . . . of words such as, therefore, *animal* and I" (33).
37. Wynter, "Unsettling the Coloniality of Being/Power/Truth/Freedom," 260.
38. Jackson, "Beyond the Limit," 57.
39. Jackson, 78.
40. On Audubon's uncertain racial identity, see Nobles, *John James Audubon,* 14–17; and Iannini, *Fatal Revolutions,* 253–80.
41. Derrida, "Eating Well," 112.
42. See, for instance, Annette Kolodny's foundational study *The Lay of the Land* (1975). Elisa New faults Kolodny for being too quick at aligning

knowledge with violence and for focusing on Audubon's "promotional writing rather than his art." By ignoring the paintings, New argues, Kolodny "loses sight" of the unique force of Audubon's sketches and the specific economy and ecology of attention at play in his "sightings" (New, *Line's Eye,* 78–79).

43. Irmscher remarks that Audubon himself "was well aware that some birds, such as the grouse, were 'decreasing at a rapid rate' and were threatened with extinction, like the original inhabitants of the American continent. 'When I first removed to Kentucky, the Pinnated Grouse were so abundant, that they were held in no higher estimation as food than the most common flesh, and no "hunter of Kentucky" deigned to shoot them.' In those days, grouse would walk in the very streets of the villages, enter the farmyards, and mingle with the poultry. Now they 'have abandoned the state of Kentucky, and removed (like the Indians) every season farther to the westward, to escape from the murderous white man'" (Irmscher, *Poetics of Natural History,* 216). The manner in which Audubon dissociates himself from "the murderous white man" can be read as a return of the repressed anxieties surrounding his own possible biracialism.
44. New, *Line's Eye,* 80.
45. Audubon claims the incident took place in Nantes, but Rhodes notes that "Saint Domingue is more likely" (*John James Audubon,* 21).
46. Audubon, *Writings and Drawings,* 765–66.
47. Michael Ziser speculates that although the passage in question "was not published until fifty years after the 'Murders in the Rue Morgue' and there is no existing record in Poe's biographies or the Poe log of the two men ever having crossed paths, the possibility of a direct historical connection between Audubon's 'man of the woods' and Poe's orangutan (literally 'man of the forest') or between the 'Du pain' of Audubon's parrot and Dupin (whose seal is made 'of bread') cannot be entirely ruled out" ("Animal Mirrors," 22).
48. Iannini, *Fatal Revolutions,* 261. Iannini reads Audubon's identification as "creole"—a term used both for subjects of mixed black and European descent and for French citizens born in the Caribbean—as a repressed heritage that the naturalist negotiated throughout his writings and

paintings and that returned to haunt him especially after his bankruptcy following the Panic of 1819, when he was afraid of losing the social and racial capital he had accrued since moving to the United States. Iannini compares the episode of the murderous ape to passages from *The Mississippi River Journal* where Audubon finds himself in Louisiana, in a "semitropical region shaped by plantation slavery, hemispheric mobility, French colonial métissage, and incipient slave revolution" (Iannini, *Fatal Revolutions,* 257). His racial anxieties were justified by a broader context in which "French creoles as a class became an object of racialist scrutiny" after the Louisiana Purchase, "as commentators asked whether they could be incorporated as citizens into the United States without rendering untenable the important legal category of whiteness—or exposing its fictionality" (258).

49. Mirzoeff, "It's Not the Anthropocene," 130–33.
50. Irmscher, *Poetics of Natural History,* 206–7; and Ziser, "Animal Mirrors," 23.
51. Mirzoeff notes that in his chosen names, Audubon irreconcilably identified himself both with the French-speaking bird and with the "man of the woods" ("It's Not the Anthropocene," 131).
52. Ziser, "Animal Mirrors," 23.
53. Ziser, 23.
54. Mbembe, "Necropolitics," 25. Setting side by side Hegel's *Phenomenology of Spirit* and Paul Du Chaillu's *Explorations and Adventures in Equatorial Africa,* Mbembe establishes a direct "connection between the *act of colonizing* and the *act of hunting*" (*On the Postcolony,* 196). He highlights the persistence of necropolitical strategies that European governmentality disavows or hides when it overlooks the centrality of slavery to the development of western democracy and maintains an explicit "right to kill" in colonial spaces. Building on Mbembe's analysis, which recognizes in plantation slavery one of the first and most formative sites of biopolitical experimentation, Scott Lauria Morgensen argues that the "perpetual subjugation" of black people is indissociable from the "naturalized" extermination of the indigenous population in North America ("Biopolitics of Settler Colonialism," 58).
55. Foucault, *Society Must Be Defended,* 241.

56. Foucault, 241.
57. Foucault, 243.
58. Foucault, *Order of Things*, 15–16.
59. Wynter, "Unsettling the Coloniality of Being/Power/Truth/Freedom," 313.
60. I borrow the term *full human* from Alexander Weheliye, who turns to Wynter's reflections on the category of "the human" in Western modernity to understand the sociogenic mechanisms that distribute people into "full humans," "not-quite-humans," and "nonhumans" (*Habeas Viscus*).
61. Wynter, "Unsettling the Coloniality of Being/Power/Truth/Freedom," 318.
62. Wynter, 260.
63. Wynter, 291.
64. Wynter, 268.
65. Daston and Galison, *Objectivity*, 80.
66. Daston and Galison, 79. For a detailed account of the skepticism and criticisms with which Audubon's paintings were met by the naturalist community of the time, see Blum, *Picturing Nature*, 111–18.
67. Blum, *Picturing Nature*, 88.
68. Arsić, *Bird Relics*, 145.
69. Arsić, 408.
70. Daston and Galison, *Objectivity*, 363.
71. Irmscher, *Poetics of Natural History*, 199. Audubon knew very little about taxonomy when he began his monumental project; as Irmscher informs us, for the texts of his *Ornithological Biography*, Audubon sought the help of the Scottish ornithologist William MacGillivray, who added "taxonomical details" and "anatomical descriptions of the birds' respiratory and digestive tracts" (199).
72. Roberts, *Transporting Visions*, 81.
73. Roberts, 81.
74. Daston and Galison, *Objectivity*. Though *The Birds of America* is rarely categorized alongside modernist artworks, Roberts demonstrates that it "emerges from and responds to the same forces that underlie modernity itself—capital flows, communication technologies, and upheavals in models of subjectivity" (*Transporting Visions*, 103).

75. The idea that knowledge supposes the suspension of power is a modern idea: if knowledge is a function of power, as Foucault argues, its correlation with power is what power cannot acknowledge, in fact cannot even know. In line with a certain colonizing logic that disavows its violence, modern science typically resorts to the vocabulary of "discovery."
76. Rhodes, *John James Audubon,* 379.
77. Irmscher, *Poetics of Natural History,* 225.
78. Several years after he first published his *Ornithological Biography,* when Audubon began working on a more affordable Octavo edition of *The Birds of America* to increase his sales, his sons persuaded him to delete entirely the scene of the killing of the golden eagle. "There is killing enough to go around in the bird biographies," Daniel Patterson explains, "but this particularly heartless passage was deemed to run an unnecessary risk of alienating readers at a time when profit was the motive" (*Missouri River Journals of John James Audubon,* 212). Violence is only tolerable when presented as a necessity (e.g., scientifically justified).
79. Foucault, *Order of Things,* 376.
80. "When natural history becomes biology," Foucault explains, "and Classical *discourse,* in which being and representation found their common locus, is eclipsed, then, in the profound upheaval of such an archaeological mutation, man appears in his ambiguous position as an object of knowledge and as a subject that knows: enslaved sovereign, observed spectator, he appears in the place belonging to the king, which was assigned to him in advance by *Las Meninas,* but from which his real presence has for so long been excluded" (340).

2. LAND SPECULATIONS

1. Chad Luck reads this scene in light of the foundational 1805 case *Pierson v. Post* deciding the legal ownership of the carcass of a fox pursued by Post but killed by Pierson. "By explaining how to take possession of, and establish title to, a wild animal," writes Luck, *Pierson v. Post* "addresses the thorny problem of original acquisition" and articulates "an ideology of property through which American citizens might more comfortably justify the appropriation of 'waste' lands and all sorts of other 'unowned' properties" (*Body of Property,* 3).

2. House, *Cooper's Americans,* 265.
3. Cooper, *The Pioneers,* in *Leatherstocking Tales,* 1:22 (hereafter, *Pioneers*). "The judge compounds voting disenfranchisement together with legal prohibition on black testimony," writes Joe Lockard, "Agamemnon . . . is an official non-person; Bess is a yet-to-be person" ("Talking Guns, Talking Turkey," 327).
4. On the legal conversion of the Indian commons into private land and on the historical silencing of Native Americans in *The Pioneers,* see Cheyfitz, "Savage Law."
5. Locke, "Second Treatise," 290.
6. Castronovo, "James Fenimore Cooper and the NSA," 689. "The question of 'how should one ever come to have a property in any thing,'" Castronovo writes, "is answered by pursuit and surveillance. The mere thought of property—not property that is in hand but property that is on the run—generates the desire to secure it. It is a lesson that the Judge's black slave no doubt appreciates only too well." Castronovo does not elaborate on this, and Cooper's text does not give Agamemnon any clear insight into his own fate as he witnesses the deer's lot. The other silent witness, Bess, is granted more interiority as she finds herself "unconsciously rejoicing in the escape of the buck" (Cooper, *Pioneers,* 20). Cooper's romance registers affinities and even a tacit solidarity between the young woman, the enslaved individual, and the hunted deer, without exploiting them fully in the plot. My thanks to Audrey Bransfield for bringing this to my attention.
7. One needed to be recognized as a citizen to claim the right to capture wild game, which meant that as captives, enslaved individuals were de facto excluded from Locke's supposedly "equitable" economy. See VanderVelde, "Role of Captives and the Rule of Capture."
8. Cheyfitz, "Savage Law," 112. Basing its decision on the Doctrine of Discovery, the Supreme Court stipulated that the land could not be purchased from Indians because they did not own the land but only occupied it. Writes Cheyfitz: "For the idea of property depends on the possibility of an individual relation to the land (as the basis of wealth), either in the name of a single person or a group, such as a corporation, acting as a single person, in which this person, precisely because he

or she or it is an 'individual,' is 'free' to alienate this land in a market economy. Or we could reverse the proposition and say: there is no individuality without property, so inseparable are the two terms in the mixed material and metaphysical traditions of the West. Locke's formulation of primal individuality—'every man has a property in his own person'—succinctly states this inseparability, which is alien to Native American cultures" (112).

9. Cooper, *Pioneers,* 360.
10. The paragon of the American historical romancer, Cooper "was accustomed to present his own versions of the beau idéal of frontier life as if they were history" (Fiedler, *Love and Death in the American Novel,* 165). According to George Dekker, Cooper embraced a "stadialist" model of history (the belief that society "evolved" according to distinct modes of subsistence, from hunting to herding to farming) that proved essential when he composed *The Prairie* (*American Historical Romance,* 95–97). As early as 1829, William Apess called out this narrative of progress as an alibi for the white settler colonial agenda (see introduction). On Cooper and the genre of the historical romance, see Chase, *American Novel and Its Tradition,* 43–56; and Budick, "American Historical Romance."
11. Cooper, *Prairie,* 11; emphasis added. All future references to this work are hereafter cited parenthetically.
12. *Oxford English Dictionary Online,* s.v. "purchase (*v.*)," accessed April 30, 2020, https://www.oed.com/view/Entry/154832.
13. On the Doctrine of Discovery and its application in North America, its metamorphosis into Manifest Destiny, and the forcible preemption of Native lands and resources it sanctioned, see R. Miller, *Native America,* esp. introduction and chaps. 1 and 2; and Dunbar-Ortiz, *Indigenous People's History of the United States,* esp. chaps. 2 and 6.
14. Significantly for us, Mbembe adds that these justifications relegate the colonized to the status of "*animal,*" presenting him or her as a being "encapsulated in himself or herself, . . . a bundle of drives but not of *capacities*" with whom the only possible relation is one of domination or domestication (*On the Postcolony,* 25–27). We recognize in this being, which is forever "enclosed" in its instinctual drives, Heidegger's captivated animal, to which Mbembe explicitly refers.

15. Deleuze and Guattari borrow the idea of "magic capture" from French philologist Georges Dumézil, who uses it to describe the operations of the State apparatus (Deleuze and Guattari, *Thousand Plateaus,* 427). In the opening paragraph of *The Pioneers,* Cooper tellingly feels compelled to add a footnote intended to account for the implausible speed by which the "wilderness" was brought "under the dominion of mild laws": "Our tale begins in 1793, about seven years after the commencement of one of the earliest of those settlements which have conduced to effect that *magical change* in the power and condition of the State to which we have alluded" (19; emphasis added).
16. *Taxis,* media theorist Bernhard Siegert notes, refers to "an order of things in which each and every object is located in a fixed place where it can be found. Humans, however, differ from things . . . because for them 'no place of meeting has been fixed'" (*Cultural Techniques,* 97). For Siegert, this distinction crumbles in modernity, which "is characterized by the invention of a *taxis* technique capable of also turning humans into retrievable objects" (97). Although evidently, this technique was already applicable and applied to human subjects, as slaves were forcibly instructed to "know their place" but without being granted a place of their own (on the taxonomy of race and the "insidious ascription of place" for black subjects, see Hartman, *Scenes of Subjection,* 193–96). The advent of surveillance societies toward the end of the eighteenth century marks the extension to those recognized as humans of a logic originally targeting nonhuman beings and dehumanized subjects. "This modern *taxis* is implemented by means of a new cultural technique which takes into account that something may be missing from its place," Siegert continues. "In other words, it encompasses the notion of an empty space. The technique in question is the grid or lattice. Its salient feature is its ability to merge operations geared toward *representing humans and things with those of governance*" (*Cultural Techniques,* 97; emphasis added).
17. Coding, overcoding, and decoding are three systems of representation that correspond to three social formations identified by Deleuze and Guattari in *Anti-Oedipus.* These three systems—the tribal, the imperial, and the capitalist—are respectively centered around the Earth, the

Sovereign, and Money as the imagined sources of production. Coding is associated with a process of territorialization; overcoding with deterritorialization immediately followed by reterritorialization; decoding with a radical deterritorialization.

18. Cooper, *The Prairie,* in *Leatherstocking Tales,* 1:884.
19. For Fiedler, Natty Bumppo is the paragon of a new species able to "orient" itself in the West without turning it into the East, and thereby to forgo the colonial violence recalled by the appellation "Indians" for the Native Americans. In Fiedler's view, the Westerner is not the emissary of Western culture but the white man remade in the Indian's image (*Return of the Vanishing American,* 49).
20. On the strategic tensions between romance and realism in frontier narratives, see Nelson, *Word in Black and White,* 38–64.
21. Pratt, *Imperial Eyes,* 61. The passive voice in *The Prairie*'s first paragraph presents this as a self-evident truth: "Much was said and written, at the time, concerning the policy of adding the vast regions of Louisiana, to the already immense and but half-tenanted territories of the United States. As the warmth of controversy however subsided, and party considerations gave place to more liberal views, the wisdom of the measure began to be generally conceded. It soon became apparent to the meanest capacity, that, while nature had placed a barrier of desert to the extension of our population in the west, the measure had made us the masters of a belt of fertile country. . . . It gave us the sole command of the great thoroughfare of the interior, and placed the countless tribes of savages, who lay along our borders, entirely within our control; it reconciled conflicting rights, and quieted national distrusts; it opened a thousand avenues to the inland trade, and to the waters of the Pacific; and, if ever time or necessity shall require a peaceful division of this vast empire, it assures us of a neighbour that will possess our language, our religion, our institutions, and it is also to be hoped, our sense of political justice" (9). On the transformation of "indigenous peoples into the *homo nullius* inhabitants of lands emptied and awaiting arrival," see Byrd, *Transit of Empire,* xxi. See also Annette Kolodny's *The Lay of the Land* on the widespread trope of the "virgin" continent, with the term's attendant sexual and gendered dimensions, in relation to Cooper's

Leatherstocking romances (89–114). On the colonial ideologies of vision in early America, see Pease, *Visionary Compacts*; and Cheyfitz, *Poetics of Imperialism.*

22. New, *Line's Eye,* 44.
23. New, 49.
24. New, 48.
25. Purdy, *After Nature,* 23.
26. Bernhard Siegert clearly articulates the growing complementarity of financial and imaginative speculations and the links between these and gridding, mapping, and surveying: "Although the rectangular survey prescribed by the Land Ordinance of 1785 only concerned territories between the Appalachians and the Mississippi, it became the model for the subsequent appropriation and colonization of the entire continent. Congress was confronted with a situation virtually unprecedented in history: It was empowered to 'make the law governing the survey and distribution of a vast territory before it was occupied.' . . . Grid patterns, colonization, and real estate speculation coincided. . . . Although the surveyors were instructed to maintain field notes on soil quality, water, and natural resources, purchasers could end up owning a swamp, a sandbank, or a piece of Native American territory. Financial and mental speculation became synonymous" (*Cultural Techniques,* 112–14). The efficacy of Jefferson's survey system was tested and confirmed by the acquisition of the Louisiana territories in 1803, which ratified the virtually limitless mechanism of control and surveillance that would power the U.S. colonial enterprise. Because of its projective dimension, the grid illustrates the new form that conquest took in North America. Cronon notes that "the grid turned the prairie into a commodity, and became the foundation for all subsequent land use" (*Nature's Metropolis,* 102).
27. The term *species,* like *speculation,* derives from *specere,* and species classification (in its modern iteration) is predicated on comparative anatomy—i.e., on the dissection of bodies in the name of their assumed commensurability. I develop this in chapter 4.
28. The scientist's slapstick quality is deceptive. The naturalist often presents himself as a deeroticized "insect hunter," Mary Louise Pratt argues: "Unlike such antecedents as the conquistador and the

hunter, the figure of the naturalist-hero often has a certain impotence or androgyny about him. . . . The naturalist-heroes are not, however, women—no world is more androcentric than that of natural history. . . . In the literature of the imperial frontier, the conspicuous innocence of the naturalist acquires meaning in relation to an assumed guilt of conquest, a guilt the naturalist figure eternally tries to escape" (*Imperial Eyes,* 56–57).

29. Kelly, *Plotting America's Past,* 105.
30. Bat's quixotic character is underlined by his being inseparable from his stubborn companion throughout the novel—at one point he is even tied up to Asinus by the Sioux who capture him: "the legs of the Naturalist were attached to the beast in such a manner that the two animals might be said to be incorporated and to form a new order" (304). But Asinus is not just the correlative of the scientist's ludicrousness. The donkey is also recruited to underline the contrast between Bumppo's pragmatic view and the scientist's sentimental idealism. Twice, Bat and Bumppo argue over the lot of Asinus, whom the trapper, for safety reasons, wishes to put to death. The compassionate naturalist ends up saving in extremis the life of his companion, who then proves crucial in helping the two men out of a perilous situation. Thus, the course of action vindicates Battius and seems to justify his (selective) compassion.
31. Derrida, *Animal That Therefore I Am,* 31.
32. Quoted in Nobles, *John James Audubon,* 264. One of these "eccentric naturalists," an "odd-looking fellow" called "M. de T." by Audubon but identified by Nobles as European botanist Constantine Rafinesque, had traveled to Henderson, Kentucky, in 1818 specifically to look at Audubon's drawings of plants. The blatant scorn in which Audubon held the observational skills of Rafinesque led Audubon to prank his rival by describing and sketching imaginary specimens—nine wild rats, two birds, one mollusk, three snails, and eleven fish species, including one with supposedly bulletproof scales—a number of which Rafinesque took credit for discovering (Woodman, "Pranked by Audubon").
33. Quoted in Gerbi, *Dispute of the New World,* 4.
34. Humans were no exception. Buffon described the American "savage" as "feeble and small in his organs of generation." In the inhospitable

climate of the New World, "far from making himself master of this territory as his own domain, [man] ruled over nothing; where having never subjugated either animals or the elements, nor tamed the waters, nor governed the rivers, nor worked the earth, he was himself no more than an animal of the first order, existing within nature as a creature without significance" (Buffon quoted in Gerbi, 6). Buffon thus attributed nature's degeneracy to inclement weather conditions and managed in the same breath to blame Native Americans for their passivity (a corollary of their perceived impotence) in conquering the wild tracts of America. His reasoning anticipates the manner in which scientific discourse ratified the genocidal politics of white settlers in the nineteenth century.

35. Jefferson, "Notes on the State of Virginia," 167. Jefferson found his most decisive refutation of Buffon's theory in the fossil remains of the great *American incognitum*—what we recognize today as the mammoth—which boasted "five or six times the cubic volume of the elephant" (167).
36. Dutta, "Mammoths, Inc."
37. Gerbi, *Dispute of the New World,* 19. One might think that shortsightedness does not prevent one from examining objects up close, but, as Buffon affirms about his own affliction, "the more short-sighted any man is, he sees objects proportionally diminished" (Buffon, Leclerc, and Barr, *Buffon's Natural History,* 268).
38. Roberts, *Transporting Visions,* 106.
39. If we consider Foucault's partition between natural history (premised on the comparison and ordering of given organisms) and biology (predicated on the establishment of analogies between organic structures), we may infer that accrued visibility—aided by the development of mechanized technologies—can account for epistemic breaks, given that Foucault explicitly makes natural history a function of the visible while biology discovers an internal "principle alien to the domain of the visible" (*Order of Things,* 246). But it would be wrong to assume that this epochal shift is but a move from the visible to the infravisible, since the *taxinomia* of the classical age was already haunted by an irreducible invisibility (think of the vanishing point of representation in *Las Meninas*) and the invisible principle that governs modern classification (i.e., life)

is inextricable from its manifestations (Foucault, 249). Rather than an indifference to the immediately visible, the shift must be understood as a new articulation of the dialectic between the visible and the invisible. Foucault makes it explicit that "comparative anatomy is not merely a deepening of the descriptive techniques employed in the Classical age; it is not content with seeking to look underneath, more precisely and more closely; it establishes a space which is neither that of visible characters nor that of microscopic elements" (293).

40. Merleau-Ponty, *Visible and the Invisible,* 190.
41. Merleau-Ponty, 154–55.
42. Merleau-Ponty, 157.
43. Merleau-Ponty, 155.
44. Merleau-Ponty, *Nature,* 192.
45. "The postulate of classical logic is that given the observer as fallible subjectivity," explains Merleau-Ponty, "there can be appearance, but this de facto appearance is reducible de jure by a better knowledge of the apparatus and of our sensorial imperfections. The idea of 'objective truth' is not beyond reach" (93).
46. The deictic distance imposed by the scientist's "there" is strikingly (though doubtfully intentionally so) at variance with Bumppo's enigmatic last word before dying: "Here!" (385). This adverb seems to freeze Bumppo in an immobility and a presentism at odds with the west- and future-oriented ethos that drives the rest of the nation and in conflict with the progressive principles the scientist obeys.
47. There is an intriguing transference at work in the case of Battius, who does not merely want to capture the animal by means of mechanized apparatuses but also dreams of mechanizing the animal itself (a desire that prophetically anticipates the intensive modification and commodification of animal life brought about by the rapid development of factory farming): "Is the power to give life to inanimate matter the gift of man? I would it were! You should speedily see a *Historia Naturalis, Americana,* that would put the sneering imitators of the Frenchman, De Buffon, to shame! A great improvement might be made in the formation of all quadrupeds; especially those in which velocity is a virtue. Two of the inferior limbs should be on the principle of the lever; wheels,

perhaps, as they are now formed; though I have not yet determined whether the improvement might be better applied to the anterior or posterior members, inasmuch as I am yet to learn whether dragging or shoving requires the greatest muscular exertion. A natural exudation of the animal might assist in overcoming the friction, and a powerful momentum be obtained. But all this is hopeless—at least for the present!" (70–71).

48. Daston and Galison, *Objectivity,* 17, 20.
49. Daston and Galison, 130.
50. In a footnote, Cooper feels compelled to explain that "this American word means one who takes his game in a trap. It is of general use on the frontiers" (22).
51. Cooper, *Leatherstocking Tales,* 2:500.
52. In Freudian psychoanalysis, sublimation describes the elevation of instinctual animal impulses into more socially acceptable occupations, especially artistic pursuits (see Freud, *Three Contributions to the Theory of Sex*). Often credited for being the first to introduce the concept of *Sublimierung* in psychological language, Nietzsche also defines *sublimation* as the "evaporation" of animal drives but, unlike Freud, he does not always valorize sublimation; he treats it instead as a form of inhibition and repression, as the very symptom of modern falsification. Calling the bluff on the supposed "purification" of modern civilization, Nietzsche strives to revert the process of sublimation in order to retrieve the obliterated animal instincts that are still active under the polished carapace of modern civilization.
53. Audubon, *Ornithological Biography,* 266.
54. Audubon explains his calculation thus: "Let us take a column of one mile in breadth, which is far below the average size, and suppose it passing over us without interruption for three hours, at the rate mentioned above of one mile in a minute. This will give us a parallelogram of 180 miles by 1, covering 180 square miles. Allowing two pigeons to the square yard, we have One billion, one hundred and fifteen millions, one hundred and thirty-six thousand pigeons in one flock" (266).
55. Audubon, 265.
56. See Nevius's introduction to Cooper, *Prairie,* xxiv.

57. In 1875, a military commander reportedly ordered that medals "with a dead buffalo on one side and a discouraged Indian on the other side" be given to any buffalo-killer (Merchant, *American Environmental History,* 20). In a logic that calls to mind the combinatory visual of the thaumatrope, the medal bound the lot of the buffalo with that of the Native American.

58. One telling example is given by historian Mary Wingerd, who explains that the 1862 war between settlers and Plains Indians in Minnesota—which led to the public hanging of thirty-eight Dakota warriors, "the largest mass execution in U.S. history"—was sparked by a controversy over indigenous hunting life (requiring more land) and the U.S. insistence on settlement and farming (*North Country,* 327). Scott Lauria Morgensen chooses this example to underline a critical, indeed constitutive, oversight in Agambenian biopolitics, which ignores the history of American settler colonialism ("Biopolitics of Settler Colonialism," 69–70). On the resistance to the "systematic effort to assimilate Indians into farmers," see Byrd, *Transit of Empire,* 159.

59. "Hunters . . . are not simply fighters on the side of humanity against the wilderness," explains Matt Cartmill. "Their loyalties are divided. Because hunting takes place at the boundary between the human domain and the wilderness, the hunter stands with one foot on each side of the boundary, and swears no perpetual allegiance to either side" (*View to a Death in the Morning,* 31). Leatherstocking is exemplary in this regard. Cooper's hunter is never just the one who tames the wild but also the one who has an intimate knowledge of nature and hunts only what is necessary to his own subsistence.

60. The figure of the frontiersman is a tragic one, as Lukács shows in his comparison of Bumppo to the "middle-of-the-road" heroes of Walter Scott's novels (*Historical Novel*). Leslie Fiedler notes the paradoxical nature of Bumppo, who, though he incarnates the true spirit of America, must make way, along with the Indian, for the civilized man: "Cooper disconcertingly condemned his own kind of fiction to extinction by predicting the disappearance of the 'New Man'—that backwoods American neither Red nor White represented by Natty Bumppo—along with that of the Indian himself" (*Return of the Vanishing American,* 121).

61. The Native's simultaneous incorporation in the national narrative and exclusion from the nation's future is "Cooper's signature move," for Armstrong and Tennenhouse (*Novels in the Time of Democratic Writing,* 159).
62. "The Indian was an occidental invention that became a bankable simulation," writes Vizenor; "the word has no referent in tribal languages or cultures" (*Manifest Manners,* 8). "Those who 'memorialized rather than perpetuated' a tribal presence and wrote 'Indian history as obituary,'" he continues, quoting Larzer Ziff, "were unconsciously collaborating 'with those bent on physical extermination'" (8).
63. Ziff, quoted by Vizenor (8).
64. For Bumppo, civilization represents the tragic triumph of white "cunning" over the forthright "manhood" that he grants to the Native American. Hence the complex formula composed by *The Prairie*: proceeding from trickery, the inexorable advancement of white modernity precipitates an inacceptable but inevitable loss of virility and moral rectitude (223–24). This symbolic impotence is compensated by valorizing hunting as a prevalent cultural identity for Americans at the very moment when it was ceasing to be an everyday activity. On the real and symbolic collusions between hunting and imperialism, see Ritvo, *Animal Estate,* and "Destroyers and Preservers"; and Gillespie, *Hunting for Empire.* On the role played by the hunter in the popular American mythology, see Smith, *Virgin Land.* Smith articulates two dominant versions of American Empire: the mercantilist, modeled after maritime conquest and commerce, and the agrarian, which promotes the control and sedentary occupation of the land. For Smith, Cooper's hunter acts as a temporary mediator between the two.
65. Agamben, *"What Is an Apparatus?,"* 13. Agamben's characterization of biopolitics as the incorporation of *zoe* into the calculus of politics is useful, but his focus on death, Luciano argues, tends to detemporalize Foucault's framework, making it unable to account for the "sexual arrangement of the time of life," what she calls chronobiopolitics (*Arranging Grief,* 9). Luciano shows how sex, the intersection between individual and population, and more specifically the nineteenth-century "culture of sentiment" served as biopolitical instruments of population

control insofar as they made it possible to distinguish between those who could subdue the (instinctive) immediacy of sensation under the (evolved) progressive temporality of sentiment and those who could not.

66. Rifkin, "Indigenizing Agamben," 101.
67. On the notion of "bare habitance," see Rifkin, 94.
68. Cooper, *Pioneers,* 425.
69. Preface to the 1832 edition, in Cooper, *Leatherstocking Tales,* 1:884–85.
70. On the collusion between paleontology and settler colonialism, see Luciano, "Tracking Prehistory"; and Schuller, "Fossil and the Photograph." On the mutually reinforcing colonial logic of "vanishing" nature and Natives, see Wakeham, *Taxidermic Signs.*
71. Apess, "Son of the Forest," 55.
72. On this revisionist projection of peace (in which Cooper's fiction participates), see Scheckel, *Insistence of the Indian,* 15–40.
73. Consider the letter that the future President Jackson sent to his troops in 1814 to justify the massacre of the Muskogee Nation at the battle of Horseshoe Bend: "The fiends of the Tallapoosa will no longer murder our Women and Children, or disturb the quiet of our borders.... They have disappeared from the face of the Earth.... The weapons of warefare [*sic*] will be exchanged for the utensils of husbandry; and the wilderness which now withers in sterility and seems to mourn the disolation [*sic*] which overspreads it, will blossom as the rose, and become the nursery of the arts.... How lamentable it is that the path to peace should lead through blood, and over the carcases [*sic*] of the slain!!" (A. Jackson, "Andrew Jackson to Soldiers").
74. Dunbar-Ortiz, *Indigenous People's History of the United States,* 103.
75. Dunbar-Ortiz, 104.
76. Coulthard, *Red Skin, White Masks,* 7.
77. Gissen, *Subnature,* 182–83.
78. Here the continuities between hunt and capture are clear. This classic hunting technique—the basis of the modern deer stand or duck blind—is sometimes used by wildlife photographers to "invisibilize" themselves and approach wild animals. Burt, for instance, mentions the case of British naturalists Richard and Cherry Kearton hiding inside a model cow (*Animals in Film,* 98).

79. Deleuze and Guattari, *Thousand Plateaus,* 440.
80. Territory is also the category by which Deleuze and Guattari substitute a functionalist for an expressionist conception of animals. They invoke Uexküll to show how animals inhabit and build (decode and encode) territories and thenceforth operate transspecific "captures." I return to Deleuze and Guattari's unexpected use of the term *capture* to describe animal-becomings in chapter 5.
81. Glen Sean Coulthard explains that the U.S. expropriation of indigenous populations, which he reframes as primitive accumulation, in turn creates a class of mobile workers readied to sell their labor (*Red Skin, White Masks,* 8–9).
82. Noting the convergence between the policing of poor and black populations after Emancipation, Hartman notes that "a variety of everyday activities that enabled a measure of subsistence or autonomy were . . . criminalized." These activities "ranged from moving about to hunting and fishing to styles of comportment" (*Scenes of Subjection,* 146).
83. Foucault, *Order of Things,* 169–70.
84. Foucault, *Society Must Be Defended,* 255–57.
85. When Foucault makes racism the precondition of the old sovereign "right to kill" under biopower, he specifies that "killing" does "not mean simply murder as such, but also every form of indirect murder: the fact of exposing someone to death, increasing the risk of death for some people, or, quite simply, political death, expulsion, rejection, and so on" (256).
86. Morgensen, "Biopolitics of Settler Colonialism," 70. Jodi Byrd makes a similar point when she sees in the United States' relation to American Indians a privileged site for analyzing the logic of exception that Agamben sees as driving Western sovereignty (*Transit of Empire,* 187). On concentration as a biopolitical technique of colonial and racial governance, see Nemser, *Infrastructures of Race.*
87. Rifkin, "Indigenizing Agamben," 117n8.
88. Morgensen, "Biopolitics of Settler Colonialism," 71.
89. Gavin Walker recalls that the manner in which "the West" arrogates "the form of the universal" is this operation that Deleuze and Guattari call "capture" (Walker, "Schema of the West and the Apparatus of Capture," 219).

90. Hartman, *Scenes of Subjection,* 115.
91. K. Marx, *Capital,* chap. 31. For an elaboration of the role played by capture in primitive accumulation, see Walker, "Schema of the West and the Apparatus of Capture," 221.
92. Deleuze and Guattari, *Thousand Plateaus,* 448.
93. Foucault, *Birth of Biopolitics,* 56–59.
94. Quoted in Chamayou, *Manhunts,* 86.
95. "In this new context," Chamayou sums up, "the police was henceforth to be an arm of the judicial system, the penal power's apparatus for capturing" (86). Foucault's history of governmentality similarly tends to overlook, Shukin argues, the role played by "sheepdogs"—i.e., "the prosthetic strong-arm of a shepherd"—in the deployment of pastoral power ("Security Bonds," 179).
96. On the systematic hunts organized by the state against "unproductive" populations, see Chamayou, *Manhunts,* esp. chaps. 7 and 8.

3. THE FUGITIVE ANIMAL

1. Foucault, *Security, Territory, Population,* 20. Foucault summarizes the complementary dimension of disciplinary and security regimes in *The History of Sexuality,* where he explains that biopower takes two main forms that constitute "two poles of development linked together by a whole intermediary cluster of relations. One of these poles—the first to be formed, it seems—focused on the body as machine: its training (*dressage*), the optimization of its capabilities, the extortion of its forces . . . all this was ensured by the procedures of power that characterized the *disciplines*: an *anatomo-politics of the human body.* The second, formed somewhat later, around the middle of the eighteenth century, focused on the species-body, the body . . . serving as the basis of biological processes: propagation, births and mortality, the level of health, life expectancy and longevity. . . . Their supervision was effected through an entire series of interventions and *regulatory controls: a biopolitics of the population*" (139).
2. Building on Luciano's insight that nineteenth-century U.S. sentimental culture performs the biopolitical work of policing bodies through affect, Schuller examines cultural and scientific discourses that suggested

that a "good" subject—i.e., a subject whose life is worth protecting and fostering—was both malleable (receptive to external sensations and emotions) and capable of self-control. At the center of these discourses was the Lamarck-inspired "American School of Evolution," which championed the idea that the individual, though deeply informed by her milieu, was not entirely determined by it and was capable of transformation through "power of habit" (*Biopolitics of Feeling,* 36).

3. Foucault, *Security, Territory, Population,* 37; emphasis added.
4. While Foucault explicitly derives the notion of milieu from biology, his understanding of territory is primarily informed by political theories of sovereignty. Apprehending space as territory means seeing it with the eyes of a conqueror. The management of the territory is centered around ensuring the "safety" of the sovereign, while the regulation of milieu is focused on the "security" of the population that lives on it. The problematic moves away from war toward civil war, from attacking another country or warding off attack from the outside to anticipating and regulating tensions inside the State. Technologies that target population, Foucault writes, aim "to establish a sort of homeostasis . . . by achieving an overall equilibrium: the security of the whole with regards to its internal dangers" (*Society Must Be Defended,* 246).
5. Benjamin, *Arcades Project,* 439.
6. Chamayou, *Manhunts,* 8.
7. Poe's "The Murders in the Rue Morgue," which grounds this chapter's arguments, has played a central role in works such as Lippit's *Electric Animal,* Boggs's *Animalia Americana,* Peterson's *Bestial Traces,* and Ravindranathan's *Behold an Animal,* to cite only the most prominent.
8. On the ontological displacement of the enslaved, see, for instance, Spillers, "Mama's Baby, Papa's Maybe." Spillers shows how captured Africans were anonymized and "degendered" as human cargo aboard slave ships and as such were excluded from the "cultural fiction" of domesticity. "Those African persons in 'Middle Passage' were literally suspended in the 'oceanic,' if we think of the latter in its Freudian orientation as an analogy for undifferentiated identity: removed from the indigenous land and culture, and not-yet 'American' either, these captive persons, without names that their captors would recognize,

were in movement across the Atlantic, but they were also *nowhere* at all" (72).

9. Morrison, *Playing in the Dark,* 32.
10. Barrett, "Presence of Mind," 158.
11. Benjamin, "Paris of the Second Empire in Baudelaire," 78; emphasis added. See also Foucault, *Discipline and Punish,* 141.
12. Among the technologies that facilitated this transformation, Benjamin cites French criminologist Alphonse Bertillon's early biometric studies. See Tagg, *Burden of Representation,* 60–102; and Finn, *Capturing the Criminal Image,* 1–31.
13. Benjamin, "Paris of the Second Empire in Baudelaire," 79.
14. Benjamin, 79. The English term *spoor,* which designates the trail of a hunted animal, derives from the German *Spur,* which was originally a hunting term and now broadly means "trace."
15. Benjamin, *Berlin Childhood around 1900,* 53.
16. In his well-known tirade against Cooper's "literary offenses," Mark Twain proposes that the *Leatherstocking* saga should be renamed *The Broken Twig Series* because every time "a Cooper person is in peril, and absolute silence is worth four dollars a minute, he is sure to step on a dry twig" (*Collected Tales, Sketches, Speeches & Essays,* 380). Calling out the perceived paucity of Cooper's literary bag of tricks (or "little box of stage-properties" as he calls it), Twain's charge also points to *The Leatherstocking Tales'* persistently clumsy privileging of senses other than sight. When sight is privileged, however, it is not used for reading (as we know, Bumppo is illiterate). Or to quote Benjamin, it is used for "reading what was never written": the tracks of an animal, the changing position of the sun, the direction of the wind, and so on. Even as Twain pokes fun at him, he nevertheless draws attention to the fact that Cooper gives us access to another mode of reading, where different senses and faculties are used. The semiotics of Cooper's stage-properties, however ridiculous for Twain, evidences the novel's insistent somatic lexicon—that is, how the imprints made down the path or the mark left by the snapped twig offer themselves to a different kind of reading and writing.
17. Nicole Shukin explains that "Napoleon's project of modernization involved, crucially, the 'exile' of the sensoriums of slaughtering and

rendering to outlying precincts far from the eyes and noses of an urban polity." She continues: "In the nineteenth century public culture began to be sanitized and sensitized through myriad practices, disciplines, and reforms best discerned, perhaps, by Foucault. According to Vialles, the institutionalization of enclosed, monitored facilities devoted solely to animal slaughter in compliance with new regulations and sensibilities around 'suffering, violence, waste and disease, "miasmas," and finally animals themselves,' helped to materially and ideologically prepare conditions for the massification of slaughter" (*Animal Capital,* 62). On the hygiene standards and the subsequent insulation of slaughterhouses in nineteenth- and twentieth-century Europe and North America, see Lee, *Meat, Modernity and the Rise of the Slaughterhouse.*

18. The detective is no less ambivalent a figure than Cooper's hunter, who is poised on the threshold between wilderness and civilization. Although the detective exposes blind spots in the police's investigation, he also holds the promise (and raises the specter) of absolute surveillance (see Rosenheim, *Cryptographic Imagination,* 70). As D. A. Miller puts it, "Detective fiction is . . . always implicitly punning on the detective's brilliant *super-vision* and the police *supervision* that it embodies. His intervention marks an explicit bringing-under-surveillance of the entire world of the narrative. As such, it can be alarming" (*Novel and the Police,* 35).

19. Chamayou complements Foucault's study of biopower by showing that the government of populations always depends on a violent and naturalized "cynegetic power" (literally, the power to drive hunting dogs). This power is external to the state, which can thus dissociate itself from its violence, but it does not precede it, as most founding myths have it; it accompanies and subtends it. Fugitive slaves, for instance, cause nothing short of an ontological crisis by refusing to conform to their supposed essence as cattle: "To reestablish the ontological order that has been thus abused, there is ultimately only one recourse: force. Violent hunting will be carried out in the form of war on men who, being born to be commanded, refuse to be commanded. . . . Thus, in the end the answer to the theoretical problem of the manhunt is the practice of manhunting itself, with the paradox that the latter is legitimized on the basis of an allegedly natural division. . . . In fact, the natural order that is

invoked . . . as the foundation of cynegetic power can be realized only by virtue of a whole arsenal of artifices" (*Manhunts,* 8).

20. Benjamin, *Arcades Project,* 806. On the flaneur as a reflection of early capitalist culture, see Eagleton, *Walter Benjamin,* 25–26.
21. There is a long and enduring history of legal but extrainstitutional violence targeting racialized subjects in the United States, both in the context of slavery (for example, the early practice of the posse comitatus and the Fugitive Slave Acts) and after Emancipation (lynching, "Stand Your Ground"). Europeans were no strangers to the practice of catching slaves, but the hunting was for the most part taking place out of immediate sight, in the colonies.
22. Douglass, "The Internal Slave Trade," in *Autobiographies,* 438.
23. The Thirteenth Amendment outlawed slavery "except as punishment of crime where of the party shall have been duly convicted." This exception was deeply racialized, as Angela Davis notes, since the Black Codes adopted after the abolition of slavery had crimes for which only black people could be convicted (*Are Prisons Obsolete?,* 28). On the role of the Thirteenth Amendment in the criminalization of race in the United States, see Alexander, *New Jim Crow.*
24. Simone Browne and Grégoire Chamayou both show that the "hunt of black skins" institutionalized by slavery does not disappear with Emancipation, and explicit acts of violence remain the common lot of certain populations; this is evidenced today by the staggering racial discrepancy in police brutality in the United States and the guarantee of a right for private (white) individuals to "stand their ground." That these displays of violence are often characterized as anachronistic, however, speaks to the transformation of the frame within which they are perceived and justified. The use of penal law in the transition from the "slave codes" to "black codes," for instance, contributed to remaking the slave laborer in the image of the criminal (see Davis, "Race and Criminalization"). Among the effects of this transition is not just mass incarceration—the most "visible" dimension of the furtive regime of capture—but also the implementation of systematic surveillance, both of which disproportionately target racialized populations. Saidiya Hartman describes Emancipation as the "metamorphosis of 'chattel into man'" (*Scenes*

of Subjection, 116), or "transubstantiation of the captive into volitional subject" (123), to show that violent subjection did not vanish but surreptitiously saturated U.S. liberal economies and imaginaries.

25. Stowe, *Uncle Tom's Cabin,* 64.

26. Reflecting on the legal and ontological status of the fugitive slave as a "property that, paradoxically, behaved like a person" Stephen Best argues that the concept of fugitivity became central to the redefinition of the legal category of the person in the second half of the nineteenth century when new technologies like the phonograph and the camera brought traditional models of property into crisis by making reproducible what heretofore had seemed the inalienable property of a person (her image, the sound of her voice) (*Fugitive's Properties,* 16). Traditionally defined in terms of (self-)ownership, the notion of personhood flounders, Best explains, when property goes from being alienable but stable (present but able to be absent) to fugitive and immaterial (absent/abstract but able to be made present). In this context, the role of the law shifts from hunting down and seizing an as yet unowned object to capturing and securing a property that appears essentially elusive. If Poe's detective is portrayed as a hunter, as we will see, it is important to note that he is not acquiring but *returning* properties that have escaped. The detective borrows his techniques of detection from the hunter, but the hunt has become capture, a mechanism of restoration (of a property that has fled, of a certain order of things). Replete with "unreasonable" animals capable of reproducing human gestures and voices, Poe's fictions are obsessed with the possibility of tracking down and returning to their rightful owners their fugitive properties. Poe's ape in "The Murders in the Rue Morgue" has rightly been recognized as an allegory for the fugitive slave, but it is also a clear emblem of mechanical reproduction. His escape, we are told, is prompted by the sailor's fury to find it "sitting before a looking-glass, attempting the operation of shaving, in which it had no doubt previously watched its master through the key-hole of the closet" (i.e., by the sailor's recognition that his own gestures—shaving, which can be read as shedding traces of animality—are replicable, imitable, ape-able). The European sailor faces the threat of a double expropriation: that of the ape as his material property, which like the fugitive slave is "moveable by

their nature, [but] considered as immoveable by the operation of law" (Goodell, quoted in Best, 1), and that of his own personhood. Dupin will restore both: safely locked up in the Jardin des Plantes at the end of the story, the ape is converted into "a very large sum" and his owner is made whole again (in fact, he gains from the transaction).

27. Jacobs, *Incidents in the Life of a Slave Girl,* 859.

28. On the surveillance of black populations in the United States, see Browne, *Dark Matters.*

29. "Was nie geschrieben wurde, lessen." Walter Benjamin was fond of this sentence by Hofmannsthal, which he quotes in the "Paralipomena to 'On the Concept of History'" and "On the Mimetic Faculty."

30. Benjamin, *Arcades Project,* 418.

31. Poe, "The Man of the Crowd," in *Poetry and Tales,* 392. All references to Poe's tales are taken from this volume and hereafter cited parenthetically.

32. Ted Geier rightly observes that it is because the man of the crowd is "given up as a calculable and categorised object," portrayed as a "most unknowable, inscrutable, contradictory and confounding object," that he is "relegated to the grossest, deepest criminal ranks" (*Meat Markets,* 122). But this logic is surprisingly reversible: it is because the criminal is construed as essentially inscrutable—his guilty impulses emerging from an unavowable place, the dark site of animal instincts—that he becomes endlessly subject to scrutiny and susceptible to capture.

33. Finding in Poe's description of the crowd an echo of a passage from Descartes's *Metaphysical Meditations,* Kevin McLaughlin argues that the man of the crowd appears illegible to the narrator because he is "more like a machine than a man" (*Paperwork,* 31). On the relationship between Poe and Descartes, see Stanley Cavell's essay "Being Odd, Getting Even," 3–36.

34. Stephen Rachman alludes in passing to the prey-like character of the man of the crowd, comparing him to a "quarry" that the narrator pursues ("'Es lässt sich nicht schreiben,'" 56–70).

35. Benjamin, "Paris of the Second Empire in Baudelaire," 418.

36. Cuvier's orangutan, in fact, has little to do with Poe's Ourang-Outang. Cuvier attempts to demystify the ape's reputation for exaggerated

humanlikeness: he describes the animal as friendly and endearing, capable of imitating human actions, but as intellectually limited, and he notes that those who saw the ape as nearly human had only seen young specimens (*Le règne animal,* 52–53). In contrast, Poe exploits the popular misperceptions of the animal: "The gigantic stature, the prodigious strength and activity, the wild ferocity, and the imitative propensities of these mammalia are sufficiently well known to all. I understood the full horrors of the murder at once" (424). We can assume that this "misreading" was deliberate given that Poe had translated Cuvier into English and written an introduction for the anatomist's work on mollusks (*Conchologist's First Book*).

37. Boggs, *Animalia Americana,* 112.
38. Poe toys with a similar idea in "The Black Cat," which relates the confession of a murderer on the eve of his execution. By associating the narrator's murderous impulse with madness, the tale challenges the very possibility of confessing: in principle, a madman cannot recognize his own madness, for the act of recognition itself requires a self capable of reflection (one that is thus not mad). On the aporia of mad narration, see Zimmerman, *Edgar Allan Poe,* 42–43; and Benefey, *Poe and the Unreadable,* 29–30.
39. Schuller, *Biopolitics of Feeling,* 160.
40. Hartman, *Scenes of Subjection,* 80.
41. Dayan, "Poe, Persons, and Property," 108. The disappearing ape can be seen as prefiguring Ralph Ellison's invisible man (despite his protestation that he is not a "spook like those that haunted Edgar Allan Poe") and Richard Wright's Bigger Thomas, as Christopher Peterson argues. Peterson suggests that "the human criminals of subsequent detective fiction all descend from Poe's ape, thereby continuing to bear the traces of an animality that no degree of evolution can efface" (*Bestial Traces,* 25).
42. Peterson, *Bestial Traces,* 23.
43. "While 'The Murders in the Rue Morgue' does not explicitly equate blacks with apes," Peterson writes, "a number of critics have read Poe's story as a thinly disguised allegory for the doctrine of black animality. And yet, this racist ideology operated in tandem with larger naturalist and evolutionary discourses centered on ape/human affinities. Indeed,

the hierarchical relationship that whites invented in order to situate blacks as more closely related to simians not only provided a convenient justification for slavery but also disavowed the monogenic history of human and nonhuman primates. If Poe's story is to be read allegorically, then, we ought to take into account how it invokes not only the racist ideology of black animality but also those emergent scientific discourses that threatened to locate all humans squarely within the domain of the animal" (157).

44. Ginzburg, *Clues, Myths, and the Historical Method,* 93.
45. On Poe's knowledge of the recently discovered "rod cells" that enable "oblique vision" and scotopic vision, or vision in very low light, see Scheick, "Intrinsic Luminosity," 85–86.
46. It is the same brand of reasoning (and a pair of green spectacles) that allows Dupin, a recurring character in Poe's tales of detection, to recover the missing missive in "The Purloined Letter" (1844) when the microscopes of the police prove ineffective.
47. In this vitalist prose poem, Poe laments the newly accepted idea that nebulae (and in particular the "great 'nebulae' in the constellation Orion") are nothing but a cluster of individual stars derived from the recent improvement of modern telescopes ("Eureka," in *Poetry and Tales,* 1319).
48. Lippit shows that the crime itself disappears as the case unfolds: "The criminal trespass dissolves into a series of accidental encounters between two women and an ape—an arbitrary slaying of two human beings by an animal. . . . There are, in the end, no monsters, only animals" (*Electric Animal,* 28). Or perhaps animals have become monsters, in the sense Foucault gives to the word in *Discipline and Punish.* After all, the ape ends up behind bars at the Jardin des Plantes.
49. Poe restores the archaic sense of *reading* as guessing or interpreting a dream or riddle. After a somewhat laborious preface praising the powers and pleasures of the "analytical ability," the narrator of "The Murders in the Rue Morgue" offers the extraordinary homicide of the L'Espanayes as a case in point to illustrate the superiority of analysis over mere calculation, which is too prone to "oversight" and overly "by the book" (398). This superiority, however, cannot be demonstrated,

only *monstrated.* From the outset, we are told that the logical continuity between the theoretical preface and the expository narrative may in effect be misleading (400). The narrator's many precautions warn the reader against the lure of logical sequences that might ultimately prove nothing but rhetorical effects. Similarly, the very first sentence of the tale declares that the "mental features discoursed of as the analytical are, in themselves, but little susceptible to analysis. We appreciate them only in their effects" (397). Thus the continuity between the two "halves" of the narrative—the moral and the story, the head (or tail) and the body—might rest on an optical illusion, just like the apparent robustness of the nail, whose decapitation parodically duplicates Mme L'Espanaye's. So, to read "The Murders in the Rue Morgue" (as Dupin reads the murders in the rue Morgue), one must adopt a different frame, must try to get "out" of the traditional frame of reference.

50. Detective fiction is intimately tied to the rise of mass media, as Stephen Rachman shows in "Poe and the Origins of Detective Fiction."
51. Foucault, *Discipline and Punish,* 286. On the crime novel as an apparatus for normalizing crime by revealing the hidden rationality of seemingly arbitrary actions, see D. Miller, *Novel and the Police.*
52. Foucault, *Discipline and Punish,* 286; emphasis added. The notion of milieu is useful insofar as it accounts "for action at a distance of one body on another" (Foucault, *Security, Territory, Population,* 21); in a milieu, bodies continually affect one another but indirectly, through the mediation of a shared environment. For example, Dupin himself changes the opinions and responses of others without direct contact by manipulating the milieu: he captures the murderer without leaving his apartment.
53. On the racist logic that underpins Dupin's assertion, see Barrett, "Presence of Mind," 165–66; and White, "Ourang-Outang Situation," 103–4.
54. Fiedler, *Love and Death in the American Novel,* 497.
55. On the uncanny fold in which Poe's Ourang-Outang abides, see Ravindranathan, "Unequal Metrics."
56. Human and animal here do not operate binaristically. Instead, animalization is a technology for producing a "certain kind of human," as Zakiyyah Iman Jackson argues ("Beyond the Limit," 1).

57. Lippit, *Electric Animal,* 27.

58. Like Agamben's, Lippit's "modernity" is less a determined historical period than a critical gesture by which what is excluded (e.g., the animal) surreptitiously returns as constitutive of humanity. Lippit's account of the modern separation between animals and humans is not incompatible with Agamben's, which I discuss in chapter 4, only it insists on the role played by the empirical disappearance of animals in the urbanized West (Lippit, *Electric Animal,* 2–3).

59. Lippit, 53–54.

60. Lippit, 54.

61. Lippit, 36.

62. Derrida, *Glas,* 107.

63. Derrida argues that the demarcation between human and animal is predicated upon a process of interiorization, which he describes as a form of sublimated eating. Even thinkers like Heidegger and Lévinas, who deconstruct the premises of what constitutes human subjectivity, essentialize the difference between humans and animals when they maintain this assimilative gesture as constitutive of genuine comprehension. For Heidegger, Derrida suggests, the incorporation of the animal is no longer a form of ingesting but rather a handling or a capturing: "As far as Heidegger's qualified humanism is concerned, which transfers the specifically human from man's interior to his hand, the boundary between human and animal still remains something which is impossible to call into question. It is not a traditional humanism, but a determination of the location—the place (*Dasein*) where meaning can be received. The location is not explicitly determined as Man, but Heidegger nonetheless provides a description of this place that excludes animals" (Birnbaum and Olsson, "Interview with Jacques Derrida on the Limits of Digestion").

64. Hegel, *Philosophy of History,* 287.

65. Lippit, *Electric Animal,* 42.

66. The combined metaphors of crypts and digestive tracts bring to mind images of the Chicago meat lockers—the animal "morgue" of the city—described in Upton Sinclair's *The Jungle* (1906): "This slaughtering machine ran on, visitors or no visitors. It was like some horrible crime

committed in a dungeon, all unseen and unheeded, buried out of sight and of memory" (35).

67. "What speculative dialectics means (to say)," Derrida explains, "is that the crypt can still be incorporated to the system. The transcendental or the repressed, the unthought or the excluded must be assimilated by the corpus, interiorized as moments, idealized in the very negativity of their labor" (*Glas,* 166).

68. The crypt conjures up the topography of the unconscious but cannot be reduced to it. In *The Wolf Man's Magic Word,* Maria Torok and Nicolas Abraham come up with the notion of the crypt precisely because they believe that Freud's theory is unable to account for the Wolf Man's "infantile neurosis." In his foreword to *The Wolf Man's Magic Word,* Derrida describes the crypt as a nonplace, or rather a place lodged inside yet completely isolated from another place (xiii).

69. On the cat's "impression" on the narrator's bedroom wall as an evocation of the daguerreotype (invented in 1839), see Sweeney, "Death, Decay, and the Daguerreotype's Influence on 'The Black Cat.'"

70. On the notorious susceptibility and resistance of Poe's fiction to psychoanalytical interpretation, see Rosenheim, *Cryptographic Imagination*, 41, 71. For examples of psychological interpretations of "The Black Cat," see Madden, "Poe's 'The Black Cat' and Freud's 'The "Uncanny'"; and Dern, "'Problem in Detection.'"

71. Bonaparte, *Life and Works of Edgar Allan Poe,* 465. To be fair, the cat is not the only transparent signifier in Bonaparte's exegetic toolbox. In "The Murders in the Rue Morgue," Poe's mother is alternately the L'Espanayes and the room itself, while the Ourang-Outang holding the razor is the figure of the father slaying the mother during coitus (a crime that is not a crime, a crime invented in the mind of little Edgar). Poe himself is in turn Dupin, the narrator, and the sailor (Bonaparte, 429).

72. On Bonaparte's reading of Poe, see Walker, "Poe Legend," 38; and Felman, "On Reading Poetry." On the intricate history of Poe and psychoanalytical interpretation, refer to Muller and Richardson, *Purloined Poe,* esp. Lacan, "Seminar on 'The Purloined Letter;'" Derrida, "The Purveyor of Truth;" and Barbara Johnson, "The Frame of Reference."

73. The cat loses one eye in Poe's story and two in Bonaparte's interpretation, where eyes are reduced to symbols for the author's soon-to-be-castrated penis.
74. Derrida, *Animal That Therefore I Am,* 11. Derrida's protestations of reality underline the absolute singularity of his cat, whose existence cannot be conceptualized or reduced to a theorem, "something seen and not seeing" (14).
75. Poe, a master of cryptography, asserts "that human ingenuity cannot concoct a cipher which human ingenuity cannot resolve" ("Few Words on Secret Writing," 1286). However, it is now widely accepted that humans can generate codes unbreakable by humans. My thanks to Justin Joque for bringing this to my attention.
76. Monfort, "Sans les mains."
77. Monfort, "Sans les mains" (my translation).
78. In this, Monfort follows Heidegger. "Only Man has hands, says Heidegger, and, through the hand, he has access to a world of meaningful action," explains Derrida. "The ape, however, possesses only '*Greifsorgane*' [organs for grasping] and is therefore excluded from the realm of the human. This distinction between hand and organ for grasping is not something Heidegger arrived at by studying apes in the Black Forest, but rather has a purely stipulative character. Here, as always, humanism rests on the sacrifice of the animal, on the implicit swallowing up of the animal" (Birnbaum and Olsson, "Interview with Jacques Derrida on the Limits of Digestion").
79. For a more detailed elaboration on the motif and economy of the hunt in Poe's tale, see Ravindranathan and Traisnel, "What Gives (Donner le change)."
80. For an analysis of the mythical subtext crypted in the *clue/clew/clou* homonymy and archeonymy, see Irwin, "Clew to a Clue."
81. Where John T. Irwin claims that Dupin is Theseus ("Clew to a Clue," 151), however, I would like to suggest that he might as well be Ariadne. Dupin never goes after the animal, only helps to find it in the labyrinth of the city, and his rival is less the animal murderer than the prefect of police (an avatar of Minos, the ruler of Crete), whom Dupin delights in having "defeated in his own castle" (431). Moreover, in the

myth, Ariadne will quickly pass from Theseus to Dionysus—i.e., from the man who subdues Pasiphaë's monstrous progeny to the animal deity.

82. In *Civilization and Its Discontents,* Freud famously accounts for hominization by a shift of priority from smell to sight that accompanies the transition from horizontality to verticality—to the upright position. Poe's tale hints that if man is the animal that cannot smell (in the transitive sense), he can easily lure himself into thinking that he does not smell (in the intransitive sense).

83. Begotten by these three illustrious fathers, he is also sometimes taken as an allegory for philosophy, derived from different sources of knowledge. There is another possible origin where Zeus, Hermes, and Poseidon come to visit Hyrieus of Tanagra, who roasts a whole bull in their honor. When they offer him a favor in return for his hospitality, he asks for the birth of a son. The gods take the bull's hide and urinate into it, bury it in the earth, and tell him to dig it up ten months later.

84. David Van Leer erroneously affirms that "Dupin forbears to enumerate" the "pungencies" attached to Orion's name. What Van Leer fails to see is that names in Poe leave traces ("Detecting Truth," quoted in Barrett, "Presence of Mind," 163).

85. Nietzsche, *Anti-Christ,* 144. For Nietzsche, lies have an olfactory trace, a sensible trail; truth, in contrast, is a "mobile army of metaphors, metonyms and anthropormorphisms—in short, a sum of human relations" whose metaphoricity is "worn out and without sensuous power." The loss of sensuous power is a paradoxical decay, a peculiar form of entropy whereby the original scent is masked by the acquisition of *lettres de noblesse.*

86. In "Philosophy of Composition," Poe justifies his tedious rhyming choice in "The Raven" by claiming that *O* and *R* are the most "sonorous" and "producible" letters respectively. What interests me here is the poem's endowment of the titular crow, "a non-reasoning creature capable of speech," with the uncanny capacity to respond to the narrator. That the raven's monotonously vocalized "Nevermore" might qualify as a response, though it is likely a meaningless reaction, contaminates in turn the narrator's speech, whose questions appear helplessly rhetorical, mechanical. As in "The Man of the Crowd," Poe links animality with

automaticity to reflect on the loss of authenticity (or originality, *UR*) when a supposedly inalienably human property like language becomes (re)producible (*OR*).

87. Cuvier, *Le règne animal,* 87.

88. "The point of Poe's zoosemiotic lesson is that man can have 'full language' only as an animal," Ziser concludes, "and that, as 'man,' he can have language only as a chain of material signs. In both cases, humans' semiotic horizon is necessarily open to the history and presence of the non-human animal" ("Animal Mirrors," 27).

89. Foucault, *Society Must Be Defended,* 8–11.

90. Barrett, "Presence of Mind," 168. On Cuvier's function in the economy of the tale, see Rowe, *Literary Culture and U.S. Imperialism,* 72.

91. An apologist of the superiority of the white race, Cuvier posited that the African race was "the most degraded of human races, whose form approaches that of the beast and whose intelligence is nowhere great enough to arrive at regular government." Cuvier, *Recherches,* quoted in Barrett, "Presence of Mind," 169.

92. Barrett, "Presence of Mind," 169, 174.

93. On mètis as a practical modality of knowledge that applies to "fugitive . . . realities that do not lend themselves to precise measurement," see Detienne and Vernant, *Les ruses de l'intelligence,* 10 (my translation).

94. For an unequalable analysis of this epigraph, see Ravindranathan, "Unequal Metrics."

95. Unless it is the captured that winds up animalized. Poe's story anticipates late nineteenth-century criminological speculations inspired by Darwin's theory of evolution (Lombroso, Galton, Bertillon). In a fascinating chiasmus, the racialist and racist logics behind the animalization of criminals appear not merely to prolong but indeed to supplant the special and speciesist logics that undergird the decriminalization of animals. This decriminalization is by no means an exculpation, let alone a form of liberation. Quite the contrary: there is no longer any need to criminalize the animal because capture has increasingly become its empirical and existential condition (think of Nabokov's ape at the end of *Lolita,* who has internalized his guilt to the point that all he can draw are the bars of his cage).

4. FABULOUS TAXONOMY

1. Melville, *Moby-Dick,* 498 (hereafter cited in text).
2. In fact, the Basilosaurus was misidentified by American anatomist Dr. Harlan in 1834. A report dated January 9, 1839, establishes Owen's correction of Harlan's initial assumption that the skeleton was that of a saurian (*Proceedings of the Geological Society of London,* 24–28).
3. Not only did the whale leave "his pre-adamite traces in the stereotype plates of nature," but "the unmistakable print of his fin" appears upon hieroglyphic records "whose antiquity seems to claim for them an almost fossiliferous character." In an ancient Egyptian planisphere, we are told, "the old Leviathan swam as of yore" among "centaurs, griffins, and dolphins, similar to the grotesque figures on the celestial globe of the moderns." Melville also introduces alternative perspectives on the hegemonic account foisted on the skeleton by comparative anatomy, noting that "awe-stricken credulous slaves in the vicinity took [the skeleton] for one of the fallen angels" (498).
4. For "The Murders in the Rue Morgue," see Peterson, *Bestial Traces*; for *The Marble Faun,* see Mason, *Civilized Creatures.*
5. Many commentators note the exact contemporaneity of Hawthorne's romance and Darwin's masterwork, often to dismiss its meaningfulness. The year 1859 is also when Louis Pasteur put an end to a millennium-long debate over the "spontaneous generation" of living organisms; cryptogamous plants and small animals could no longer appear "of their own accord" (*sua sponte*) but always and of necessity descended from a traceable origin. Pasteur disproved the doctrine of spontaneous generation in favor of biogenesis, the notion that only life can engender life. In her brilliant study of romantic materialism and the modern life sciences, Amanda Jo Goldstein shows that spontaneous generation was not simply "erroneous," as orthodox accounts of scientific progress have it, but actively resisted the strict determinations of biological/sexual causality or the autotelism of emergent vitalist epistemologies (*Sweet Science,* 76–90). There is an undeniably "conservative" dimension in Pasteur's efforts to prove that matter could not "organize itself" and that every organism had to recognize the authority of its genitors (Farley and Geison, "Science, Politics, and Spontaneous

Generation," 188–90), a dimension that can account for the critical role his work played in the promotion of public hygiene, vaccination, and the cordoning off of populations perceived as unsanitary.

6. Hawthorne, *Marble Faun,* 10 (hereafter cited in text).
7. Hawthorne, *French and Italian Notebooks,* 179; emphasis added.
8. It is worth noting that when Hawthorne first encountered Praxiteles's faun in the Borghese gardens, he associated it with "that ugly, bearded woman, who was lately exhibited in England, and by some supposed to have been engendered betwixt a human mother and an orang-outang" (*French and Italian Notebooks,* 173–74). Hawthorne refers here to Julia Pastrana, a Mexican woman with hypertrichosis (excessive hair growth) that performed in Europe, Russia, and America while being billed as a human-orangutan hybrid.
9. See, for instance, Riss, "Art of Discrimination"; Johnson, "Classifying Donatello"; Kemp, "*Marble Faun* and American Postcolonial Ambivalence"; Bentley, "Slaves and Fauns"; and Pearson, "Bloodliness and Abortions."
10. The readings mentioned above tend to (in Steve Baker's formulation) make the animal disappear as a "transparent signifier" of the human, thereby foreclosing other equally possible—by no means incompatible or antithetical—interpretations. On this issue, see Mason, *Civilized Creatures,* 23, 42–94. Mason recalls Hawthorne's lifelong interest in and scandalized skepticism toward the possibility of a kinship between humans and nonhuman primates (in particular, orangutans). She argues that if *The Marble Faun* contributed to "the acceptance of the theory of species transformation" (24), it was not by foregrounding the anatomical resemblance between apes and humans but by highlighting humans' sympathetic affinities with pets and domesticated animals (particularly dogs, with which Donatello is repeatedly associated in the first half of the book). Mason suggestively claims that Donatello's "successful transformation from faun to human" (78)—a scenario that, she omits to say, remains entirely speculative, since the author and his characters refuse to classify Donatello with certainty—draws on Lamarck's theory of *transformisme* rather than Darwin's theory of evolution (*On the Origin of Species* was published a month after Hawthorne sent

his manuscript to the publisher). Bert Bender is equally skeptical about Darwin's possible influence on Hawthorne (*Descent of Love,* 120–21). However, I would argue that Hawthorne's "postscript," subscribed by his English publishers Smith, Elder & Co. on March 14, 1860, and published a month later, and in particular its explicit mention of Cuvier's name, constitutes enough of an invitation to read his book as a meditation on the debate prompted by Darwin's work.

11. Murphy, "'Betwixt Human and Brute Life.'"
12. "Natural history was a science of surfaces and skin," writes Rusert, "driven by the belief that racial differences were produced by varying climatic conditions in different geographical regions. Comparative anatomy went deeper, seeking to locate human differences, and inequalities, in the internal structures of the body" (*Fugitive Science,* 115).
13. The "genealogist" bent on authenticating someone's pedigree is bound to stray "in the region beyond demonstrable and definite fact"—i.e., to become a "romancer" (180). Hawthorne's genealogist, Benjamin Murphy insightfully shows, is always "a mixed breed." Romance and taxonomic science are thus not inimical, despite the latter's tendency to disavow its reliance on the former. Murphy draws a parallel between *The Marble Faun* and Foucault's account of the modern mutation of race wars in *Society Must Be Defended*: "Hawthorne's relation of Donatello's family origins echoes, at points, Foucault's account of the mythic race war discourse that generated histories and counter-histories favorable to the discourse's speaker. In the modern era, this discourse has transmuted to depict a society at war against itself, at war with its own sub-race(s). Foucault's point is that a biopolitics of life can countenance death only when a 'caesura' splits the human from a defining other—from its 'brute life,' in Hawthorne's terms, or 'bare life,' in Agamben's. The discourse of the Nondescript insists that such a labor of distinction—what Agamben calls the 'anthropological machine'—is always open-ended; taxonomizing the human and sub-human has as much if not more to do with Romance than with the ostensibly empirical strictures of realism" ("'Betwixt Human and Brute Life'").
14. Foucault, *Society Must Be Defended,* 61–62.
15. James, *Hawthorne,* 131, 134.

16. Pétillon, postface, 65.
17. James, *Hawthorne,* 132; emphasis added.
18. James, 134.
19. James, 134.
20. Without lingering on the phallic dimension of Donatello's pointed ears, we will recall that the term *point* comes from the Latin *pungere,* "to pierce or prick." In response to his shyness, Miriam teases Donatello: "'your tender point—your two tender points, if you have them—shall be safe, so far as I am concerned'" (12–13). This rejoinder can be understood as a refusal of his attempt to seduce her or, more generously, as the acceptance of Donatello's generic and gender ambiguity. On this, Emily Miller Budick writes: "The question that emerges is not only, is the faun with his ears and tail fully human, but is he fully male? Does the erect penis, perhaps, come to replace the tail as the defining feature in the evolution from male faun to human male?" ("Perplexity, Sympathy, and the Question of the Human," 242).
21. Brooks, *Bodies in Dissent,* 8. On Donatello's racial ambiguity, see Bentley, "Slaves and Fauns"; Cheyfitz, "Irresistibleness of Great Literature"; Kemp, "*Marble Faun* and American Postcolonial Ambivalence"; and Riss, "Art of Discrimination."
22. Gould, *Mismeasure of Man,* 118.
23. On gender in nineteenth-century racial science, particularly in relation to Baartman, see Wiegman, *American Anatomies,* 58–59; Rusert, *Fugitive Science,* 181–84; Fausto-Sterling, "Gender, Race, and Nation"; and Berry, *Price for Their Pound of Flesh,* 72–73.
24. Foucault, *Security, Territory, Population,* 293.
25. Jennifer Mason notes that Hawthorne "may have considered satirizing Cuvier in his fiction as early as 1842. A notebook entry for June 1 of that year records the following idea for a story: 'A young man finds a portion of the skeleton of a Mammoth; he begins by degrees to become interested in completing it; searches round the world for the means of doing so; spends youth and manhood in this pursuit; and in old age has nothing to show for his life, but this skeleton.' One of Cuvier's great claims to fame was his naming and study of the mastodon, as Hawthorne himself notes in the article 'Extinct Animals' of the Boston magazine *American*

Magazine of Useful and Entertaining Knowledge, for which he served as an editor in 1836" (*Civilized Creatures,* 200n75).

26. Budick, "Perplexity, Sympathy, and the Question of the Human," 243.
27. Hawthorne, *House of the Seven Gables,* in *Collected Novels,* 351; emphasis added.
28. Gustave Flaubert and Jules Barbey d'Aurevilly also appeal to Cuvier's unique powers of reconstitution in their novels *Salammbô* (1862) and *Le Chevalier des Touches* (1864), respectively.
29. Balzac, *Wild Ass's Skin,* 40–41; emphasis added.
30. Rancière, *Dissensus,* 163.
31. Ginzburg, "Clues: Roots of an Evidential Paradigm," in *Clues, Myths, and the Historical Method.*
32. Quoted in Ginzburg, *Clues, Myths, and the Historical Method,* 117; emphasis added.
33. "The hunter would have been the first 'to tell a story,'" Ginzburg claims, "because he alone was able to read, in the silent, nearly imperceptible tracks left by his prey, a coherent sequence of events" (103). On the novelistic dimension of Cuvier's method, see L. R. Brown, *Emerson Museum,* 126.
34. In a public lecture held in Paris in 1798, Cuvier explains that "the number, direction, and shape of the bones that compose each part of an animal's body are always in a necessary relation to all the other parts, in such a way that—up to a point—one can infer the whole from any one of them, and vice versa" (quoted in Rudwick, *Georges Cuvier, Fossil Bones, and Geological Catastrophes,* 36). Although Cuvier recognizes a limit to anatomy's powers of inference ("up to a point"), he attributes it to the imperfection of the fossil record, not of his system.
35. Ginzburg, *Clues, Myths, and the Historical Method,* 124.
36. Ginzburg, 125.
37. Ginzburg, 188. On the paradoxical "opposition" between anatomy and the diagnostic technique, see Foucault, *Order of Things,* 294; and Cohen, *La Méthode de Zadig,* 115–26. In the eulogy he delivered upon Lamarck's death, Cuvier cruelly praised his rival for the "fanciful conceptions" with which he mingled his scientific discoveries, saying that Lamarck was too prone to indulge in "what is conjectural or doubtful." Lamarck,

he deplored, belonged to a species of scientists who "laboriously constructed vast edifices on imaginary foundations, resembling the enchanted palaces of our old romances [*nos vieux romans*]." Cuvier thought that Lamarck's theory of life rested on arbitrary assumptions: "A system established on such foundations may amuse the imagination of a poet; a metaphysician may derive from it an entirely new series of systems; but it cannot for a moment bear the examination of any one who has dissected a hand, a viscus, or even a feather" ("Elegy of Lamarck").

38. Brown, *Emerson Museum.*

39. This quotation is excerpted from Cuvier's "Elegy of Lamarck." The first paragraph of Cuvier's *Lectures on Comparative Anatomy* (1802) is revealing: "The idea of Life is one of those general and obscure ideas produced in us by observing a certain series of phaenomena possessing mutual relations, and succeeding each other in a constant order. We know not indeed the nature of the link that unites these phaenomena, but we are sensible that a connexion must exist; and this conviction is sufficient to induce us to give it a name, which the vulgar are apt to regard as the sign of a particular principle, though in fact that name can only indicate the totality of the phaenomena which have occasioned its formation" (1). On the seismic transformation of the natural sciences after the invention of life, see Foucault, *Order of Things,* 287–304.

40. Foucault argues that despite his fixism, Cuvier anticipates Darwin. In contrast with classical taxonomy, in which individual variations are not worthy of a scientist's attention, Cuvier argues that the species is no longer the "minimal element" of scientific knowledge (Foucault, "Cuvier's Position in the History of Biology," 211). But if the individual is seen as carrying in itself all its specific determinations (and thus in theory contains within itself the entire history of its species)—if it acquires a reality hitherto denied by classical science—it now runs the risk of being mechanically abolished as individual in an "anatomo-physiological" structure that binds the infra-individual (the organ, the molecule) to the supra-individual (the species, genus, order . . .): "The individual in its real existence, in its life, is nothing other than the totality of both taxonomic and anatomo-physiological structures, and

this totality is also present in some way in the individual, within a given milieu" (214).

41. Foucault, *Order of Things*, 291.
42. Rancière, *Dissensus*, 19. Already in *The Order of Things*, Foucault shows that modern grammar and biology have in common a nonrepresentational paradigm (*Order of Things*, 305).
43. Ritvo, *Platypus and the Mermaid*, 178–86.
44. Ritvo, 179.
45. Bernard Heuvelmans, the founder of cryptozoology, berates Cuvier for declaring in 1812 that there remained "little hope of discovering new species of large quadrupeds" (*On the Tracks of Unknown Animals*, 18). As his title indicates, Heuvelmans rejects Cuvier's proclamation that the hunt was over.
46. L. R. Brown, *Emerson Museum*, 102–3.
47. In his 1861 history *The Sea*, Jules Michelet conjectures that we will be able to find "whole, or even partial, skeletons of these creatures" when "the Museums of Europe shall throw open to our view the whole of their immense collections" (245). Michelet hints that the siren's disappearance is not the result of scientific demystification but of a calculated attempt to hide (and thus continue) the sirens' extermination. He imputes this intentional extinction to the human's repugnance at recognizing his own "form" in an animal and (more importantly) to the idea that sirens were evolving toward humanity: "In such horror and hate were they held in the eyes of the middle ages that their appearance was considered a prodigy, an omen that God permitted to terrify sinners. People scarcely dared to name them, and made haste to get rid of them. Even the bold sixteenth century still believed them to be men and women in shape, but Devils in reality, and not even to be touched, excepting with the harpoon. They had become very rare when miscreants made a profit of keeping and exhibiting them" (245). Michelet implies that the newly dominant scientific tradition led by the tyrannical Cuvier, "the great descriptor," was complicit with this programmed extermination (*Histoire du dix-neuvième siècle*, 79–81). We also remember that Foucault opens *The Order of Things* with the irrepressible laughter caused by a Borges story in which sirens are impossibly juxtaposed with

stray dogs in "a certain Chinese encyclopaedia." "It is not the 'fabulous' animals that are impossible" in Borges's tale, Foucault notes, "but the narrowness of the distance separating them from (and juxtaposing them to) the stray dogs." Some of the categories "do certainly involve fantastic entities—fabulous animals or sirens—but, precisely because it puts them into categories of their own, the Chinese encyclopedia localizes their powers of contagion. . . . The possibility of dangerous mixtures has been exorcized, heraldry and fable have been relegated to their own exalted peaks: no inconceivable amphibious maidens, no clawed wings, no disgusting, squamous epidermis" (xvi–xvii).

48. Cuvier precipitates the Classical Age's "old flat world of animals and plants" into "history" by accounting for the extinction of species and by "substituting anatomy for classification" (Foucault, *Order of Things,* 150), thereby laying the foundations for the theory of evolution. In that respect, his fixism seems paradoxical, but for Foucault it could "arise only against a historical background" incompatible with the general stability of classical taxonomy (301).

49. Foucault, "Cuvier's Position in the History of Biology," 210.

50. The *Lepidosiren* is also the specimen chosen by Richard Owen as the exemplary "archetype" of all vertebrates. For Owen, archetypes account for the unity of diverse life-forms without assuming (as Cuvier does) that organisms obey immutable laws of composition determined by a principle of functionality.

51. Darwin, *On the Origin of Species,* 100.

52. Carlo Ginzburg notes that "Thomas Huxley, on a lecture tour to publicize Darwin's discoveries, defined as 'Zadig's method' that procedure which combined history, archaeology, geology, physical astronomy, and paleontology: namely, the ability to forecast retrospectively" (*Clues, Myths, and the Historical Method,* 117).

53. Darwin, *Descent of Man,* 155; emphasis added.

54. Darwin, 15.

55. On the influence of anatomists on Western art, see Kuriyama, *Expressiveness of the Body,* 118. On the anatomists who inspired the Pre-Raphaelites in particular, see Hartley, *Physiognomy and the Meaning of Expression,* 80–81.

56. Darwin, *Expression of the Emotions in Man and Animals,* 183.
57. Darwin, *Descent of Man,* 17.
58. Darwin specifies that these "points not only project *inwards* towards the center of the ear, but often a little *outwards* from its plane, so as to be visible when the ear is viewed from directly in front or behind" (Darwin, 31).
59. Hawthorne, *French and Italian Notebooks,* 179.
60. Agamben, *Open,* 37.
61. Agamben, 37.
62. Foucault, *Society Must Be Defended,* 255.
63. For a succinct account of Lombroso's "criminal anthropology," its racist motivations and colonialist implications, and its twentieth-century legacies, see Gould, "The Criminal as Nature's Mistake, or the Ape in Some of Us," in *Ever Since Darwin,* 222–28.
64. Sims, *Adam's Navel,* 87.
65. In anthropometric studies, Allan Sekula shows that ears occupy a unique position as both insignificant and determinant details: "In his search for a type, Galton did not believe that anything significant was lost in underexposure. This required an unacknowledged presupposition: only the gross features of the head mattered. Ears, for example, which were highly marked as signs in other physiognomic systems, both as individuating and as typical features, were not registered at all by the composite process. (Later Galton sought to 'recapture' small differences or 'unimportant details' by means of a technique he called 'analytical photography,' which superimposed positive and negative images, thereby isolating their unshared elements)" ("Body and the Archive," 48).
66. Ginzburg, *Clues, Myths, and the Historical Method,* 123. Galton was inspired by the discovery of the British officer Sir William Herschel, who used fingerprinting to manage and control the Bengali population under his supervision. "As Galton observed retrospectively," Ginzburg notes, "there was a real need for an efficient method of identification in the British colonies, and not in India alone: natives were illiterate, quarrelsome, cunning, deceitful, and, in the eyes of a European, indistinguishable" (122). On the invention of fingerprinting, see Sengoopta, *Imprint of the Raj.*

67. Nietzsche, *Gay Science,* 109–10.

68. Agamben describes "the anthropological machine" as a dispositif that is simultaneously inclusionary and exclusionary: "Insofar as the production of man through the opposition man/animal, human/inhuman, is at stake here, the machine necessarily functions by means of an exclusion (which is also always already a capturing) and an inclusion (which is also always already an exclusion). Indeed, precisely because the human is already presupposed every time, the machine actually produces a kind of state of exception, a zone of indeterminacy in which the outside is nothing but the exclusion of an inside and the inside is in turn only the inclusion of an outside" (*Open,* 37). At issue for Agamben is the exposure of the "irony" of the self-perpetuating mechanisms that define the ontological status of the human. In fact, Agamben seems to say, it is the chase and not the arrest—the capturing and not the capture—that determines who deserves to be labeled human and what is left over. *The Open* insists on the interminability, from the point of view of anthropogenesis, of the twofold movement of capture and exclusion at work in the co-constitutive making of Man and of "the animal" but also tells us that this interminability operates according to historically differentiated modalities.

69. Mel Y. Chen perfectly sums up the way in which certain "kinds of animality are racialized not through nature's or modernity's melancholy but through another temporalized map: that of pseudo-Darwinian evolutionary discourses tied to colonialist strategy and pedagogy that superimposed phylogenetic maps onto synchronic human racial typologies, yielding simplistic promulgating equations of 'primitive' people with prehuman stages of evolution" (*Animacies,* 101–2).

70. Darwin, *On the Origin of Species,* 82.

71. In a section titled "Monsters and Fossils," Foucault explains that aberrant forms simultaneously condition and belie the concept of life as unified and continuous that we inherit from Cuvier's paleontological studies: "Just as the geological catastrophe was necessary to enable us to work back from the taxonomic table to the continuum, through a blurred, chaotic, and fragmented experience, so the proliferation of monsters *without a future* is necessary to enable us to work down again

from the continuum, through a temporal series, to the table. . . . The monster ensures in time, and for our theoretical knowledge, a continuity that, for our everyday experience, floods, volcanoes, and subsiding continents confuse in space. . . . How . . . are we to recognize that nature, starting from a primitive prototype, has never ceased to work towards the provisionally terminal form that is man? By the fact that it has abandoned on the way thousands of forms that provide us with a picture of the rudimentary model. *How many fossils are there, for man's ear, or skull, or sexual parts, like so many plaster statues, fashioned one day and dropped the next in favour of a more perfected form?*" (*Order of Things*, 170; emphasis added). "Rather than indicating the triumph of life in man," Lynne Huffer explains, "Foucault's rendering of this part-animal, part-mineral, fragmented evidence of the spatial disruption of temporal continuity returns evolutionary human parts to another space-time as other-than-human characters in a taxonomic table we cannot fully know" ("Foucault's Fossils," 82).

72. Wynter shows how, in the transition from sovereign to biopolitical power and the attendant mutation from what she calls Man1 (rational political subject) to Man2 (bioeconomic subject), colonized populations were conceptualized as "fossil Others," thus "dysselected by Evolution until proven otherwise" ("Unsettling the Coloniality of Being/Power/Truth/Freedom," 266–67). Here Wynter enables us to think together the lots of enslaved individuals declared unfit to be full humans and of indigenous populations calculatedly destined to extinction. Critics have traditionally seen in Donatello a figure of the African, but Clayton Zuba shows that the racialized tropes that Hawthorne uses to describe Donatello can also position him "as a descendant of an indigenous people colonized by settler-invaders" ("Hawthorne's Empire," 161).
73. Hawthorne, *House of the Seven Gables*, 2.
74. Agamben, *Open*, 2.
75. Agamben, 21.
76. Agamben, 3.
77. LaCapra, *History and Its Limits*, 166.
78. LaCapra, 189.
79. LaCapra, 165–67.

80. LaCapra, 170.
81. Agamben, *Open,* 80.
82. Agamben, 16.
83. Agamben, 92.
84. Agamben, 91.
85. Arsić, *Bird Relics,* 164.
86. "The 'general outline' of Cuvier's science," Arsić explains, "concerned the nature of life. What life is, Cuvier claimed, will be revealed only once we learn how to read the structure of fossils. The centrality of fossils for disclosing the secret of life lay in the fact that they never include contemporaneous living forms . . . but are instead relics of a life form now completely extinct" (164).
87. Jennifer Mason quotes this passage to establish a link between the sculptor's "fossilizing" art and Cuvier's paleontology, showing that Kenyon finally breaks the rigid mold of ideality that defines his aesthetics when he finds himself, in the Carnival, surrounded by "absurd figures" that "embody the kind of permeability between species against which Cuvier inveighed" (*Civilized Creatures,* 200).
88. Deleuze and Guattari, *Thousand Plateaus,* 47.

5. THE STOCK IMAGE

1. When a virus attacks bacteria, the latter release an enzyme that breaks down and memorizes the virus's genetic makeup to prepare for future infections. The Harvard team hacked the immunitary system of E. coli bacteria to force them to integrate into their genome a manufactured DNA sequence with the pixel values of a short movie.
2. Ledford, "Lights, Camera, CRISPR."
3. Kolata, "Living Hard Drive."
4. Kolata, "Living Hard Drive."
5. Muybridge, *Descriptive Zoopraxography,* 2.
6. "In the writings of Soviet filmmaker and theorist Sergei Eisenstein," Akira Mizuta Lippit observes, "the process of editing, or montage, is frequently likened to a genetic code in which dominant as well as recessive links are made between convergent strings of information" (*Electric Animal,* 23–24).

7. On the relationship between cinematic recording techniques and genetics, see Thurtle, *Emergence of Genetic Rationality.* Phillip Thurtle uses Deleuze's transition from the movement-image to the time-image to account for a change in biology: "the use of recording technologies [enabled] researchers [to] juxtapose data from disparate times and places, allowing them to gain a more straightforward glimpse at the workings of time itself as it informed the workings of the body." The study of genetics, he explains, used its "ability to fold different times to 'plunge' into the body and literally find a space within the cellular nucleus that acted much like these recording technologies" (13–14).
8. In the second half of the nineteenth century, Doane observes, time becomes divisible, rationalized, and thus rendered valuable by capitalist standards: "This rationalized time is a time in complicity with notions of the inevitability of a technologically induced historical progress. It is Benjamin's 'homogeneous, empty time.' It is also time's abstraction—its transformation into discrete units, its consolidation as a value, its crucial link to processes of pure differentiation and measurability. No longer a medium in which the human subject is situated (it is no longer *lived* or experienced in quite the same way), time is externalized and must be consulted. . . . Karl Marx, more thoroughly than anyone, delineated the precise way in which time, in capitalism, has become the measure of value. A commodity has value because it is the objectification of abstract human labor. . . . Qualityless, the labor can be measured only by its duration" (*Emergence of Cinematic Time,* 7).
9. On Muybridge and the "melancholy of horsepower," see Ravindranathan, *Behold an Animal,* 13–54.
10. Uexküll, *Foray into the Worlds of Animals and Humans,* 41.
11. Sebeok, *Signs,* 122.
12. When Foucault develops the concept of "milieu" in *Security, Territory, Population,* as we saw in chapter 3, he refers to Canguilhem's "The Living and Its Milieu," in which Canguilhem extols the milieu as a capital contribution to the modern understanding of life: "The notion of the milieu," he writes, "is in the process of becoming a universal and obligatory mode to capture the experience and existence of living beings" (quoted in Buchanan, *Onto-ethologies,* 7).

13. Canguilhem, *Knowledge of Life,* 103–6.
14. Canguilhem, 111–12.
15. Uexküll's introduction of the notion of subject in biology owes a debt to Kant, whose *Critique of Pure Reason* he read and discussed with Rainer Maria Rilke: "Without a living subject," he writes, "there can be neither space nor time. With this observation, biology has once and for all connected with Kant's philosophy, which biology will now utilize through the natural sciences by emphasizing the decisive role of the subject" (Uexküll, *Foray into the Worlds of Humans and Animals,* 52). Uexküll shares Kant's view that what is experienced as objective reality is conditioned by the subject's perceptual dispositions. But he expands Kant's foundational gesture by insisting on the embodied dimension of subjectivity and by focusing on the role played by sensory organs in the construction of this reality. He thus logically extends subjectivity to all living beings, where Kant had made it a human prerogative. If time and space constitute a priori forms of sensation, they are nonetheless experienced differently depending on the perceptual capacities of different bodies, human and nonhuman (the difference is operative at the level of the species but also of the individual). On Kant's influence on Uexküll, see Buchanan, *Onto-Ethologies,* 12–15; and Gens, *Jakob von Uexküll,* 15–17, 64–70. On Uexküll's "shaky" understanding of Kant's epistemology, see Geoffrey Winthrop-Young's afterword to Uexküll, *Foray into the Worlds of Humans and Animals,* 230–31.
16. Benjamin, "Work of Art in the Age of Its Technological Reproducibility," 254. For a perceptive analysis of Uexküll's use of chronophotography and his influence on Benjamin's concept of "optical unconscious," see Pollmann, "Invisible Worlds, Visible."
17. For Deleuze, cinema operates its Kantian revolution after the Second World War, when the movement-image gives way to the time-image—that is, when time emancipates itself from sensorimotor schemas, when movement is subordinated to time and no longer to a moving body. In the first volume of his study of cinema, Deleuze chooses Muybridge's galloping mare as paradigmatic of the movement-image in that movement appears "dissected" into instants, all equal to one another, "which relate to the whole of the [horse's] canter to any-point-whatever" (*Cinema 1,* 5).

These sections of time make visible "remarkable or singular points that belong to movement"—a movement inextricable from the moving bodies that produce it. Remembering that Muybridge's first apparatuses were activated by the horses themselves, there is perhaps a history of the movement-image that can itself be said to operate a Kantian revolution, one that reveals movement to be subjectively experienced.

18. Like Audubon—born Jean Rabin, then renamed Jean-Jacques Fougère Audubon before migrating to the United States—Eadweard Muybridge is a man of many avatars. Born Edward James Muggeridge, he changed his surname on several occasions, first to Muggridge, then Muygridge, before adopting the spelling by which he is now remembered. He also used the pseudonym Helios when he worked as a photographer in California and briefly changed his first name to Eduardo Santiago when he traveled to Central America. Quite appropriately, on his headstone his name is misspelled as Maybridge.
19. On Stanford and eugenics, see Thurtle, *Emergence of Genetic Rationality,* 29–72.
20. Stanford, quoted in Ott, "Iron Horses," 414.
21. Stillman, *Horse in Motion,* 16.
22. Muybridge, *Animals in Motion,* 13.
23. The zoetrope differs from the thaumatrope mentioned in the introduction precisely because, like cinema, it creates movement from still images; the thaumatrope, in contrast, blends two still images into one still image (as when the bird and the cage blended to show the bird inside the cage).
24. This new system was put in place to avoid accidents such as what happened to Sallie Gardner, a mare that Muybridge photographed on June 15, 1878, in front of a large press contingent invited by Stanford. "Rather than triggering the shutters electrically," Marta Braun writes, "'Sallie Gardner' tripped them manually by breaking strings that had been stretched across her path. Spooked by her repeated bumping into the strings as she ran, after breaking the eighth or ninth, she 'gave a wild bound in the air, breaking the saddle girth she left the ground.' The accident was caught in the negatives, soon viewed by the invited guests" (*Picturing Time,* 142).

25. Muybridge, *Descriptive Zoopraxography,* 14.
26. Rabinbach, *Human Motor,* 107.
27. Doane, *Emergence of Cinematic Time,* 60.
28. "For the velocity of the horse not being quite uniform," Marey writes, "the equidistant wires were not reached at equal intervals of time. Besides, the wire was more or less stretched before rupture took place. From these causes there was *a certain inequality in the rates of succession* which Muybridge did not succeed in satisfactorily overcoming by letting off the shutters independently of the horse's motion" (quoted in Rabinbach, *Human Motor,* 330–31n107; emphasis added). Likewise, John Ott notes that when Muybridge "could not initially synchronize the animals and the arsenal of cameras, the railroad executive [Stanford] complained that 'the horse would not keep the correct time'" ("Iron Horses," 415).
29. Crary, *Suspensions of Perception,* 140.
30. Quoted in Crary, *Suspensions of Perception,* 142. "Muybridge seems to present the semblance of a classical tabular organization," Crary elaborates, "but what is arrayed in his rows and columns has none of the immutable identities on which the intelligibility of a table depends. *The Horse in Motion* has to be understood as an uprooting of perception from any stable space-time coordinates. Muybridge's work is a significant instance of what Deleuze and Guattari described as processes of capitalist deterritorialization and decoding—infelicitous terms perhaps, but they suggest how anything with a permanent stable location in space is incapable of being inserted into a system of exchange and circulation and how anything that is part of a code (a traditional or established pattern of behavior or representation) will resist being deployed in networks of abstract relations" (143–44).
31. Quoted in Solnit, *River of Shadows,* 58.
32. Hawthorne, *The Blithedale Romance,* in *Collected Novels,* 802. "There are forces in operation," Douglass writes, "which must inevitably work the downfall of slavery. . . . Walled cities and empires have become unfashionable. The arm of commerce has borne away the gates of the strong city. . . . Oceans no longer divide, but link nations together. . . . Space is comparatively annihilated" ("What to the Slave Is the Fourth of July?," 220).

33. Adams, *Education of Henry Adams,* quoted in L. Marx, *Machine in the Garden,* 345.
34. Crary, *Suspensions of Perception,* 144.
35. Ott, "Iron Horses," 414.
36. Ott, 416.
37. M. Lawrence, "Muybridgean Motion/Materialist Film," 75.
38. Lawrence rightfully notes that it is crucial to recognize how patterns of domination are perpetuated by technological innovations, but it is equally critical to discern the qualitative thresholds that punctuate this larger history of exploitation. I see technological reproducibility as one such threshold insofar as it introduces a new stage in which animals are not merely exploited as livestock; in this period, animality itself becomes a stocking technology (as the genes in the introduction were). In *Animals as Biotechnology,* Richard Twine recognizes that breeding is an "old" animal technology, but he warns against dismissing biotechnology as a transhistorical phenomenon. In fact, he shows that the Biotechnology Innovation Organization has a vested interest in claiming that modern biotechnology at the molecular level is but the continuation of older practices like domestication. Presenting modern genetic operations as "enhancements" of older techniques makes it possible to disavow any substantial transformation in the treatment of animal life. Twine marks a stronger break when it comes to how contemporary biology assists breeding and genetic selection. He identifies the past century's transition from a breeding mostly based on animals' appearance and performance toward a modern concern for invisible genetic attributes, echoing the break identified by Foucault in *The Order of Things.*
39. M. Lawrence, "Muybridgean Motion/Materialist Film," 79.
40. M. Lawrence, 81.
41. In fact, the concept of "livingness" that Lawrence borrows from film scholar Jonathan Burt invites precisely this reading. Burt defines *livingness* as "the mode of active coexistence whereby an individual's ability to live (or die) depends on the nature of its interaction with others" ("Morbidity and Vitalism," 169). He argues that the invisibilization of killing in industrial farming and the fragmentation of the living

wrought by modern biosciences demand an analysis that is not centered on questions of death and (self-)identity—in which he finds Derrida helplessly mired—but based on a renewed "attention to life." Arguing via Deleuze that film makes livingness apparent, Burt sees in cinema the possibility to conceive living beings as co-constituted organisms rather than autonomous individuals.

42. Shukin, *Animal Capital,* 72–73.
43. In a more recent essay titled "Netted Together," Ott considers the contribution to the nascent ecological consciousness made by Muybridge, as well as what Ott sees as his animal collaborators (he lists pigeons, horses, and kangaroos as "coauthors" of *Animal Locomotion*).
44. Agre, "Surveillance and Capture," 101.
45. Agre, 121; emphasis added.
46. Agre, 110.
47. Muybridge and Marey are commonly perceived as reducing animals to mere data (see, for instance, Corkin, *Realism and the Birth of the Modern United States,* 57). But the verb *reducing* is misleading, as it suggests a simple minimization of something instead of its transformation. It would be more accurate to say these photographers made animals susceptible to capture. Johanna Drucker invites us to "reconceive all data as capta"—i.e., to adopt a constructivist approach that recognizes that knowledge is "taken, not simply given as a natural representation of pre-existing fact" ("Humanities Approaches to Graphical Display").
48. Braun, *Eadweard Muybridge,* 193.
49. On the anthropometric grid in Muybridge's work, see E. Brown, "Racialising the Virile Body."
50. Muybridge, *Animal Locomotion,* plates 537–40.
51. Finn, *Capturing the Criminal Image,* 42.
52. Lawrie, *Forging a Laboring Race,* 2–3, 6–7.
53. Lawrie, 2–3, 6–7.
54. Solnit, *River of Shadows,* 194.
55. Solnit, 194–95. Ott, likewise, situates Muybridge's grids "in the context of the growing bureaucratization of urban America" ("Netted Together," 90).

56. Marta Braun disputes the scientificity of Muybridge's grids, lamenting that they "give us no way to measure anything real." She insists that Muybridge's photographs have been "misread" as scientific and that they are instead only "fictions" (*Eadweard Muybridge,* xvi). Such strict partition between art and science is untenable, of course, and Braun's judgment endorses a dominant but limited idea of science, even if she lucidly contrasts Muybridge's unsystematic experiments with the rigorous protocols observed by Marey.
57. The idea originally came from the invention of an "astronomical revolver" by Jules Janssen, an astrophysicist director of the observatory at Meudon (Dagognet, *Etienne-Jules Marey,* 91–93). As I mentioned in the introduction, Marey's photographic gun is exemplary of the desire to capture the animal image with as little interference as possible. Marey wished to be rid of the contingency of living bodies even as he sought to understand them in action. He was looking for "the most 'immaterial,' the most self-effacing, link between the body and the recording instrument," Doane explains, hence he initially idealized photography as a medium that promised to eliminate the "corruptive effects of mediation" (*Emergence of Cinematic Time,* 48). He would ultimately be disappointed by chronophotography, however, because it is predicated on intermittency; the interval of the exposure was, for him, "lost time" (68).
58. Blum, *Picturing Nature,* 113. "In principle," Blum comments, "professional naturalists—the new 'zoologists'—described observations that others should be able to reproduce; an observation that could not be repeated had little scientific credibility" (133–14).
59. Muybridge deplored that he was not able "to have photographed many of the animals while they were enjoying more freedom of movement than that afforded by the Gardens of the Zoological Society," admitting that "the difficulties attending a satisfactory investigation under their natural conditions of life were, at the time, too great to be surmounted" (*Animals in Motion,* 67).
60. Doane, *Emergence of Cinematic Time,* 60.
61. Snyder, "Visualization and Visibility," 387.
62. Braun, *Picturing Time,* 12.

63. Burt, *Animals in Film,* 112.
64. Dagognet, *Etienne-Jules Marey,* 102.
65. Braun, *Picturing Time,* 155.
66. The influence of Muybridge's work on modern perception is often described (first by Muybridge himself) in terms of the correction of human senses, which are thus retroactively conceived as innately defective, or at least limited. On the one hand, envisioning technology as a prosthetic compensation for our perceptual limitations compels us to draw new frontiers beyond which lies a nonhuman "real" that is (as yet) unapproachable. On the other hand, the enhanced perception promised by Muybridge's stop-motion apparatuses presents this infravisible real as infinitely atomizable and susceptible to manipulation.
67. Krauss, *Grids,* 50.
68. Krauss, 52.
69. Lippit, *Electric Animal,* 185.
70. To be fair, Muybridge did complain about having to work with domesticated or zoo animals with limited "freedom of movement" (*Animals in Motion,* 67). In that sense, he was aware that his experiments were contingent on the profound "marginalization" of animals described by Berger.
71. The phrase is Burt's (*Animals in Film,* 43).
72. Bousé, *Wildlife Films,* 42.
73. The animal, for Shukin, is the repressed substrate or "stock" of industrial capitalism (*Animal Capital,* 45). Gelatin is a perfect example of animal rendering, in the double sense of contributing materially to the carnal and semiotic powering of capitalism while at the same time disappearing—being reproduced in order to disappear—at an unprecedented scale and speed. Gelatin, interestingly, is the forgotten analogy used by Marx to designate the abstraction of human labor; Keston Sutherland shows that the two most influential translations of *Das Kapital* mistranslate the term *Gallerte* into "congelation," which implies that labor appears to be merely "frozen" in commodities. However, *Gallerte* "is not an abstract noun [but the name] of a specific commodity. Marx's German readers will not only have bought *Gallerte,* they will have eaten it" ("Marx in Jargon," 7). Sutherland claims that Marx intended

to disgust his readers by reminding them that what they consumed was a quivering substance made of undifferentiated animal remains. This figure created an innuendo of cannibalism, for workers, too, became an undifferentiated mass. *Gallerte,* for Sutherland, "is the paradigmatic commodity" because it does not just index the occultation of production but also shows that the process of occultation is inherently disgusting and irreversible (9). When we combine Marx's use of the term with Shukin's analysis of the transformation of livestock into film stock, we see how enriched a reading of Marx is when it is attuned to the (animal) material that constitutes capital's technological and ideological mechanisms. If we take seriously Sutherland's foray into Marxist lexicon, however, we must not make animals mere stand-ins for the figure of the worker; workers might just as well stand in for the figure of the animal, for their lot criticizes the process by which animals come to us as commodities.

74. This insight is already true of capital, as Marx observes that the "conditions of production are at the same time the conditions of reproduction" (*Capital,* 711).
75. Shukin, *Animal Capital,* 20.
76. Shukin, 20, 51.
77. Shukin, 7.
78. Lippit, *Electric Animal,* 195.
79. Lippit, 196.
80. Shukin, *Animal Capital,* 41.
81. Shukin, 52–59.
82. Menely, *Animal Claim,* 215n41.
83. On the selection of reproducible animals, the attendant dysselection of feral or "wandering" animals, and their consequences for indigenous farmers, see Anderson, *Creatures of Empire.*
84. On the mechanisms put in place to justify and perpetuate the killing of animals on an industrial scale, see Vialles, *Animal to Edible.* Mass slaughter, Vialles explains, involves not only a major overhaul of slaughter techniques (sanitization and standardization of the handling and slaughter of animals and hyperfragmentation of unskilled tasks so that it becomes virtually impossible to identify the person responsible for

the killing) but also a profound reconceptualization of the slaughtered animals, turning them from feeling beings into unfeeling objects. This is accomplished, in part, on a semantic level; death is euphemized and the animals are anonymized. Interestingly for us, Vialles turns to hunting to elucidate the symbolic and material transformations undergone by animals in her discussion of the "trap" (*piège* in French, "stunning pen" in English), a mechanism that she sees as paradigmatic of a new type of human/animal relation that obtains in modern abattoirs. She frames this transformation as a shift from cynegetics (the art of hunting) to ceptology (the logic of capture) (111–21).

85. On the biopolitics of conservation, see Braverman, *Wild Life,* 226–32.
86. C. Wolfe, *Before the Law,* 53–54.
87. Writes Muybridge: "It is impressed on our minds in infancy that a certain arbitrary symbol indicates an existing fact; if this same association of emblem and reality is reiterated at the preparatory school, insisted upon at college, and pronounced correct at the university; symbol and fact—or supposed fact—becomes [*sic*] so intimately blended that it is extremely difficult to disassociate them, even when reason and personal observation teaches [*sic*] us they have no true relationship. So it is with the conventional galloping horse; . . . we think the representation to be unimpeachable, until we throw all our preconceived impressions on one side, and seek the truth by independent observations from Nature herself" (*Animals in Motion,* 57).
88. On the converging political, economic, and technological circumstances that brought about the near-extinction of the bison in 1860s and 1870s, see Solnit's section "The Transubstantiation of the Bison" (*River of Shadows,* 62–66). Solnit highlights the perverse circularity with which bison hides were used for the belts operating the trains that contributed to the bison's disappearance: they were shot for sport from the trains, and the same trains brought them to the Chicago slaughterhouses. *Transubstantiation* ultimately refers to the conversion of an overexploited nature into myth and imagery.
89. Brower, *Developing Animals,* xvii. Focusing on the "historical moment when photographic technology allowed photographing animals in nature to become a practice," Brower contends that wildlife photography

must be understood as altering the epistemic conditions in which animals are seen and, consequently, their very "conception" (xvii). Brower sees wildlife photography and its attendant rhetoric and technologies as a paradoxically artificial means of positing and "naturalizing" an unbridgeable divide between humans and animals (nostalgically construed as metonyms of a nature untouched by society).

90. Kittler, *Gramophone, Film, Typewriter,* 5. On the affinities between death and photography, see Barthes, *Camera Lucida.*
91. The association of cinema with the stilling of life is but one—of three, according to Raymond Bellour—of the origin stories of cinema, to which Muybridge and Marey's names are commonly attached. The singularity of cinema, according to this narrative, "is the principle of invisibility internal to the machines that capture life by producing its death, according to the interruption of movement upon which photography is premised" (*Le Corps du cinéma,* 40; my translation). In his work on cinema, Deleuze forcefully contests this association of cinema with death.
92. Crary, *Suspensions of Perception,* 144.
93. Agamben, "Notes on Gesture," 55.
94. Agamben, 58.
95. Benjamin, quoted in Pollmann, "Invisible Worlds, Visible," 808.
96. Crary draws a parallel between the technologization of the observer and that of the worker in the nineteenth century. The worker becomes a tool among others in the factory, and man assumes a relation of contiguity to the machine—a relation that before had been merely metaphorical. Similarly, the observer is no longer the source or ideal standard for vision, as had been the case in the seventeenth and eighteenth centuries, but a technology among others (*Techniques of the Observer,* 129).
97. Crary, *Suspensions of Perception,* 140.
98. Benjamin, "Work of Art in the Age of Its Technological Reproducibility," 265.
99. Benjamin, 265; emphasis added.
100. Uexküll, *Foray into the Worlds of Animals and Humans,* 63.
101. Pollmann, "Invisible Worlds, Visible," 790.
102. "Time, which frames all events, seemed to us to be the only objectively consistent factor, compared to the variegated changes of its contents,

but now we see that the subject controls the time of its environment. . . . 'Without a living subject, there can be no time'" (Uexküll, *Foray into the Worlds of Animals and Humans,* 52).

103. Uexküll, 72.
104. Uexküll, 70–71.
105. Pollmann, "Invisible Worlds, Visible," 803.
106. On Spinoza's ethics as ethology, see Deleuze, *Spinoza.* "Ethology," writes Deleuze, "is first of all the study of the relations of speed and slowness, of the capacities for affecting and being affected that characterize each thing. For each thing these relations and capacities have an amplitude, thresholds (maximum and minimum), and variations or transformations that are peculiar to them" (125).
107. *Nietzsches Werkes,* quoted in Kofman, *Nietzsche and Metaphor,* 72. Nietzsche praises Spinoza's philosophy for challenging the system of abstract causality that organizes Cartesian thought. Playing on the phonetic similarity between Spinoza and *Spinne*—"spider," in German, the animal that *spins* webs by producing a viscous thread from its spinneret glands—Nietzsche compares the architecture of Spinoza's philosophy to a spider web. "Spinoza's geometrical order," Sarah Kofman sums up, "is in the last resort an arachnidan one" (69).
108. Uexküll, *Foray into the Worlds of Animals and Humans,* 53.
109. Uexküll, *Theory of Meaning,* in *Foray into the Worlds of Animals and Humans,* 158–59.
110. Uexküll, 191; trans. modified.
111. Deleuze and Guattari, *What Is Philosophy?,* 185.
112. Uexküll, *Theory of Meaning,* 193.
113. Merleau-Ponty, *Nature,* 183.
114. Doane, *Emergence of Cinematic Time,* 218.
115. Deleuze, *Spinoza,* 125.
116. Deleuze and Guattari, *Thousand Plateaus,* 275.
117. Kafka, "Report to an Academy," 253. Kari Weil fascinatingly connects Kafka's insistence that Red Peter's forced "evolution" into humanhood is nothing but a "way out [*Ausweg*]" with Foucault's reminder that, for Kant, the Enlightenment is just that: a "way out [*Ausgang*]" thanks to which "humans will escape their former subjection to despotic rule or

irrational authority and find their rightful status as autonomous subjects" (*Thinking Animals,* 13).

118. Doane, *Emergence of Cinematic Time,* 70.

CONCLUSION

1. In *Hope Is the Thing with Feathers,* Christopher Cokinos notes that the last wild passenger pigeon was sighted in 1900 by a young boy from Ohio, who killed it with a shotgun (228–57). Of course, it is impossible to know with certainty whether the boy's victim (posthumously nicknamed "Buttons" because the amateur taxidermist who mounted it used shoe buttons instead of glass eyes) truly was the last wild passenger pigeon. Joel Greenberg has recently found evidence that a wild pigeon was sighted—and again, killed—in 1902 by a young boy in Indiana (*Feathered River across the Sky,* 166–77).
2. Audubon, *Ornithological Biography,* 268.
3. Cooper, *The Pioneers,* in *Leatherstocking Tales,* 1:251. Cooper explicitly links the organized massacre of the passenger pigeon to the programmed decimation of indigenous populations and, more broadly, to irreversible transformations of the land by new transportation and communication technologies. Historians have shown that the convergence of several technological innovations contributed to the pigeon's erasure: the telegraph informed professional "pigeoners" when and where to expect the flocks; trains transported the pigeoners to these locations; refrigerated cars made it possible to conserve the meat and feed the more and more populous cities. But these increasingly automated ways to trap, harvest, and stock large quantities of pigeons only sped up the extinction process that had already become inevitable since the settlers began clearing the forests and transforming them into farmland. William Cronon provocatively ties the extinction of certain species to the overproduction of others in his analysis of the "new livestock economy" developed in the Chicago stockyards (via the shift from open range to feedlot and enclosure, the incursion of the railroad and the concomitant increase in access to previously nearly closed areas, and the systematic destruction of nonscalable habitats) (*Nature's Metropolis,* 207–59).
4. Braverman, *Wild Life,* 158.

5. The Lacey Act, the first federal law to criminalize poaching and restrict interstate transportation of game, was signed into law by President William McKinley in 1900. When Congressman John F. Lacey introduced the bill on the floor, he mournfully hinted at the passenger pigeon's fate: "It is late. It is too late as to the wild pigeon. The buffalo is almost a thing of the past, but there still remains much to preserve, and we must act earnestly if we would accomplish such things." The passenger pigeon's extinction, however, cannot be simply excused as ignorance. Beside Bumppo's exhortation to kill with discernment and restraint in *The Pioneers* ("Use, but don't waste"; Cooper, *The Pioneers,* in *Leatherstocking Tales,* 1:250), there had been numerous warnings about the consequences of overhunting pigeons. In 1847, after witnessing the massacre of a pigeon roost, the French writer Benedict Revoil predicted that the amateur ornithologist of the next century would "find no more wild pigeons, except those in the Museums of Natural History"; in 1869, Henry Bergh—the same Bergh of the Society for the Prevention of Cruelty to Animals referenced in Kilburn's ad for the gun camera—was campaigning against the wasteful carnage of pigeon-shooting matches; in his 1895 essay on "The Wild Pigeon of North America," Chief Simon Pokagon of the Potawatomi tribe remembers rebuking white hunters for the brutal techniques they had invented for harvesting ever-larger quantities of birds (see Greenberg, *Feathered River across the Sky,* 210, 116–17).
6. The last pair of pigeons were named after the first First Couple, George and Martha Washington.
7. Shufeldt, "Published Figures and Plates of the Extinct Passenger Pigeon," 465. "As a story filled with romance, prodigality, cruelty and short-sightedness," Shufeldt writes of the passenger pigeon's journey toward extinction, "it outranks the most unbelievable fables. . . . We can now only regretfully look back on the picture and systematize the data at hand" (458).
8. Haraway, "Teddy Bear Patriarchy," 42.
9. Braverman, *Wild Life,* 81.
10. Twine, *Animals as Biotechnology,* 153; and C. Wolfe, *Before the Law,* 15.
11. Dickinson, "I Held It So Tight That I Lost It," 1659. The youth of the

poem's subject denotes less innocence than male recklessness, as the manuscript shows that Dickinson hesitated between "Child" and "Boy," and Sharon Cameron teaches us not to choose between Dickinson's variants (*Choosing Not Choosing,* 63). In appearance grammatically secure, the subject becomes strangely tied to its object when we read the preposition "of" not as expressing intent ("said the child *about* the butterfly") but indicating filiation ("the butterfly's child"). If the butterfly engenders its captor, its disappearance at the child's hands in turn threatens the child's very existence.

12. Uexküll, *Foray into the Worlds of Animals and Humans,* 69–70.

BIBLIOGRAPHY

Adams, Carol J. *The Sexual Politics of Meat: A Feminist-Vegetarian Critical Theory.* London: Continuum, 2010.

Agamben, Giorgio. *Homo Sacer: Sovereign Power and Bare Life.* Translated by Daniel Heller-Roazen. Stanford, Calif.: Stanford University Press, 1998.

Agamben, Giorgio. "Notes on Gesture." In *Means without End: Notes on Politics,* 49–62. Minneapolis: University of Minnesota Press, 2000.

Agamben, Giorgio. *The Open: Man and Animal.* Translated by Kevin Attell. Stanford, Calif.: Stanford University Press, 2003.

Agamben, Giorgio. *"What Is an Apparatus?" and Other Essays.* Translated by David Kishik and Stephan Pedatella. Stanford, Calif.: Stanford University Press, 2009.

Agre, Philip. "Surveillance and Capture: Two Models of Privacy." *Information Society* 10, no. 2 (1994): 101–27.

Alexander, Michelle. *The New Jim Crow: Mass Incarceration in the Age of Colorblindness.* New York: New Press, 2010.

Allewaert, Monique. *Ariel's Ecology: Plantations, Personhood, and Colonialism in the American Tropics.* Minneapolis: University of Minnesota Press, 2013.

Altschuler, Sari. *The Medical Imagination: Literature and Health in the Early United States.* Philadelphia: University of Pennsylvania Press, 2018.

Anderson, Virginia DeJohn. *Creatures of Empire: How Domestic Animals Transformed Early America.* Oxford: Oxford University Press, 2004.

Apess, William. "Son of the Forest." In *On Our Own Ground: The Complete Writings of William Apess, a Pequot,* edited by Barry O'Connell, 1–98. Amherst: University of Massachusetts Press, 1992.

Armstrong, Nancy, and Leonard Tennenhouse. *Novels in the Time of Democratic Writing: The American Example.* Philadelphia: University of Pennsylvania Press, 2018.

Armstrong, Philip. "'Leviathan Is a Skein of Networks': Translations of Nature and Culture in *Moby-Dick.*" *ELH* 71, no. 4 (Winter 2004): 1039–63.

Arnheim, Rudolf. *New Essays on the Psychology of Art.* Berkeley: University of California Press, 1986.

Arsić, Branka. *Bird Relics: Grief and Vitalism in Thoreau.* Cambridge, Mass.: Harvard University Press, 2016.

Audubon, John James. *Ornithological Biography; or, An Account of the Habits of the Birds of the United States of America.* Edinburgh: A. & C. Black, 1831.

Audubon, John James. *Writings and Drawings.* New York: Library of America, 1999.

Bailly, Jean-Christophe. *Le visible est le caché.* Illustrated by Gilles Aillaud. Paris: Gallimard—Musée de la Chasse et de la Nature, 2009.

Baker, Steve. *The Postmodern Animal.* London: Reaktion Books, 2000.

Balzac, Honoré de. *The Wild Ass's Skin.* Translated by Herbert J. Hunt. London: Penguin Classics, 1977.

Baratay, Eric, and Elisabeth Hardouin-Fugier. *Zoos : Histoire Des Jardins Zoologiques En Occident (XVIe-XXe Siècle).* Paris: La Découverte, 1998.

Barnard, John Levi. "The Cod and the Whale: Melville in the Time of Extinction." *American Literature* 89, no. 4 (2017): 851–79.

Barrett, Lindon. "Presence of Mind: Detection and Racialization in 'The Murders in the Rue Morgue.'" In *Romancing the Shadow: Poe and Race,* edited by J. Gerald Kennedy and Liliane Weissberg, 157–76. Oxford: Oxford University Press, 2001.

Barthes, Roland. *Camera Lucida: Reflections on Photography.* Translated by Richard Howard. New York: Hill and Wang, 1982.

Bates, Ralph S. *Scientific Societies in the United States.* New York: Technological Press, 1945.

Bellour, Raymond. *Le Corps du cinéma: Hypnoses, émotions, animalités.* Paris: P.O.L., 2009.

Bender, Bert. *The Descent of Love: Darwin and the Theory of Sexual Selection in American Fiction, 1871–1926.* Philadelphia: University of Pennsylvania Press, 1996.

Benefey, Christopher. *Poe and the Unreadable: "The Black Cat" and "The Tell-Tale Heart."* Cambridge: Cambridge University Press, 1993.

Benjamin, Walter. *The Arcades Project.* Translated by Howard Eiland and Kevin McLaughlin. Cambridge, Mass.: Harvard University Press, 1999.

Benjamin, Walter. *Berlin Childhood around 1900.* Translated by Howard Eiland. Cambridge, Mass.: Harvard University Press, 2006.

Benjamin, Walter. "On the Mimetic Faculty." In *Selected Writings,* vol. 2, edited by Howard Eiland, Michael W. Jennings, and Gary Smith, 720–22. Cambridge, Mass.: Harvard University Press, 2003.

Benjamin, Walter. "Paralipomena to 'On the Concept of History.'" In *Selected Writings,* vol. 4, edited by Howard Eiland and Michael W. Jennings, 401–11. Cambridge, Mass.: Harvard University Press, 2003.

Benjamin, Walter. "The Paris of the Second Empire in Baudelaire." In *Selected Writings,* vol. 4, edited by Marcus Bullock and Michael W. Jennings, 3–92. Cambridge, Mass.: Harvard University Press, 2003.

Benjamin, Walter. "The Work of Art in the Age of Its Technological Reproducibility (Third Edition)." In *Selected Writings,* vol. 4, edited by Howard Eiland and Michael W. Jennings, 251–83. Cambridge, Mass.: Harvard University Press, 2003.

Bentham, Jeremy. *Introduction to the Principles of Morals and Legislation.* 1789. Reprint, Oxford: Clarendon Press, 1823.

Bentley, Nancy. "Slaves and Fauns: Hawthorne and the Uses of Primitivism." *ELH* 57, no. 4 (1990): 901–37.

Berger, John. *About Looking.* New York: Pantheon Books, 1980.

Berry, Daina Ramey. *The Price for Their Pound of Flesh: The Value of the Enslaved, from Womb to Grave, in the Building of a Nation.* Boston: Beacon Press, 2017.

Best, Stephen. *The Fugitive's Properties: Law and the Poetics of Possession.* Chicago: University of Chicago Press, 2004.

Birnbaum, Daniel, and Anders Olsson. "An Interview with Jacques Derrida on the Limits of Digestion." Translated by Brian Manning Delaney. *e-flux journal* 2 (2009): https://www.e-flux.com/journal/02/68495/an-interview-with-jacques-derrida-on-the-limits-of-digestion/.

Blanchard, Pascal, Nicolas Bancel, Eric Deroo, and Sandrine Lemaire, eds. *Human Zoos: Science and Spectacle in the Age of Colonial Empires.* Liverpool: Liverpool University Press, 2009.

Blum, Ann Shelby. *Picturing Nature: American Nineteenth-Century Zoological Illustration.* Princeton, N.J.: Princeton University Press, 1993.

Boggs, Colleen Glenney. *Animalia Americana: Animal Representations and Biopolitical Subjectivity.* New York: Columbia University Press, 2013.

Boisseron, Bénédicte. *Afro-Dog: Blackness and the Animal Question.* New York: Columbia University Press, 2018.

Bonaparte, Marie. *The Life and Works of Edgar Allan Poe: A Psycho-analytic Interpretation.* Translated by John Rodker. London: Imago Publishing, 1949.

Bousé, Derek. *Wildlife Films.* Philadelphia: University of Pennsylvania Press, 2000.

Braun, Marta. *Eadweard Muybridge.* London: Reaktion Books, 2010.

Braun, Marta. *Picturing Time: The Works of Étienne-Jules Marey.* Chicago: University of Chicago Press, 1992.

Braverman, Irus. *Wild Life: The Institution of Nature.* Stanford, Calif.: Stanford University Press, 2015.

Broglio, Ron. *Beasts of Burden: Biopolitics, Labor, and Animal Life in British Romanticism.* Albany: State University of New York Press, 2017.

Brooks, Daphne A. *Bodies in Dissent: Spectacular Performances of Race and Freedom, 1850–1910.* Durham, N.C.: Duke University Press, 2006.

Brower, Matthew. *Developing Animals: Wildlife and Early American Photography.* Minneapolis: University of Minnesota Press, 2011.

Brown, Elspeth H. "Racialising the Virile Body: Eadweard Muybridge's Locomotion Studies 1883–1887." *Gender & History* 17, no. 3 (November 2005): 627–56.

Brown, Lee Rust. *The Emerson Museum: Practical Romanticism and the Pursuit of the Whole.* Cambridge, Mass.: Harvard University Press, 1997.

Browne, Simone. *Dark Matters: On the Surveillance of Blackness.* Durham, N.C.: Duke University Press, 2015.

Bryden, Henry Anderson. *Gun and Camera in Southern Africa; A Year of Wanderings in Bechuanaland, the Kalahari Desert, and the Lake River Country,*

Ngamiland with Notes on Colonisation, Natives, Natural History, and Sport. London: Edward Stanford, 1893.

Buchanan, Brett. *Onto-ethologies: The Animal Environments of Uexküll, Heidegger, Merleau-Ponty, and Deleuze.* Albany: State University of New York Press, 2008.

Budick, Emily Miller. "The American Historical Romance: From James Fenimore Cooper and Nathaniel Hawthorne to Toni Morrison, Louise Erdrich, and E. L. Doctorow." In *A Companion to the American Novel,* edited by Alfred Bendixen, 147–69. Blackwell Companions to Literature and Culture. Malden, Mass.: Wiley Blackwell, 2012.

Budick, Emily Miller. "Perplexity, Sympathy, and the Question of the Human: A Reading of *The Marble Faun.*" In *The Cambridge Companion to Nathaniel Hawthorne,* edited by Richard Millington, 230–50. Cambridge: Cambridge University Press, 2004.

Buffon, Georges, Louis Leclerc, and James Smith Barr. *Buffon's Natural History: Containing a Theory of the Earth, a General History of Man, of the Brute Creation, and of Vegetables, Minerals, &c. &c.* London: Printed for the Proprietor, and sold by H. D. Symonds, 1797.

Burgat, Florence. *Une autre existence: La condition animale.* Paris: Éditions Albin Michel, 2012.

Burt, Jonathan. *Animals in Film.* London: Reaktion Books, 2002.

Burt, Jonathan. "Morbidity and Vitalism: Derrida, Bergson, Deleuze, and Animal Film Imagery." *Configurations* 14, no. 1 (2006): 157–79.

Byrd, Jodi A. *The Transit of Empire: Indigenous Critiques of Colonialism.* Minneapolis: University of Minnesota Press, 2011.

Calarco, Matthew. *Zoographies: The Question of the Animal from Heidegger to Derrida.* New York: Columbia University Press, 2008.

Cameron, Sharon. *Choosing Not Choosing: Dickinson's Fascicles.* Chicago: University of Chicago Press, 1993.

Canetti, Elias. *Crowds and Power.* London: Continuum, 1978.

Canguilhem, Georges. *Knowledge of Life.* Translated by Stefanos Geroulanos and Daniela Ginsburg. New York: Fordham University Press, 2008.

Cartmill, Matt. *A View to a Death in the Morning: Hunting and Nature through History.* Cambridge, Mass.: Harvard University Press, 1993.

Casarino, Cesare. *Modernity at Sea: Melville, Marx, Conrad in Crisis.* Minneapolis: University of Minnesota Press, 2002.

Castronovo, Russ. "James Fenimore Cooper and the NSA: Security, Property, Liberalism." *American Literary History* 28, no. 4 (2016): 677–701.

Cavell, Stanley. "Being Odd, Getting Even (Descartes, Emerson, Poe)." In *The American Face of Edgar Allan Poe,* edited by Shawn Rosenheim and Stephen Rachman, 3–36. Baltimore: Johns Hopkins University Press, 1995.

Chamayou, Grégoire. *Manhunts: A Philosophical History.* Translated by Steven Rendall. Princeton, N.J.: Princeton University Press, 2012.

Chase, Richard. *The American Novel and Its Tradition.* Baltimore: Johns Hopkins University Press, 1980.

Chen, Mel Y. *Animacies: Biopolitics, Racial Mattering, and Queer Affect.* Durham, N.C.: Duke University Press, 2012.

Chevalier, Charles. *Guide du photographe.* Paris: Palais-Royal, 1854.

Cheyfitz, Eric. "The Irresistibleness of Great Literature: Reconstructing Hawthorne's Politics." *American Literary History* 6, no. 3 (1994): 539–58.

Cheyfitz, Eric. *The Poetics of Imperialism: Translation and Colonization from "The Tempest" to "Tarzan."* New York: Oxford University Press, 1991.

Cheyfitz, Eric. "Savage Law: The Plot against American Indians in *Johnson and Graham's Lessee v. M'Intosh* and *The Pioneers.*" In *The Cultures of United States Imperialism,* edited by Donald Pease and Amy Kaplan, 109–28. Durham, N.C.: Duke University Press, 1993.

Chomel, Noël. *Dictionnaire oeconomique contenant divers moyens d'augmenter son bien, et de conserver sa santé. . . .* Paris: Chez L. Bruyset, 1718.

Chow, Rey. *Entanglements, or Transmedial Thinking about Capture.* Durham, N.C.: Duke University Press, 2012.

Chun, Wendy Hui Kyong. "Race and/as Technology; or, How to Do Things to Race." *Camera Obscura* 24, no. 1 (2009): 7–35.

Cioc, Mark. *The Game of Conservation: International Treaties to Protect Migratory Animals.* Athens: Ohio University Press, 2009.

Coetzee, J. M. *Elizabeth Costello.* New York: Viking, 2003.

Cohen, Claudine. *La Méthode de Zadig: La trace, le fossile, la preuve.* Paris: Seuil, 2011.

Cokinos, Christopher. *Hope Is the Thing with Feathers.* New York: Penguin, 2000.

Cooper, James Fenimore. *The Leatherstocking Tales.* 2 vols. New York: Library of America, 1985.

Cooper, James Fenimore. *The Prairie: A Tale.* Introduction by Blake Nevius. New York: Penguin Classics, 1987.

Corkin, Stanley. *Realism and the Birth of the Modern United States: Literature, Cinema, and Culture.* Athens: University of Georgia Press, 1996.

Coulthard, Glen Sean. *Red Skin, White Masks: Rejecting the Colonial Politics of Recognition.* Minneapolis: University of Minnesota Press, 2014.

Crary, Jonathan. *Suspensions of Perception: Attention, Spectacle, and Modern Culture.* Cambridge, Mass.: MIT Press, 1999.

Crary, Jonathan. *Techniques of the Observer: On Vision and Modernity in the Nineteenth Century.* Cambridge, Mass.: MIT Press, 1990.

Cronon, William. *Nature's Metropolis: Chicago and the Great West.* New York: W. W. Norton, 1991.

Cuvier, Georges. "Elegy of Lamarck." *Edinburgh New Philosophical Journal* 20 (1836): 1–22, http://www.victorianweb.org/science/science_texts/cuvier/cuvier_on_lamarck.htm.

Cuvier, Georges. *Le règne animal distribué d'après son organisation pour servir de base à l'histoire naturelle des animaux et d'introduction à l'anatomie comparée.* Vol 1. 3rd ed. Brussels: Louis Hauman, 1836.

Cuvier, Georges. *On the Origins of Sensation.* Vol. 2, *Lectures on Comparative Anatomy.* Translated by William Ross. London: Oriental Press, 1802.

Cuvier, Georges, F.-É Guérin-Méneville, and Auguste Henri André Duméril. *Recherches anatomiques sur les reptiles regardés encore comme douteux par les naturalistes, faites à l'occasion de l'axolotl, rapporté par m. de Humbolt du Mexique.* Manuscript. 1807.

Dagognet, François. *Etienne-Jules Marey: A Passion for the Trace.* Translated by Robert Galeta. New York: Zone Books, 1992.

Daintith, Terence. *Finders Keepers? How the Law of Capture Shaped the World Oil Industry.* Washington, D.C.: RFF Press, 2010.

d'Alembert, Jean Le Rond, and Diderot, Denis. *Encyclopédie : Ou Dictionnaire Raisonné Des Sciences, Des Arts et Des Métiers.* Lausanne, Switzerland: Sociétés typographiques, 1778.

Darwin, Charles. *The Descent of Man, and Selection in Relation to Sex.* London: Penguin Classics, 2004.

Darwin, Charles. *The Expression of the Emotions in Man and Animals.* London: J. Murray, 1872.

Darwin, Charles. *On the Origin of Species by Means of Natural Selection.* Oxford: Oxford University Press, 1998.

da Silva, Denise Ferreira. "Before *Man*: Sylvia Wynter's Rewriting of the Modern Episteme." In *Sylvia Winter: On Being Human as Praxis,* edited by Katherine McKittrick, 90–105. Durham, N.C.: Duke University Press, 2015.

Daston, Lorraine, and Peter Galison. *Objectivity.* New York: Zone Books, 2010.

Davis, Angela Y. *Are Prisons Obsolete?* New York: Seven Stories Press, 2003.

Davis, Angela Y. "Race and Criminalization: Black Americans and the Punishment Industry." In *The House That Race Built: Original Essays by Toni Morrison, Angela Y. Davis, Cornel West, and Others on Black Americans and Politics in America Today,* edited by Wahneema Lubiano, 264–79. New York: Vintage, 1998.

Dayan, Colin. "Poe, Persons, and Property." In *Romancing the Shadow: Poe and Race,* edited by J. Gerald Kennedy and Liliane Weissberg, 106–26. Oxford: Oxford University Press, 2001.

Dayan, Colin. *With Dogs at the Edge of Life.* New York: Columbia University Press, 2015.

Dekker, George. *The American Historical Romance.* Cambridge: Cambridge University Press, 1984.

Deleuze, Gilles. *Cinema 1: The Movement-Image.* London: Athlone Press, 1986.

Deleuze, Gilles. *Desert Islands: And Other Texts, 1953–1974.* Edited by David Lapoujade. Translated by Mike Taormina. Cambridge, Mass.: MIT Press, 2004.

Deleuze, Gilles. *Spinoza: Practical Philosophy.* San Francisco: City Lights, 1988.

Deleuze, Gilles, and Félix Guattari. *Anti-Oedipus: Capitalism and Schizophrenia.* Translated by Robert Hurley, Mark Seem, and Helen R. Lame. Minneapolis: University of Minnesota Press, 2000.

Deleuze, Gilles, and Félix Guattari. *A Thousand Plateaus: Capitalism and Schizophrenia.* Translated by Brian Massumi. Minneapolis: University of Minnesota Press, 2003.

Deleuze, Gilles, and Félix Guattari. *What Is Philosophy?* Translated by Hugh Tomlinson and Graham Burchell. New York: Columbia University Press, 1994.

Dern, John A. "'A Problem in Detection': The Rhetoric of Murder in 'The Black Cat.'" *Edgar Allan Poe Review* 18, no. 2 (Autumn 2017): 163–82.

Derrida, Jacques. *The Animal That Therefore I Am (Following).* Translated by David Wills. New York: Fordham University Press, 2008.

Derrida, Jacques. "'Eating Well,' or the Calculation of the Subject: An Interview with Jacques Derrida." In *Who Comes after the Subject?,* edited by Eduardo Cadava, Peter Connor, and Jean-Luc Nancy, 96–119. New York: Routledge, 1991.

Derrida, Jacques. "Foreword: Fors: The Anglish Words of Nicholas Abraham and Maria Torok," translated by Barbara Johnson. In *The Wolf Man's Magic Word: A Cryptonymy,* edited by Nicholas Abraham and Maria Torok, translated by Nicholas Rand, xi–xlviii. Minneapolis: University of Minnesota Press, 1986.

Derrida, Jacques. *Glas.* Translated by John P. Leavy Jr. and Richard Rand. Lincoln: University of Nebraska Press, 1986.

Detienne, Marcel, and Jean-Pierre Vernant. *Les ruses de l'intelligence: La* mètis *des Grecs.* Paris: Flammarion, 1974.

Dickinson, Emily. "I Held It So Tight That I Lost It." In *The Poems of Emily Dickinson: Including Variant Readings Critically Compared with All Known Manuscripts,* edited by Thomas H. Johnson. Cambridge, Mass.: Belknap, 1955.

Doane, Mary Ann. *The Emergence of Cinematic Time: Modernity, Contingency, the Archive.* Cambridge, Mass.: Harvard University Press, 2002.

Douglass, Frederick. *Autobiographies: Narrative of the Life of Frederick Douglass, My Bondage and My Freedom, Life and Times of Frederick Douglass.* Edited by Henry Louis Gates Jr. New York: Library of America, 1994.

Douglass, Frederick. "What to the Slave Is the Fourth of July?" In *The Portable Frederick Douglass,* edited by John Stauffer and Henry Louis Gates Jr., 195–222. New York: Penguin, 2016.

Drucker, Johanna. "Humanities Approaches to Graphical Display." *Digital Humanities Quarterly* 5, no. 1 (2011): www.digitalhumanities.org/dhq/vol/5/1/000091/000091.html.

Dunaway, Finis. "Hunting with the Camera: Nature Photography, Manliness, and Modern Memory—1890–1930." *Journal of American Studies* 34, no. 2 (2000): 207–30.

Dunbar-Ortiz, Roxanne. *An Indigenous Peoples' History of the United States.* Boston: Beacon, 2014.

Dutta, Arindam. "Mammoths, Inc.: Nature, Architecture, and the Debt, Part 1." Aggregate. Accessed January 19, 2015. http://we-aggregate.org/piece/mammoths-inc-nature-architecture-and-the-debt-part-1.

Eagleton, Terry. *Walter Benjamin; or, Towards a Revolutionary Criticism.* London: Verso, 1981.

Edison, Thomas. "The Phonograph and Its Future." *North American Review* 26, no. 262 (May–June 1878): 527–36.

Fabbri, Lorenzo. "From Inoperativeness to Action: On Giorgio Agamben's Anarchism." *Radical Philosophy Review* 14, no. 1 (2011): 85–100.

Farley, John, and Gerald L. Geison. "Science, Politics, and Spontaneous Generation in Nineteenth-Century France: The Pasteur-Pouchet Debate." *Bulletin of the History of Medicine* 48, no. 2 (1974): 161–98.

Fausto-Sterling, Anne. "Gender, Race, and Nation: The Comparative Anatomy of 'Hottentot' Women in Europe, 1815–1817." In *Deviant Bodies: Critical Perspectives on Difference in Science and Popular Culture,* edited by Jennifer Terry and Jacqueline Urla, 19–48. Bloomington: Indiana University Press, 1995.

Felman, Shoshana. "On Reading Poetry: Reflections on the Limits and Possibilities of Psychoanalytical Approaches." In *The Purloined Poe: Lacan, Derrida, and Psychoanalytical Reading,* edited by John P. Muller and William J. Richardson, 133–56. Baltimore: Johns Hopkins University Press, 1988.

Fiedler, Leslie A. *Love and Death in the American Novel.* Champaign, Ill.: Dalkey Archive, 2003.

Fiedler, Leslie A. *The Return of the Vanishing American.* New York: Stein and Day, 1968.

Finn, Jonathan M. *Capturing the Criminal Image: From Mug Shot to Surveillance Society.* Minneapolis: University of Minnesota Press, 2009.

Flusser, Vilem. *Towards a Philosophy of Photography.* London: Reaktion Books, 2000.

Foucault, Michel. *The Birth of Biopolitics: Lectures at the Collège de France, 1978–1979.* Translated by Graham Burchell, edited by Michel Senellart. London: Palgrave Macmillan, 2010.

Foucault, Michel. "Cuvier's Situation in the History of Biology." Translated by Lynne Huffer. *Foucault Studies* 22 (January 2017): 208–37.

Foucault, Michel. *Discipline and Punish: The Birth of the Prison.* Translated by Alan Sheridan. New York: Vintage, 1995.

Foucault, Michel. *The History of Sexuality.* Vol. 1, *An Introduction.* Translated by Robert Hurley. New York: Vintage, 1990.

Foucault, Michel. "The Mesh of Power." *Viewpoint Magazine.* Last modified September 12, 2012. Last accessed August 10, 2019. https://www.viewpointmag.com/2012/09/12/the-mesh-of-power/.

Foucault, Michel. *The Order of Things: An Archaeology of the Human Sciences.* New York: Routledge, 2005.

Foucault, Michel. *Security, Territory, Population: Lectures at the Collège de France, 1977–1978.* Edited by Michel Senellart. Translated by Graham Burchell. New York: Picador, 2007.

Foucault, Michel. *Society Must Be Defended: Lectures at the Collège de France, 1975–1976.* Edited by Mauro Bertani and Allesandro Fortano. Translated by David Mace. New York: Picador, 2003.

Freud, Sigmund. *Civilization and Its Discontents.* Garden City, N.Y.: Doubleday, 1958.

Freud, Sigmund. *Three Contributions to the Theory of Sex.* New York: Dutton, 1962.

Frost, John. *Heroes and Hunters of the West.* Philadelphia: H. C. Peck and Theo Bliss, 1860.

Geier, Ted. *Meat Markets: The Cultural History of Bloody London.* Edinburgh: Edinburgh University Press, 2017.

Gens, Hadrien. *Jakob von Uexküll, explorateur des milieux vivants: Logique de la signification.* Paris: Hermann, 2014.

Gerbi, Antonello. *The Dispute of the New World: The History of a Polemic, 1750–1900.* Translated by Jeremy Moyle. Pittsburgh: University of Pittsburgh Press, 2010.

Gillespie, Greg. *Hunting for Empire: Narratives of Sport in Rupert's Land, 1840–70.* Seattle: University of Washington Press, 2007.

Ginzburg, Carlo. *Clues, Myths, and the Historical Method.* Translated by John Tedeschi and Anne C. Tedeschi. Baltimore: Johns Hopkins University Press, 1992.

Gissen, David. *Subnature: Architecture's Other Environments.* Princeton, N.J.: Princeton's Architectural Press, 2009.

Goldstein, Amanda Jo. *Sweet Science: Romantic Materialism and the New Logics of Life.* Chicago: University of Chicago Press, 2017.

Gould, Stephen Jay. "A Biological Homage to Mickey Mouse." In *The Panda's Thumb: More Reflections in Natural History,* 95–107. New York: W. W. Norton, 1980.

Gould, Stephen Jay. *Ever Since Darwin: Reflections on Natural History.* New York: W. W. Norton, 2007.

Gould, Stephen Jay. *The Mismeasure of Man.* New York: W. W. Norton, 1996.

Greenberg, Joel. *A Feathered River across the Sky: The Passenger Pigeon's Flight to Extinction.* New York: Bloomsbury USA, 2014.

Greene, John C. *American Science in the Age of Jefferson.* Ames: Iowa State University Press, 1984.

Gunning, Tom. "The Play between Still and Moving Images: Nineteenth-Century 'Philosophical Toys' and Their Discourse." In *Between Stillness and Motion : Film, Photography, Algorithms,* edited by Eivind Røssaak, 27–44. Amsterdam : Amsterdam University Press, 2011.

Haraway, Donna. *Primate Visions: Gender, Race, and Nature in the World of Modern Science.* New York: Routledge, 1989.

Haraway, Donna. *Staying with the Trouble: Making Kin in the Chthulucene.* Durham, N.C.: Duke University Press, 2016.

Haraway, Donna. "Teddy Bear Patriarchy: Taxidermy in the Garden of Eden, New York City, 1908–36." *Social Text* 4, no. 2 (1984/1985): 19–64.

Haraway, Donna. *When Species Meet.* Posthumanities 3. Minneapolis: University of Minnesota Press, 2008.

Hartley, Lucy. *Physiognomy and the Meaning of Expression in Nineteenth-Century Culture.* Cambridge: Cambridge University Press, 2005.

Hartman, Saidyia V. *Scenes of Subjection: Terror, Slavery, and Self-Making in Nineteenth-Century America.* Oxford: Oxford University Press, 1997.

Hawthorne, Nathaniel. *Collected Novels: Fanshawe, The Scarlet Letter, The House of the Seven Gables, The Blithedale Romance, The Marble Faun.* Library of

America Nathaniel Hawthorne Edition. New York: Library of America, 1983.

Hawthorne, Nathaniel. *French and Italian Notebooks.* The Centenary Editions of the Works of Nathaniel Hawthorne, vol. 14. Columbus: Ohio State University Press, 1956.

Hawthorne, Nathaniel. *The Marble Faun; or, The Romance of Monte Beni.* The Centenary Editions of the Works of Nathaniel Hawthorne, vol. 4. Columbus: Ohio State University Press, 1971.

Hegel, G. W. F. *Philosophy of History.* Translated by J. Sibree. New York: Collier and Son, 1901.

Heidegger, Martin. *The Fundamental Concepts of Metaphysics: World, Finitude, Solitude.* Translated by William McNeill and Nicholas Walker. Bloomington: Indiana University Press, 1995.

Herman, Daniel Justin. *Hunting and the American Imagination.* Washington, D.C.: Smithsonian Institution Scholarly Press, 2003.

Heuvelmans, Bernard. *On the Tracks of Unknown Animals.* Translated by Richard Garnett. Illustrated by Alika Lindbergh. New York: Routledge, 2014.

Holloway, Lewis, and Carol Morris. "Exploring Biopower in the Regulation of Farm Animal Bodies: Genetic Policy Interventions in UK Livestock." *Genomics, Society and Policy* 3, no. 2 (2007): 1–17.

House, Kay Seymour. *Cooper's Americans.* Columbus: Ohio State University Press, 1965.

Huffer, Lynne. "Foucault's Fossils: Life Itself and the Return to Nature in Feminist Philosophy." In *Anthropocene Feminism,* edited by Richard Grusin, 65–88. Minneapolis: University of Minnesota Press, 2017.

Iannini, Christopher P. *Fatal Revolutions: Natural History, West Indian Slavery, and the Routes of American Literature.* Chapel Hill: University of North Carolina Press, 2012.

Irmscher, Christopher. *The Poetics of Natural History: From John Bartram to William James.* New Brunswick, N.J.: Rutgers University Press, 1999.

Irwin, John T. "A Clew to a Clue: Locked Rooms and Labyrinths in Poe and Borges." In *The American Face of Edgar Allan Poe,* edited by Shawn Rosenheim and Stephen Rachman, 139–52. Baltimore: Johns Hopkins University Press, 1995.

Jackson, Andrew. "Andrew Jackson to Soldiers, April 2." April 2, 1814. Manuscript/Mixed Material. https://www.loc.gov/item/maj002801/.

Jackson, Zakiyyah Iman. "Beyond the Limit: Gender, Sexuality, and the Animal Question in (Afro)Modernity." PhD diss., University of California Berkeley, 2012.

Jacobs, Harriet. *Incidents in the Life of a Slave Girl.* Edited by Frances Smith Foster and Richard Yarborough. Second Norton Critical Edition. New York: W. W. Norton, 2019.

James, Henry. *Hawthorne.* Ithaca, N.Y.: Cornell University Press, 1997.

Jefferson, Thomas. "Notes on the State of Virginia." In *Writings: Autobiography, Notes on the State of Virginia, Public and Private Papers, Addresses, Letters.* New York: Library of America, 2011.

Johnson, Kendall. "Classifying Donatello: The Visual Aesthetics of American Exceptionalism." In *Henry James and the Visual,* 25–59. Cambridge: Cambridge University Press, 2007.

Jones, Karen R. *Epiphany in the Wilderness: Hunting, Nature, and Performance in the Nineteenth-Century American West.* Boulder: University Press of Colorado, 2015.

Kafka, Franz. "A Report to an Academy." In *Collected Stories,* edited by Gabriel Josipovici. New York: Knopf, 1993.

Kelly, William P. *Plotting America's Past: Fenimore Cooper and the Leatherstocking Tales.* Carbondale: Southern Illinois University Press, 1983.

Kemp, Mark A. R. "*The Marble Faun* and American Postcolonial Ambivalence." *Modern Fiction Studies* 43, no. 1 (Spring 1997): 209–36.

Kilburn, Benjamin K. Photographic Camera. U.S. Patent 286,447, issued October 9, 1883.

Kittler, Friedrich A. *Gramophone, Film, Typewriter.* Translated by Geoffrey Winthrop-Young and Michael Wutz. Stanford, Calif.: Stanford University Press, 1999.

Kofman, Sarah. *Nietzsche and Metaphor.* Translated by Duncan Large. Stanford, Calif.: Stanford University Press, 1994.

Kolata, Gina. "A Living Hard Drive That Can Copy Itself." *New York Times,* July 13, 2017.

Kolbert, Elizabeth. *The Sixth Extinction: An Unnatural History.* New York: Henry Holt, 2014.

Kolodny, Annette. *The Lay of the Land: Metaphor as Experience and History in American Life and Letters.* Chapel Hill: University of North Carolina Press, 1984.

Krauss, Rosalind. *Grids: Format and Image in 20th Century Art: The Pace Gallery.* Pace Gallery, New York, 1980. Exhibition catalog.

Kuriyama, Shigehisa. *The Expressiveness of the Body and the Divergence of Greek and Chinese Medicine.* New York: Zone Books, 1999.

LaCapra, Dominick. *History and Its Limits: Human, Animal, Violence.* Ithaca, N.Y.: Cornell University Press, 2009.

Lawrence, David Herbert. *Studies in Classic American Literature.* Cambridge: Cambridge University Press, 2003.

Lawrence, Michael. "Muybridgean Motion/Materialist Film: Malcolm Le Grice's Berlin Horse." In *Animal Life and the Moving Image,* edited by Michael Lawrence and Laura MacMahon, 67–85. London: BFI/Palgrave, 2015.

Lawrie, Paul. *Forging a Laboring Race: The African American Worker in the Progressive Imagination.* New York: New York University Press, 2016.

Ledford, Heidi. "Lights, Camera, CRISPR: Biologists Use Gene Editing to Store Movies in DNA." *Nature,* July 12, 2017. Accessed June 7, 2019. https://www.nature.com/news/lights-camera-crispr-biologists-use-gene-editing-to-store-movies-in-dna-1.22288.

Lee, Paula Young. *Meat, Modernity, and the Rise of the Slaughterhouse.* Durham: University of New Hampshire Press, 2008.

Lewis, Andrew J. *A Democracy of Facts: Natural History in the Early Republic.* Philadelphia: University of Pennsylvania Press, 2011.

Lippit, Akira Mizuta. *Electric Animal: Toward a Rhetoric of Wildlife.* Minneapolis: University of Minnesota Press, 2000.

Lockard, Joe. "Talking Guns, Talking Turkey: Racial Violence in Early American Law and James Fenimore Cooper." In *Making America, Making American Literature: Franklin to Cooper,* edited by Robert Lee and W. M. Verhoeven, 313–36. Amsterdam: Rodopi, 1995.

Locke, John. "Second Treatise." In *Two Treatises of Government.* Cambridge: Cambridge University Press, 1988.

Luciano, Dana. *Arranging Grief: Sacred Time and the Body in Nineteenth-Century America.* New York: New York University Press, 2007.

Luciano, Dana. "Tracking Prehistory." *J19: The Journal of Nineteenth-Century Americanists* 3, no. 1 (Spring 2015): 173–81.

Luck, Chad. *The Body of Property: Antebellum American Fiction and the Phenomenology of Possession.* New York: Fordham University Press, 2014.

Lukács, Georg. *The Historical Novel.* Translated by Hannah Mitchell and Stanley Mitchell. Lincoln: University of Nebraska Press, 1983.

Lundblad, Michael. "From Animal to Animality Studies." *PMLA* 124, no. 2 (2009): 496–502.

MacKenzie, John. *The Empire of Nature: Hunting, Conservation, and British Imperialism.* Manchester: Manchester University Press, 1988.

Madden, Fred. "Poe's 'The Black Cat' and Freud's 'The Uncanny.'" *Literature and Psychology* 39, nos. 1–2 (1993): 52–62.

Marx, Karl. *Capital.* Vol. 1. Translated by Ben Fowkes. Introduction by Ernest Mandel. London: Penguin Classics, 1992.

Marx, Leo. *The Machine in the Garden: Technology and the Pastoral Ideal in America.* New York: Oxford University Press, 1964.

Mason, Jennifer. *Civilized Creatures: Urban Animals, Sentimental Culture, and American Literature, 1850–1900.* Baltimore: Johns Hopkins University Press, 2005.

Mbembe, J.-A. "Necropolitics." Translated by Libby Meintjes. *Public Culture* 15, no. 1 (Winter 2003): 11–40.

Mbembe, J.-A. *On the Postcolony.* Berkeley: University of California Press, 2001.

McCracken, Peggy. *In the Skin of a Beast: Sovereignty and Animality in Medieval France.* Chicago: University of Chicago Press, 2017.

McHugh, Susan. *Animal Stories: Narrating across Species Lines.* Minneapolis: University of Minnesota Press, 2011.

McLaughlin, Kevin. *Paperwork: Fiction and Mass Mediacy in the Paper Age.* Philadelphia: University of Pennsylvania Press, 2005.

Megill, Allan, ed. *Rethinking Objectivity.* Durham, N.C.: Duke University Press, 1994.

Melville, Herman. *Moby-Dick; or, The Whale.* Introduction by Andrew Delbanco. Notes and explanatory commentaries by Tom Quirk. London: Penguin Classics, 1992.

Menely, Tobias. *The Animal Claim: Sensibility and the Creaturely Voice.* Chicago: University of Chicago Press, 2015.

Merchant, Carolyn, ed. *American Environmental History: An Introduction.* New York: Columbia University Press, 2007.

Merleau-Ponty, Maurice. *Nature: Course Notes from the Collège de France.* Translated by Robert Vallier. Evanston, Ill.: Northwestern University Press, 2003.

Merleau-Ponty, Maurice. *The Visible and the Invisible.* Translated by Alphonso Lingis. Evanston, Ill.: Northwestern University Press, 1968.

Michelet, Jules. *Histoire du dix-neuvième siècle.* Paris: Flammarion, 1898.

Michelet, Jules. *The Sea.* New York: Rudd & Carleton, 1861.

Miller, D. A. *The Novel and the Police.* Berkeley: University of California Press, 1988.

Miller, Robert J. *Native America, Discovered and Conquered: Thomas Jefferson, Lewis and Clark, and Manifest Destiny.* Lincoln: University of Nebraska Press, 2008.

Mirzoeff, Nicholas. "It's Not the Anthropocene, It's the White Supremacy Scene; or, The Geological Color Line." In *After Extinction,* edited by Richard Grusin, 123–50. Minneapolis: University of Minnesota Press, 2016.

Monfort, Bruno. "Sans les mains: vérité achéiropoiète chez Poe." *Théorie, Littérature, Épistémologie* 28 (2011).

Morgan, Jennifer L. "*Partus sequitur ventrem*: Law, Race, and Reproduction in Colonial Slavery." *Small Axe: A Caribbean Journal of Criticism* 22, no. 1 (March 2018): 1–17.

Morgensen, Scott Lauria. "The Biopolitics of Settler Colonialism: Right Here, Right Now." *Settler Colonial Studies* 1 (2011): 52–76.

Morrison, Toni. *Playing in the Dark: Whiteness and the Literary Imagination.* New York: Vintage, 1992.

Muller, John P., and William J. Richardson, eds. *The Purloined Poe: Lacan, Derrida, and Psychoanalytical Reading.* Baltimore: Johns Hopkins University Press, 1988.

Murphy, Benjamin. "'Betwixt Human and Brute Life': Romancing the Biopolitical in Hawthorne's *The Marble Faun.*" Paper presented at the Society for Literature, Science, and the Arts, Tempe, Ariz., November 2017.

Muybridge, Eadweard. *Animals in Motion.* New York: Dover Publications, 1957.

Muybridge, Eadweard. *Descriptive Zoopraxography; or, The Science of Animal Locomotion Made Popular.* Philadelphia: University of Pennsylvania, 1893.

Nash, Roderick. *Wilderness and the American Mind.* 3rd ed. New Haven, Conn.: Yale University Press, 1982.

Nealon, Jeffrey T. *Plant Theory: Biopower and Vegetable Life.* Stanford, Calif.: Stanford University Press, 2015.

Nelson, Dana D. *The Word in Black and White: Reading "Race" in American Literature, 1638–1867.* Oxford: Oxford University Press, 1993.

Nemser, Daniel. *Infrastructures of Race: Concentration and Biopolitics in Colonial Mexico.* Austin: University of Texas Press, 2017.

New, Elisa. *The Line's Eye: Poetic Experience, American Sight.* Cambridge, Mass.: Harvard University Press, 1998.

Ngai, Sianne. "The Cuteness of the Avant-Garde." *Critical Inquiry* 31, no. 4 (Summer 2005): 811–47.

Nietzsche, Friedrich. *The Anti-Christ, Ecce Homo, Twilight of the Idols, and Other Writings.* Translated by Judith Norman. Cambridge: Cambridge University Press, 2005.

Nietzsche, Friedrich. *The Gay Science: With a Prelude in German Rhymes and an Appendix of Songs.* Translated by Josefine Nauckhoff. Poems translated by Adrian del Caro. Cambridge: Cambridge University Press, 2003.

Nobles, Gregory. *John James Audubon: The Nature of the American Woodsman.* Philadelphia: University of Pennsylvania Press, 2017.

Novek, Joel. "Pigs and People: Sociological Perspectives on the Discipline of Nonhuman Animals in Intensive Confinement." *Society & Animals* 13, no. 3 (2005): 221–44.

Ott, John. "Iron Horses: Leland Stanford, Eadweard Muybridge, and the Industrialised Eye." *Oxford Art Journal* 28, no. 3 (2005): 407–28.

Ott, John. "Netted Together: Eadweard Muybridge's *Animal Locomotion* at the Dawn of Comparative Biology." In *Greene Country Towne: Philadelphia, Ecology, and the Material Imagination,* edited by Alan C. Braddock and Laura Turner Igoe, 81–95. University Park: Penn State University Press, 2017.

Parrish, Susan Scott. *American Curiosity: Cultures of Natural History in the Colonial British Atlantic World.* Chapel Hill: University of North Carolina Press, 2005.

Patterson, Daniel, ed. *John James Audubon's Journal of 1826: The Voyage to the Birds of America.* Lincoln: University of Nebraska Press, 2011.

Patterson, Daniel, ed. *The Missouri River Journals of John James Audubon.* Lincoln: University of Nebraska Press, 2016.

Pearson, Maeve. "Bloodliness and Abortions: Heredity and Childhood in Hawthorne." In *The Materials of Exchange between Britain and North-East America, 1750–1900,* edited by Daniel Maudlin and Robin Peel, 17–36. New York: Routledge, 2016.

Pease, Donald. *Visionary Compacts: American Renaissance Writings in Cultural Context.* Madison: University of Wisconsin Press, 1987.

Peterson, Christopher. *Bestial Traces: Race, Sexuality, Animality.* New York: Fordham University Press, 2012.

Pétillon, Pierre-Yves. Postface to *Contes et Récits,* by Nathanial Hawthorne. Translated by Muriel Zagha. Paris: Imprimerie Nationale Éditions, 1996.

Pick, Anat. *Creaturely Poetics: Animality and Vulnerability in Literature and Film.* New York: Columbia University Press, 2011.

Poe, Edgar Allan. *The Conchologist's First Book: A System of Testaceous Malacology, Arranged Expressly for the Use of Schools, in Which the Animals, According to Cuvier, Are Given with the Shells, a Great Number of New Species Added, and the Whole Brought Up, as Accurately as Possible, to the Present Condition of the Science.* Philadelphia: Haswell, Barrington, and Haswell, 1839.

Poe, Edgar Allan. "A Few Words on Secret Writing." In *Essays and Reviews: Theory of Poetry, Reviews of British and Continental Authors, Reviews of American Authors and American Literature,* 1277–91. New York: Library of America, 1984.

Poe, Edgar Allan. "The Philosophy of Composition." In *Essays and Reviews: Theory of Poetry, Reviews of British and Continental Authors, Reviews of American Authors and American Literature,* 13–25. New York: Library of America, 1984.

Poe, Edgar Allan. *Poetry and Tales.* New York: Library of America, 1984.

Pollmann, Inga. "Invisible Worlds, Visible: Uexküll's *Umwelt,* Film, and Film Theory." *Critical Inquiry* 39, no. 4 (Summer 2013): 777–816.

Pratt, Mary Louise. *Imperial Eyes: Travel Writing and Transculturation.* New York: Routledge, 2003.

Proceedings of the Geological Society of London. Vol. 3. November 1838–June 1842. London: R. & J. E. Taylor, 1842.

Purdy, Jedediah. *After Nature: A Politics for the Anthropocene.* Cambridge, Mass.: Harvard University Press, 2015.

Puskar, Jason. "Pistolgraphs: Liberal Technoagency and the Nineteenth-Century Camera Gun." *Nineteenth-Century Contexts* 36, no 5 (2014): 517–34.

Rabinbach, Anson. *The Human Motor: Energy, Fatigue, and the Origins of Modernity.* New York: Basic Books, 1990.

Rachman, Stephen. "'Es lässt sich nicht schreiben': Plagiarism and 'The Man of the Crowd.'" In *The American Face of Edgar Allan Poe,* edited by Shawn Rosenheim and Stephen Rachman, 49–90. Baltimore: Johns Hopkins University Press, 1995.

Rachman, Stephen. "Poe and the Origins of Detective Fiction." In *The Cambridge Companion to American Crime Fiction,* edited by Catherine Ross Nickerson, 17–28. Cambridge: Cambridge University Press, 2010.

Rancière, Jacques. *Dissensus: On Politics and Aesthetics.* Translated by Steven Corcoran. London: Continuum, 2010.

Ravindranathan, Thangam. *Behold an Animal: Four Exorbitant Readings.* Evanston, Ill.: Northwestern University Press, 2020.

Ravindranathan, Thangam. "Unequal Metrics: Animals Passing in La Fontaine, Poe, and Chevillard." *differences* 24, no. 3 (2013): 1–35.

Ravindranathan, Thangam, and Antoine Traisnel. "What Gives (Donner le change)." *SubStance* 45, no. 2 (2016): 143–61.

Reiger, John F. *American Sportsmen and the Origins of Conservation.* 3rd ed. Corvallis: Oregon State University Press, 2000.

Rhodes, Richard. *John James Audubon: The Making of an American.* New York: Knopf, 2004.

Rieppel, Lukas. *Assembling the Dinosaur: Fossil Hunters, Tycoons, and the Making of a Spectacle.* Cambridge, Mass.: Harvard University Press, 2019.

Rifkin, Mark. *Fictions of Land and Flesh: Blackness, Indigeneity, Speculation.* Durham, N.C.: Duke University Press, 2019.

Rifkin, Mark. "Indigenizing Agamben: Rethinking Sovereignty in Light of the 'Peculiar' Status of Native Peoples." *Cultural Critique* 73 (Fall 2009): 88–124.

Riss, Arthur. "The Art of Discrimination." *ELH* 71, no. 1 (2004): 251–87.

Ritvo, Harriet. *The Animal Estate: The English and Other Creatures in the Victorian Age.* Cambridge, Mass.: Harvard University Press, 1989.

Ritvo, Harriet. "Destroyers and Preservers: Big Game in the Victorian Empire." *History Today* 52, no. 1 (2002): 33–39.

Ritvo, Harriet. *The Platypus and the Mermaid: And Other Figments of the Classifying Imagination.* Cambridge, Mass.: Harvard University Press, 1998.

Roberts, Jennifer L. *Transporting Visions: The Movement of Images in Early America.* Berkeley: University of California Press, 2014.

Rosenheim, Shawn. *The Cryptographic Imagination: Secret Writing from Edgar Poe to the Internet.* Baltimore: Johns Hopkins University Press, 1997.

Rothfels, Nigel. *Savages and Beasts: The Birth of the Modern Zoo.* Baltimore: Johns Hopkins University Press, 2002.

Rowe, John Carlos. *Literary Culture and U.S. Imperialism: From the Revolution to World War II.* Oxford: Oxford University Press, 2000.

Rudwick, Martin, J. S. *Georges Cuvier, Fossil Bones, and Geological Catastrophes.* Chicago: University of Chicago Press, 1997.

Rusert, Britt. *Fugitive Science: Empiricism and Freedom in Early African American Culture.* New York: New York University Press, 2017.

Ryan, James R. *Picturing Empire: Photography and the Visualization of the British Empire.* Chicago: University of Chicago Press, 1998.

Scheckel, Susan. *The Insistence of the Indian: Race and Nationalism in Nineteenth-Century American Culture.* Princeton, N.J.: Princeton University Press, 1998.

Scheick, William J. "An Intrinsic Luminosity: Poe's Use of Platonic and Newtonian Optics." In *American Literature and Science,* edited by Robert J. Scholnick, 77–93. Lexington: University Press of Kentucky, 1992.

Schuller, Kyla. *The Biopolitics of Feeling: Race, Sex, and Science in the Nineteenth Century.* Durham, N.C.: Duke University Press, 2018.

Schuller, Kyla. "The Fossil and the Photograph: Red Cloud, Prehistoric Media, and Dispossession in Perpetuity." *Configurations* 24, no. 2 (2016): 229–61.

Schuller, Kyla. "Specious Bedfellows: Ethnicity, Animality, and the Intimacy of Slaughter in *Moby-Dick.*" *Leviathan* 12, no. 3 (2010): 3–20.

Sebeok, Thomas. *Signs: An Introduction to Semiotics.* Toronto: University of Toronto Press, 1994.

Sekula, Allan. "The Body and the Archive." *October* 39 (1986): 3–64.

Sengoopta, Chandak. *The Imprint of the Raj: How Fingerprinting Was Born in Colonial India.* London: Pan Macmillan, 2004.

Seshadri, Kalpana Rahita. *HumAnimal: Race, Law, Language.* Minneapolis: University of Minnesota Press, 2012.

Shufeldt, Robert Wilson. "Published Figures and Plates of the Extinct Passenger Pigeon." *Scientific Monthly* 12, no. 5 (May 1921): 458–481.

Shukin, Nicole. *Animal Capital: Rendering Life in Biopolitical Times.* Minneapolis: University of Minnesota Press, 2009.

Shukin, Nicole. "Security Bonds: On Feeling Power and the Fiction of an Animal Governmentality." *English Studies in Canada* 39, no. 1 (2013): 177–98.

Siegert, Bernhard. *Cultural Techniques: Grids, Filters, Doors, and Other Articulations of the Real.* Oxford: Oxford University Press, 2015.

Sims, Michael. *Adam's Navel: A Natural and Cultural History of the Human Form.* New York: Viking, 2003.

Sinclair, Upton. *The Jungle.* New York: Bantam, 1981.

Slotkin, Richard. *The Fatal Environment: The Myth of the Frontier in the Age of Industrialization, 1800–1890.* New York: Atheneum, 1985.

Slotkin, Richard. *Regeneration through Violence: The Mythology of the American Frontier, 1600–1800.* Norman: University of Oklahoma Press, 1973.

Smith, Henry Nash. *Virgin Land: The American West as Symbol and Myth.* Cambridge, Mass.: Harvard University Press, 1971.

Snyder, Joel. "Visualization and Visibility." In *Picturing Science, Producing Art,* edited by Caroline A. Jones and Peter Galison, 379–400. New York: Routledge, 1998.

Solnit, Rebecca. *River of Shadows: Eadweard Muybridge and the Technological Wild West.* New York: Viking, 2003.

Sontag, Susan. *On Photography.* New York: Picador, 2011.

Spillers, Hortense. "Mama's Baby, Papa's Maybe: An American Grammar Book." *Diacritics* 17, no. 2 (1987): 65–81.

Stanescu, James. "Beyond Biopolitics: Animal Studies, Factory Farms, and the Advent of Deading Life." *PhaenEx* 8, no. 2 (Fall/Winter 2013): 135–60.

Stebbins, Theodore E., Jr. "Audubon's Drawings of American Birds, 1805–38." In *John James Audubon: The Watercolors for the Birds of America,* edited by Annette Blaugrund and Theodore E. Stebbins, 3–26. New York: Villard, 1993.

Stillman, J. D. B. *The Horse in Motion: As Shown by Instantaneous Photography: With a Study on Animal Mechanics: Founded on Anatomy and the Revelations of the Camera: In Which Is Demonstrated the Theory of Quadrupedal Locomotion.* Boston: James R. Osgood, 1882.

Stoler, Ann Laura. *Race and the Education of Desire: Foucault's History of Sexuality and the Colonial Order of Things.* Durham, N.C.: Duke University Press, 1995.

Stowe, Harriet Beecher. *Uncle Tom's Cabin; or, Life among the Lowly.* New York: W. W. Norton, 2018.

Sutherland, Keston. "Marx in Jargon." *World Picture* 1 (2008): 1–25.

Sweeney, Susan Elizabeth. "Death, Decay, and the Daguerreotype's Influence on 'The Black Cat.'" *Edgar Allan Poe Review* 19, no. 2 (2018): 206–32.

Tagg, John. *The Burden of Representation: Essays on Photographies and Histories.* Minneapolis: University of Minnesota Press, 1993.

Taylor, Chloe. "Foucault and Critical Animal Studies: Genealogies of Agricultural Power." *Philosophy Compass* 8, no. 6 (2013): 539–51.

Taylor, J. Traill. *The Photographic Amateur.* 2nd ed. New York: Scovill Manufacturing, 1883.

Thierman, Stephen. "Apparatuses of Animality: Foucault Goes to a Slaughterhouse." *Foucault Studies* 9, no. 9 (2010): 89–110.

Thoreau, Henry David. *Walden; or, Life in the Woods.* New York: Library of America, 1989.

Thurtle, Phillip. *The Emergence of Genetic Rationality: Space, Time, and Information in American Biological Science, 1870–1920.* Seattle: University of Washington Press, 2007.

Tocqueville, Alexis, de. *Democracy in America: Historical-Critical Edition of De la démocracie en Amérique.* 2 vols. Edited by Eduardo Nolla. Translated by James T. Schleifer. Indianapolis: Liberty Fund, 2010. Last accessed August 10, 2019. https://oll.libertyfund.org/titles/2284.

Twain, Mark. *Collected Tales, Sketches, Speeches & Essays 1852–1890.* New York: Library of America, 1992.

Twine, Richard. *Animals as Biotechnology: Ethics, Sustainability, and Critical Animal Studies.* Abingdon, U.K.: Earthscan, 2010.

Uexküll, Jakob, von. *A Foray into the Worlds of Animals and Humans, with A Theory of Meaning.* Translated by Joseph D. O'Neil. Introduction by Dorion

Sagan. Afterword by Geoffrey Winthrop-Young. Posthumanities 12. Minneapolis: University of Minnesota Press, 2010.

VanderVelde, Lea. "The Role of Captives and the Rule of Capture." *Environmental Law* 35, no. 4 (2005): 649–71.

Vialles, Noëlie. *Animal to Edible.* Cambridge: Cambridge University Press, 1994.

Vizenor, Gerald Robert. *Fugitive Poses: Native American Indian Scenes of Absence and Presence.* Lincoln: University of Nebraska Press, 1998.

Vizenor, Gerald Robert. *Manifest Manners: Postindian Warriors of Survivance.* Lebanon, N.H.: University Press of New England, 1994.

Wakeham, Pauline. *Taxidermic Signs: Reconstructing Aboriginality.* Minneapolis: University of Minnesota Press, 2008.

Walker, Gavin. "The Schema of the West and the Apparatus of Capture: Variations on Deleuze and Guattari." *Deleuze and Guattari Studies* 12, no. 2 (May 2018): 210–35.

Walker, Ian. "The Poe Legend." In *A Companion to Poe Studies,* edited by Eric W. Carlson, 19–42. Westport, Conn.: Greenwood Press, 1996.

Warren, Louis S. *The Hunter's Game: Poachers and Conservationists in Twentieth-Century America.* New Haven, Conn.: Yale University Press, 1999.

Weheliye, Alexander G. *Habeas Viscus: Racializing Assemblages, Biopolitics, and Black Feminist Theories of the Human.* Durham, N.C.: Duke University Press, 2014.

Weil, Kari. *Thinking Animals: Why Animal Studies Now?* New York: Columbia University Press, 2012.

White, Ed. "The Ourang-Outang Situation." *College Literature* 30, no. 3 (Summer 2003): 88–108.

Wiegman, Robyn. *American Anatomies: Theorizing Race and Gender.* Durham, N.C.: Duke University Press, 1995.

Wingerd, Mary. *North Country: The Making of Minnesota.* Minneapolis: University of Minnesota Press, 2010.

Wolfe, Cary. *Before the Law: Humans and Other Animals in a Biopolitical Frame.* Chicago: University of Chicago Press, 2013.

Wolfe, Patrick. *Settler Colonialism and the Transformation of Anthropology: The Politics and Poetics of an Ethnographic Event.* London: Cassell, 1999.

Woodman, Neil. "Pranked by Audubon: Constantine S. Rafinesque's Description of John James Audubon's Imaginary Kentucky Mammals." *Archives of Natural History* 43, no. 1 (2016): 95–108.

Wynter, Sylvia. "The Ceremony Found: Towards the Autopoetic Turn/Overturn, Its Autonomy of Human Agency and Extraterritoriality of (Self-) Cognition." In *Black Knowledges/Black Struggles: Essays in Critical Epistemology,* edited by Jason R Ambroise and Sabine Broeck, 184–252. Liverpool: Liverpool University Press, 2015.

Wynter, Sylvia. "Unsettling the Coloniality of Being/Power/Truth/Freedom: Towards the Human, after Man, Its Overrepresentation—An Argument." *CR: The New Centennial Review* 3, no. 3 (2003): 257–337.

Zimmerman, Brett. *Edgar Allan Poe: Rhetoric and Style.* Montreal: McGill-Queen's University Press, 2005.

Ziser, Michael. "Animal Mirrors: Poe, Lacan, Von Uexküll, and Audubon in the Zoosemiosphere." *Angelaki* 12, no. 3 (2007): 11–33.

Zuba, Clayton. "Hawthorne's Empire: Sculpture and the Indigenous in *The Marble Faun.*" *Studies in American Fiction* 43, no. 2 (Fall 2016): 161–82.

INDEX

Page references in italics refer to illustrations

ANTOINE TRAISNEL is assistant professor of English and comparative literature at the University of Michigan. He is author of *Hawthorne: Blasted Allegories,* coauthor with Thangam Ravindranathan of *Donner le change: L'impensé animal,* and coeditor with Thomas Constantinesco of *Littérature et politique en Nouvelle-Angleterre.* He is translator of Robert Montgomery Bird's gothic novel *Sheppard Lee*.